THE STORM IS HERE

ALSO BY LUKE MOGELSON

These Heroic, Happy Dead: Stories

THE
STORM
IS
HERE

AN AMERICAN CRUCIBLE

LUKE MOGELSON

PENGUIN PRESS
NEW YORK
2022

PENGUIN PRESS
An imprint of Penguin Random House LLC
penguinrandomhouse.com

Portions of this book were originally published in different form in *The New Yorker* as
"The Heart of the Uprising in Minneapolis," "The Militias Against Masks,"
"In the Streets with Antifa," and "Among the Insurrectionists."

Grateful acknowledgment is made to *The New Yorker* for permission to reprint
an adapted version of "In Minneapolis, Protesters Confront the Police—and One Another,"
by Luke Mogelson, copyright © 2020 by Condé Nast. Reprinted by permission.

LIBRARY OF CONGRESS CATALOGING-IN-PUBLICATION DATA

Names: Mogelson, Luke, author.
Title: The storm is here : an American crucible / Luke Mogelson.
Description: New York : Penguin Press, 2022. | Includes bibliographical references and index. |
Identifiers: LCCN 2022008423 (print) | LCCN 2022008424 (ebook) |
ISBN 9780593489215 (hardcover) | ISBN 9780593489222 (ebook)
Subjects: LCSH: Political culture—United States—History. |
COVID-19 Pandemic, 2020——Social aspects—United States. |
United States—Politics and government—2017–2021. |
United States—Social conditions—2020–
Classification: LCC E912 .M64 2022 (print) |
LCC E912 (ebook) | DDC 973.933—dc23/eng/20220518
LC record available at https://lccn.loc.gov/2022008423
LC ebook record available at https://lccn.loc.gov/2022008424

Printed in the United States of America
1st Printing

DESIGNED BY MEIGHAN CAVANAUGH

CONTENTS

FALL

WINTER

INTRODUCTION

Hoping to stave off an encroaching despair on the morning of January 7, 2021, I left my hotel in Washington, D.C., and caught a taxi to the Lincoln Memorial. I was looking for sanctuary, and the open-air chamber, designed to resemble a temple, seemed as likely a place to find it as any. I'd been there once or twice before; passing between the marble columns, you weren't humbled into silence so much as welcomed by it. When I arrived this time, however, the monument was closed. Squad cars were pulling up. Officers expelled a braying mob.

Many of the people wore red MAGA hats and TRUMP 2020 shirts. I asked someone what had happened. It seemed that a woman had been posing for pictures with a Gadsden flag—DON'T TREAD ON ME below a hissing snake, on a yellow field—when an officer advised that such displays were not allowed. A fracas had ensued. Now the Trump supporters converged at the bottom of the steps—the same steps from which, in 1963, Martin Luther King delivered his "I Have a Dream" speech—and began calling the officers Nazis, Marxists, pigs. Young men in blazers waved their middle fingers. "Christ is king!" they chanted. "Aren't we the pussies?" a little bald man asked. "Honestly, we're not overrunning them?"

"That's when they just start executing people," said a woman in her thirties, glaring hatefully at the police.

It occurred to me that some of the officers impassively absorbing this abuse probably had friends in the hospital. Less than twenty-four hours earlier, I had watched Donald Trump tell a similar though much larger mob, assembled on the far end of the reflecting pool that extended behind us, "If you don't fight like hell, you're not going to have a country anymore." Thousands of people—many armed with bats, clubs, whips, and other rudimentary weapons—had proceeded to march up the National Mall. At the Capitol, they had wounded around 180 law enforcement agents, charged past clouds of pepper spray and volleys of rubber bullets, smashed through doors and windows, and frantically hunted for politicians, determined to sabotage the peaceful transition of power. Some carried nooses, barked racial epithets, assaulted journalists, and called for the vice president to be lynched. On the Senate floor, I watched Trump supporters ransack desks and steal confidential documents. A bare-chested man in a horned headdress, wielding a spear, pronounced Mike Pence "a fucking traitor." Then he led the rioters in prayer. An officer who suffered a stroke after being maced would later die.

Now, it was not the police but the Trump supporters who were outraged. Once again, they believed they had been wronged. Once again, their sense of injury was blistering.

The woman with the Gadsden flag was a pastor from Los Angeles. "I know that had to be Antifa," she said of the attack on the Capitol. "I *know* it did. Because everyone here"—she gestured at the livid crowd berating the police—"there's such a spirit of community." She began to weep. "How *dare* they?" she demanded of the officers. "What is *wrong* with this country? This is *not* my America. I don't *understand*."

That made two of us. I could think of only one question to ask. "Where do we go from here?"

The pastor wiped her tears. Her suffering was vast. "I will tell you this," she sobbed. "I will not turn the other cheek to what's not right. This is not right. *This is not right*."

THE FIRST EPIDEMIC I reported on was in West Africa, in 2014. Although Ebola was far more deadly and contagious than COVID-19, the international response had been woefully inadequate. Liberia's largest slum, a dense warren of crude squatter dwellings on a narrow peninsula that jutted into the Atlantic from downtown Monrovia, was a formidable early hot zone. Below a canopy of rusty sheet metal, some eighty thousand denizens lacked running water, relieved themselves in the cramped gaps between walls, and repurposed detritus as a bulwark against eroding riverbanks. As the virus wiped out whole families, the Liberian military sealed off the encampment with ramparts and barbed wire. Gunships patrolled the coast. Crime spiked. Panic spread. Soldiers fired on people trying to escape. The community looked doomed.

After ten days, emissaries from the slum prevailed on the government to end the blockade. In exchange, they agreed to implement a suite of precautions: identifying and isolating sick people in their homes, tracking down their recent contacts, and vigilantly monitoring each individual for a period of three weeks (the maximum amount of time that the virus was known to incubate before manifesting symptoms). Normally, all this should have been the responsibility of medical professionals and epidemiologists. In the slum, the job fell to locals. Against most expectations, within a month the outbreak had been contained.

Monrovia was not an aberration. In the absence of rescue—by the world and by their own governments, which were among the poorest on earth—West Africans proved remarkably adept at helping one another to survive. Neighborhoods mobilized. Health-care workers volunteered. Secluded villages formed ad hoc task forces to oversee sanitation, quarantines, and mandatory social distancing. Education was crucial. Initially, conspiracy theories abounded. Some West Africans embraced a rumor that the virus was a ploy to solicit foreign donor money. Spiritual healers proffered metaphysical explanations for the vagaries of death and illness. At one remote hamlet that I visited in Sierra Leone, where the virus had killed more than thirty people, the chief had been told that somewhere a commercial plane had crashed: for every passenger who'd died a villager must as well.

"This was the information we were given," he explained with some embarrassment. "We have our culture, and we believed." As soon as Sierra Leonean health officials reached the chief and apprised him of the epidemic, he'd immediately recognized that the information he'd been given was bad. Following the advice of experts, he forbade the anointment of corpses and other traditional burial rituals, quarantined potential vectors, and assembled a team to conduct stringent contact tracing. By the time I visited the village, no one was sick.

At the height of the epidemic, the US Centers for Disease Control and Prevention warned that Ebola could infect a million and a half West Africans within a couple of months. The dire forecast assumed no "changes in community behavior." Because West Africans proved this assumption false, fewer than thirty thousand people contracted the virus. As I encountered story after story of courageous resilience and ingenuity in the face of implacable cataclysm, a question nagged at me. How would *my* country bear up under similar pressure? National hysteria provoked by four Ebola cases in Texas and New York did not augur well. But then, perhaps we'd rise to the occasion if confronted with a real disaster. Perhaps, like West Africans, who had only recently emerged from years of civil war, we'd set aside our differences to ally against a common enemy.

When the real disaster came, this is precisely what Donald Trump asked us to do. "Now is our time," he declared from the White House, in March 2020. "We must sacrifice together, because we are all in this together." Over the next year, COVID-19 would kill half a million people in the US, far more than in any other nation. Legions of Americans would join a millenarian internet cult prophesying righteous mass murder. Political tribalism, incipient fascism, and unrestrained demagoguery would pit citizens against one another, online and in the streets. A raging blizzard of propaganda would completely blot out reality. Banks, post offices, and police stations would burn. Thousands of soldiers would be deployed in dozens of cities. Religious extremism would proliferate. Gun violence would claim nearly twenty thousand victims, the highest toll in decades. Hate crimes would skyrocket. So would drug overdoses and domestic abuse. Trust in the press would disintegrate, along with confidence in our system of governance. Talk of war, revolution, and even the apocalypse would become almost commonplace. Elected officials would attempt a coup.

Before the pandemic, I had mainly covered the wars in Afghanistan, Syria, and Iraq. My impression was that most Americans, regardless of their political persuasion, assumed that some intrinsic flaw, which we were not afflicted by and could not remedy, predisposed those societies to turmoil and strife. I had never doubted that the US, under the wrong circumstances, could succumb to spiraling cycles of violence as intractable as any I'd seen abroad. But what were those circumstances? Over the course of 2020, while on assignment for *The New Yorker*, I witnessed frustration with COVID-19 policies grow into a fanatical anti-government movement, which became a militarized opposition to demands for racial justice, which became an organized crusade against democracy. January 6 was not the apotheosis of that evolution: it was another stage. The evolution is ongoing.

AFTER I LEFT THE PASTOR at the Lincoln Memorial, I took a car back to my hotel. The driver was a recent immigrant from Ethiopia. As we made small talk, he had a lot of questions. Not just about the insurrection—so much of the past year was so incompatible with everything he'd imagined when moving to America.

"How did this happen?" he wanted to know.

I stammered and searched for a reply. What was I supposed to say? "We have our culture, and we believed"? I wanted to tell him something true. I had been in his position. I had asked the same thing—on many occasions, in many places. An honest answer, though, would have taken more time than we had.

SPRING

ONE

LET US IN

It started in Michigan. On April 15, 2020, thousands of vehicles convoyed to Lansing and clogged the streets surrounding the state capitol for a protest that had been advertised as "Operation Gridlock." Drivers leaned on their horns, men with guns got out and walked. Signs warned of revolt. Someone waved an upside-down American flag. Already—nine months before January 6, seven months before the election, six weeks before a national uprising for police accountability and racial justice—there were a lot of them, and they were angry. Gretchen Whitmer, Michigan's Democratic governor, had recently extended a stay-at-home order and imposed additional restrictions on commerce and recreation, obliging a long list of businesses to close. Around thirty thousand Michiganders had tested positive for COVID-19—the third-highest rate in the country, after New York and California—and almost two thousand had died. Most of the cases, however, were concentrated in Detroit, and the predominantly rural residents at Operation Gridlock resented the blanket lockdown. On April 30, with Whitmer holding firm as deaths continued to rise, they returned to Lansing.

This time, more were armed and fewer stayed in their cars. Michigan is an open-carry state, and no law prohibited licensed owners from bringing loaded weapons inside the capitol. Men with assault rifles filled the rotunda and approached the barred doors of the legislature, squaring off against police. Others accessed the gallery that overlooked the Senate. Dayna Polehanki, a Democrat from southern Michigan, tweeted a picture of a heavyset man with a Mohawk and a long gun in a scabbard on his back. "Directly above me, men with rifles yelling at us," she wrote.

The next day, a security guard in Flint turned away an unmasked customer from a Family Dollar. The customer returned with her husband, who shot the guard in the head. Later that week, a clerk in a Dollar Tree outside Detroit asked a man to don a mask. The man replied, "I'll use this," grabbed the clerk's sleeve, and wiped his nose with it. By then, the movement that had begun with Operation Gridlock had spread to more than thirty states. In Kentucky, the governor was hanged in effigy outside the capitol; in North Carolina, a protester hauled a rocket launcher through downtown Raleigh; in California, a journalist covering an anti-lockdown demonstration was held at knifepoint; ahead of a rally in Salt Lake City, a man wrote on Facebook, "Bring your guns, the civil war starts Saturday . . . The time is now."

I was living in Paris, where, since late March, we had been permitted to go outside for a maximum of one hour per day, and to stray no farther than a kilometer from our homes. Most businesses were closed (except those "essential to the life of the nation," such as bakeries and wine and cigarette shops). Few complained. Every night at eight o'clock, we opened our windows and banged metal pots with wooden spoons to celebrate French medical workers; down the block from my apartment, a pharmacist stepped into the street and waved. I'd been a foreign correspondent for nearly a decade and during that time had not spent more than a few consecutive months in the US. The images of men in desert camo, flak jackets, and ammo vests, carrying military-style carbines through American cities, portrayed a country I no longer recognized. One viral photograph struck me as particularly exotic. It showed a man with a shaved head and a blond beard, mid-scream, his gaping mouth inches away from two officers gazing stonily past him, in the capitol in Lansing. What accounted for such exquisite rage? And why was it so widely shared?

In early May, I took an almost-empty flight to New York, then a slightly fuller one to Michigan.

My FIRST STOP WAS OWOSSO, a small town on the banks of the Shiawassee River, in the bucolic middle of the state. I arrived at Karl Manke's barbershop a little before nine a.m. The neon Open sign was dark; a crowd loitered in the parking lot. Spring had not yet made it to Owosso, and people sat in their trucks with the heaters running. Some, dressed in fatigues and packing sidearms, belonged to the Michigan Home Guard, a civilian militia. A week before, Manke, who was seventy-seven, had reopened his business in defiance of Governor Whitmer's prohibition on "personal care services." That Friday, Michigan's attorney general, Dana Nessel, had declared the barbershop an imminent danger to public health and dispatched state troopers to serve Manke with a cease-and-desist order. Over the weekend, Home Guardsmen had warned that they would not allow Manke to be arrested. Now it was Monday, and the folks in the parking lot had come to see whether Manke would show up.

"He's a national hero," Michelle Gregoire, a twenty-nine-year-old school bus driver, mother of three, and Home Guard member, told me. She was five feet four but hard to miss. Wearing a light fleece jacket emblazoned with Donald Trump's name, she waved a Gadsden flag at the passing traffic. Car after car honked in support. Michelle had driven ninety miles, from her house in Battle Creek, to stand with her comrades. She'd been at the capitol on April 30, and did not regret what happened there. When I mentioned that officials were considering banning guns inside the statehouse, she laughed: "If they go through with that, they're not gonna like the next rally."

Manke appeared at nine thirty, to cheers and applause. He had a white goatee and wore a blue satin smock, black-rimmed glasses, and a rubber bracelet with the words "When in Doubt, Pray." He climbed the steps to the front door stiffly, his posture hunched. The previous week, he'd strained his back working fifteen-hour days, pausing only to snack on hard-boiled eggs brought to him on paper plates by his wife. When the Open sign flickered on, people crowded inside. Manke had been cutting hair in town for half a century and at his current location since the eighties. The phone was rotary, the clock analog. An out-of-service gumball machine stood beside a row of chairs. Black-and-white photographs of Owosso occupied cluttered shelves alongside old radios and bric-a-brac. Also on display were flashy paperback copies of the ten novels that Manke had written. *Unintended Consequences* featured an antiabortion activist who "stands on his convictions"; *Gone to Pot* offered readers "a daring view into the underbelly of the sixties and seventies." As Manke fastened a cape around the first customer's neck, a man in foul-weather gear picked out a book and deposited a wad of bills in a wicker basket on the counter. "My father was a barber," he told Manke. "He believed in everything you believe in. Freedom. We're the last holdout in the world."

Manke nodded. "We did this in seventeen seventy-six, and we're doing it again now."

Like the redbrick buildings and decorative parapets of Owosso's historic downtown, there was something out of time about him. During several days that I would spend at the barbershop, I'd hear Manke offer countless customers and journalists subtle variations of the same stump speech. He'd lived under fourteen presidents, survived the polio epidemic, and never witnessed such "government oppression." Governor Whitmer was not his mother. He'd close his business when they dragged him out in handcuffs, or when he died, or when Jesus came— "whichever happens first." He had a weakness for pat aphorisms, his delight in them undiminished by repetition. "I got one foot in the grave, the other on a banana peel"; "Politicians come to do good and end up doing well"; "You can't fool me, I'm too ignorant." Nearly every interview Manke gave concluded with a recitation of the serenity prayer, which he delivered with theatrical élan, as if oblivious to the possibility that anyone might have heard it before.

"You're getting a scoop," he assured me when I introduced myself. "American rebellion."

Customers continued to arrive, and the phone did not stop ringing. Some people had traveled hundreds of miles. They left cards, bumper stickers, leaflets, brochures. A security contractor offered his services, free of charge. So did a scissors sharpener. (Manke: "You do corrugations?" Sharpener: "Of course. God bless you, and God bless America.") A local TV crew squeezed into the shop, struggling to social-distance in the crush of waiting men, recording Manke with a boom mic as he sculpted yet another high-and-tight. Around noon, Glenn Beck called, live on the air. "It's hardly my country anymore, in so many different ways," Manke told him. "You remind me of my father," Beck responded, with a wistful sigh.

Manke seemed to remind everybody of something or someone that no longer existed. Hence the people with guns outside, ready to do violence on those who threatened what he represented. You could not have engineered a more quintessential paragon of that mythical era when America was great.

ONE DAY AT THE BARBERSHOP, I was approached by a man clad from head to toe in hunting gear, missing several teeth. He hadn't realized I was press. Manke had first come to the attention of the attorney general, the man informed me, because of a reporter from Detroit. He held out his arms to indicate the woman's girth.

"A big Black bitch."

In the 1950s, when Manke was in high school, Owosso was a "sundown town": African Americans were not welcome. Like much of rural Michigan, it remained almost exclusively white. Detroit, an hour and a half to the south, was 80 percent Black. Because politics broke down along similar lines—less-populated counties voted Republican; urban centers, Democrat—partisan rancor in the state could often look like racial animus. While conservatives tended to ridicule any such interpretation as liberal cant, the pandemic had created two new discrepancies that were hard to ignore. The first was that COVID-19 disproportionately affected Black communities, in Michigan as well as nationwide. The second was that the people mobilizing against containment measures were overwhelmingly white.

On April 30, the state representative Sarah Anthony had watched from her office across the street as anti-lockdown protesters filled the capitol lawn. Anthony had been born and raised in Lansing. In 2012, at the age of twenty-nine, she'd become the youngest Black woman in America to serve as a county commissioner. Six years later, a landslide victory made her the first Black woman to represent Lansing in the state legislature. As Anthony walked from her office to the capitol, she had to navigate a heavily armed white mob. She noticed a Confederate flag.

A man waved a fishing rod with a naked Barbie doll—brunette, like Whitmer—dangling from a mini noose. Men screamed insults. A sign declared: TYRANTS GET THE ROPE.

Anthony was in the House of Representatives when the mob entered the building. "It just felt like, if they had come through that door, I would've been the first to go down," she recalled.

We were in the rotunda, where she had insisted on giving me a tour. Her eyes brightened above her mask as she pointed out the star-speckled oculus in the apex of the dome 160 feet above us. "It's designed to inspire," Anthony explained. "There's a sense of awe." At seventeen, she had participated in an after-school internship program at the statehouse, "for nerdy kids who had too many credits and needed something productive to do." After shadowing Mary Waters, a Black representative from Detroit, she had resolved to become a politician. "To see a woman that looked like me in a leadership position—I didn't know we could do that," she said. As we strolled in a circle beneath the dome, it was easy to imagine the dazzled intern, gazing up.

Anthony's reverence for the building had made April 30 that much more unsettling. A sanctum had been violated—its meaning changed. The structure was an equally potent symbol for the people whose cries she'd heard on the other side of the door, however. On the eve of the rally, Michelle Gregoire, the school bus driver and Home Guard member, had visited the capitol. Wearing a neon safety vest scrawled with COVID-1984, she and two friends filming on their phones had climbed a marble staircase to the gallery in the House of Representatives. A sergeant at arms informed them that the legislature was not in session, the chamber closed. "This is our house," responded one of them, striding past him and sitting on a bench. The chief sergeant at arms, David Dickson, arrived and grabbed the woman by her arm, attempting to remove her.

"You are not allowed to touch me!" the woman howled.

Dickson turned his attention to Michelle. When she also resisted, he dragged her into the hallway, through a pair of swinging doors.

"Stay out," he told her.

That night, the women posted their footage on Facebook, with the caption "We are living in NAZI Germany!!!" Many of the protesters at the capitol the next day had watched the clips, including the man with the shaved head and blond beard in the viral photograph. He was not accosting the two officers in the image, it turns out—he was shouting at Dickson, who stood behind them, outside the picture's frame. "You gonna throw me around like you did that girl?" the man was shouting. Other protesters called Dickson and his colleagues "traitors" and "filthy rats."

I left several messages for Dickson at his office, but he never called me back. Eventually, I returned to the capitol and found him standing guard outside the legislature. His hair was starting to gray, and beneath his blazer his collared shirt strained a little at the midriff. In 1974, Dickson had become the first Black deputy in Eaton County. He'd gone on to serve for twenty-five years as an officer in Lansing. After some polite conversation, I asked whether he thought that any of the visceral acrimony directed at him on April 30 might have been connected to his skin color and to that of the white women he'd ejected the day before.

Dickson frowned. "I don't play the race card," he said. Given his deprecating tone, I wondered if he'd been dodging my calls out of concern that I would raise this question. It was a question you could not really help raising in Michigan. To what extent was the exquisite rage behind the anti-lockdown fervor *white* rage? Dickson had no interest in discussing it. Of his encounter with Michelle, he told me, "I didn't sleep for weeks. You don't feel good about those kinds of things." In his opinion, the white men who had threatened and belittled him had simply failed to grasp that he was duty bound to enforce the state-house rules. "I love my job," he stated with finality, putting an end to the interview.

For others, the answer to the question was self-evident. After April 30, Sarah Anthony acquired a bulletproof vest. Though she was an optimist by nature, her outlook had dimmed. "People are angry about being unemployed, about having to close their businesses—I get that," she said. "But there are elements, extremists, who are using this as an opportunity to ignite hate. Hate toward our governor, hate toward government, and also hate toward Black and brown people. These conditions are creating a perfect storm."

CAMOUFLAGE

The April 30 protest had been organized by a few men on Facebook calling themselves the American Patriot Council. Two and a half weeks later, they held a second demonstration, in Grand Rapids, at a plaza known as Rosa Parks Circle. This time, there were no Confederate flags. A video from the Lansing rally, which had sparked backlash online, showed two adolescent girls dancing in rubber masks: one of Trump, the other of Obama with exaggeratedly dark skin. In Grand Rapids, the same two girls danced to "Bleed the Same," by the gospel singer Mandisa. "Are you Black? Are you white?" Mandisa crooned. "Aren't we all the same inside?"

The optics felt effortful, to say the least. I saw one person of color in the crowd. On the periphery, dozens of armed white men in tactical apparel surveilled the plaza. A few held flags with the Roman numeral III—a reference to the dubious contention that only 3 percent of colonists fought the British, and a generic emblem signifying readiness to do the same against the US government. (Americans who displayed the symbol and embraced the mentality that it represented often identified as "Three Percenters.") Some were Home Guard. Others belonged to the Michigan Liberty Militia, including the heavyset man with the Mohawk whose picture Dayna Polehanki had tweeted from the Senate floor. He wore a sleeveless shirt and a black vest laden with ammunition. A laminated badge read SECURITY. His habit of pressing a small gadget embedded in his ear with his index and middle fingers felt like an imitation of something he had seen on-screen. He appeared to be having an excellent time.

A general atmosphere of cheerful make-believe was accentuated by the presence and intense engagement of actual children. One of them, materializing suddenly, interrupted my conversation with a Home Guardsman: "Excuse me, what kinds of guns are those?"

We looked down to find a ten-year-old boy with a businesslike expression.

"This is an AK-47," the Home Guardsman told him.

"With a flashlight or a suppressor?"

"That's a suppressor. This is a flashlight with a green dot."

"What pistol is that?"

"That is a Glock. A nine-millimeter."

The boy seemed underwhelmed. "I've heard a lot of people say that," he said.

"Before you ever pick up a gun, you have to have your hundred hours of safety classes, right?" admonished the Home Guardsman, bristling a little.

"I already have them."

The keynote speaker was Dar Leaf, a sheriff from nearby Barry County who had refused to enforce Governor Whitmer's executive orders. Diminutive, plump, and bespectacled, with a startling falsetto and an unruly mop of bright yellow hair, Leaf cut an unlikely figure in his uniform, the baggy brown trousers of which bunched around his ankles. Nevertheless, he promptly captivated his audience by inviting it to imagine an alternate version of the past—one in which Alabama officers, upholding the Constitution, had not arrested Rosa Parks.

To facilitate the thought experiment, Leaf channeled a hypothetical deputy boarding the bus on which Parks—in the real world—was detained. "Hey, Ms. Parks," said the sheriff, playing the part. "I'm gonna make sure nobody bothers you, and you can sit wherever you want."

The crowd cheered.

"Thank you!" a white man cried out.

In Alabama, during the sixties, sheriffs and deputies were often more ruthless than their municipal counterparts toward Black citizens. The sheriff Jim Clark led a horseback assault against peaceful marchers on the Edmund Pettus Bridge, in Selma, and habitually terrorized African Americans with a cattle prod that he wore on his belt. Dar Leaf, though, saw himself as heir to a different legacy. According to him, the weaponization of law enforcement to suppress Black activism arose from the same infidelity to American principles of individual freedom that in our time defined the political left. "I got news for you," Leaf said. "Rosa Parks was a rebel." And then, for those minds not yet wrapped around what he was telling them: "Owosso has their little version of Rosa Parks, don't they? Karl Manke!"

The equivalence was all the more incredible given that Leaf belonged to the Constitutional Sheriffs and Peace Officers Association, or CSPOA. The notion of the "constitutional sheriff" had been first promulgated by William Potter Gale, a Christian Identity minister from California. Christian Identity theology held that Europeans were the true descendants of the lost tribes of Israel; that Jews were the diabolic progeny of Eve and the serpent; and that all non-whites were subhuman "mud people." In the seventies, Gale developed a movement of rural resistance to federal authority that expanded the model of white vigilantism in the South to a national scale, adding to the fear of Black integration the specter of governmental infiltration by Communists and Jews. He called his organization Posse Comitatus, which is Latin for "power of the county," and it recognized elected sheriffs as "the only legal law enforcement" in America. Posse Comitatus groups across the country were instructed to convene "Christian common-law grand juries," indict public officials who violated the Constitution, and "hang them by the neck." Gale's guidance on what offenses merited such punishment was straightforward: any enforcement of federal tax regulations or of the Civil Rights Act.

The CSPOA argued that county sheriffs retained supreme authority within their jurisdictions to interpret the law, and that their primary responsibility was to defend their constituents from state and federal overreach. In Grand Rapids, Sheriff Dar Leaf told the anti-lockdowners, "We're looking at common-law grand juries. I'd like to see some indictments come out of that." At the end of his speech, he called the Michigan Liberty Militia onto the stage. "This is our last home defense right here," he said. Glancing at the heavyset man with the Mohawk, Leaf added, "These guys have better equipment than I do. I'm lucky they got my back."

NAZI TIMES

Later, while reviewing my videos from Rosa Parks Circle, I noticed a woman with a toothbrush mustache painted on her upper lip. Looking closer, I saw that she also wore a wig. It was brunette and wavy, intended to resemble Governor Whitmer's hair. The woman wasn't doing Hitler, in other words: she was doing Whitmer doing Hitler. She would probably have said that she was doing "Whitler."

While comparing pandemic measures to the atrocities of the Third Reich might have constituted its own kind of antisemitism, it also suggested how desperate many anti-lockdowners understood the situation to be. Nazis were a frequent topic of conversation in the barbershop— which, for Karl Manke's supporters, represented a bulwark against the kind of creeping authoritarianism that had gradually engulfed Germany in the 1930s. Manke himself had a lot to say on the subject. His great-grandfather had immigrated from Germany, and Manke had grown up attending a Lutheran church with services in German. He often cited the Jewish victims of the Holocaust as a cautionary tale. "They would trade their liberty for security," he told a customer one afternoon. "Because the Nazis said to them, 'Get in these cattle cars, and we're gonna take you to a nice, safe place. Just get in.'"

"I would rather die than have the government tell me what to do," the man in the chair responded.

In mid-May, when Attorney General Nessel suspended his business license, Manke exclaimed, "It's tyrannical! I'm not getting in the cattle car!" His 2015 novel, *Age of Shame*, recounts the travails of Rhena Nowak, a thirteen-year-old Polish Jew who is raped by a German sergeant and loaded into a cattle car during the Second World War. "Millions of Jews have already been moved through this process with little to no resistance," Manke writes, "holding true to their centuries-old compliance to their weakness toward fatalism." Just a few outliers "are not cut out to become willing participants in this collapse of strength." Rhena pries loose the slats nailed over a window and leaps from the train, earning her freedom. When I bought a copy of *Age of Shame*, Manke inscribed the title page with one of his timeworn maxims: "History unheeded is history repeated."

A few days later, a customer in striped knee-length shorts caught my eye. While in line, he'd become intensely absorbed in a thick hardcover book—the seminal evangelical treatise *How Should We Then Live?* When it was his turn, he told Manke that he was from Hamburg and they proceeded to talk in German. After the man paid, I followed him out and asked what they'd discussed. "We were just talking about how it was back in the Nazi times," he said.

A meme shared widely at the beginning of the pandemic had juxtaposed a picture of American police enforcing social-distancing restrictions with an image of gestapo officers interrogating Jews in a European ghetto. At the time, I'd assumed that it was deliberate hyperbole, meant to provoke. But the longer I stayed in Michigan, the clearer it became that many anti-lockdowners sincerely placed mask mandates and concentration camps on the same continuum. "This has nothing to do with the virus," a sixty-eight-year-old retiree told me outside the barbershop. "They want to take power away from the people, and they want to control us. We're never gonna get our freedoms back from this if we don't stop it now." Given the stakes, violence was inevitable. "We're a trigger pull away," he said. "You're gonna see it. We're getting to the point where people have had enough."

We had to raise our voices to hear each other over a Christian family loudly singing hymns. But I had the sense that the retiree would have been yelling anyway. "You got storm troopers coming in here!" he shouted, referencing the officers who'd served Manke with a cease-and-desist order. "They weren't cops, they were storm troopers! They deserve to wear the Nazi emblem on their sleeves."

When I went back inside, the phone was ringing. An anonymous caller wanted Manke to know that the National Guard was on its way. "We need more people," a customer in a pressed shirt announced. I'd met him earlier. A self-described "citizen scientist," he'd given me a flier explaining that masks prevented the body from detoxifying and therefore did more harm than good. "If we get more people, we can stand them off," he told Manke.

"I would hope it's a rumor," Manke said.

"Whatever it is, we could use more people."

"Well, if they come with a tank . . ."

"Like Tiananmen Square!" the citizen scientist agreed. He lapsed into pensive silence, as if calculating how many people it would take to stand off a tank. Finally, a solution occurred to him: "The sheriff can stop them. The sheriff has the power to stop the National Guard, the federal government, everybody."

Someone looked up the number. Reaching a voice mail, the citizen scientist left a message: "Attention, Sheriff. We need you over here at the barbershop. Please come here immediately to attend to a situation. We need your help here to defend our constitutional rights. Please hurry up."

After a while, it became apparent that neither the sheriff nor the National Guard was coming. I went back outside. The family had stopped singing and was now reciting scripture. Psalm 2: "Why do the nations conspire and the peoples plot in vain?" The patriarch was joined by his son, daughter, and one-year-old grandson. "If there's children, they won't shoot tear gas," he said. "That's my hope, anyway—if we're here, they back off."

"Who backs off?" I asked.

"The Nazis."

TWO

WORK

A stylist named Anne had volunteered to help Manke with the onslaught of customers. She'd installed herself in a back room, her face concealed by an American flag bandanna. A mother of three, she was understandably worried about losing her license. Still, she felt a moral obligation to support Manke. "He's opening the door for all of us to get back to work," she said.

I asked if she was eligible for unemployment.

"I am," Anne responded. "But I don't want to be socialist. I don't want somebody feeding me. That's the point. The point is: that's not America."

A man with grease-stained palms and a whirling cowlick entered the room. "Short as possible," he told Anne. He was a tow-truck driver named Rusty Wheeler. So was his son. His grandson, Rusty Wheeler III, was not yet old enough to drive.

"I junk cars," Rusty said. "The mills just opened back up because of the lack of metal for ventilators and what have you. I've towed five cars since then, and honestly? It felt awesome. Just working. I don't know how to explain it."

"That's how it is for me," said Anne.

"A month and a half inside—I never did that my entire life," Rusty said. To my astonishment, he had begun to cry. "I always been out working."

Anne nodded. "That's why I'm here. I'm here because I think we should be free."

I also liked to work. That's what I was doing while talking to Anne and Rusty. I could hardly judge them. But if the conflation of work and freedom—the idea of work as an act of liberty as sacrosanct as the right to speech—sounded like a conveniently profitable ethos for ultra-rich industrialists, it was probably because that's who had come up with it. The first "right to work" campaign was launched in the 1940s, by the Christian American Association, an oil lobby firm dedicated to crippling organized labor. In 2012, the billionaires David and Charles Koch resurrected the phrase while spearheading a similar effort in Michigan. They were joined by the DeVos family, which helped create the Michigan Freedom Fund to promote a right-to-work bill that would curb the collective bargaining powers of blue-collar employees. Richard DeVos was the heir to Amway, a multilevel marketing company that has been likened to a pyramid scheme. While the Michigan Freedom Fund presented the right to work as a matter of individual autonomy, detractors saw a cynical ploy to sacrifice the common good for select financial gain. The governor at the time, Rick Snyder, was a Republican. The day he signed the right-to-work bill into law, thousands of factory workers descended on the capitol. Among them was Representative Sarah Anthony's father, a benefits rep for the

United Auto Workers union at a General Motors plant in Lansing. Gretchen Whitmer, then a state senator, delivered a rousing speech to the protesters.

The pandemic had pitched these same ideological camps against each other, and it was unsurprising that those who had equated work with liberty in 2012 would frame the suspension of private business as a form of tyranny in 2020. Trump had made Richard DeVos's wife, Betsy, his secretary of education, but the couple still contributed to the Michigan Freedom Fund. It had been the Michigan Freedom Fund that organized Operation Gridlock, the first anti-lockdown demonstration in the country.

A month later, the group held a second event: Operation Haircut. The weather had thawed. The sky was rich, bright, and empty. A dozen stylists had set up improvised stations on the capitol lawn—scissors immersed in Tupperware containers of blue Barbicide, clippers connected by extension cords to diesel generators—and hundreds of people waited in long lines for complimentary trims. Karl Manke, in his satin smock and thick-rimmed glasses, addressed them from the capitol steps. On the dome above him, a flag flew at half-mast. Almost ninety thousand Americans had died from COVID-19.

"It brought me to my knees," Manke said of the six weeks his shop had been closed. He cited bills, credit, rent. "I could not afford to go without work," he claimed.

I don't know, maybe I'd been in Europe too long. The whole scene felt grotesquely backward. Here was an organization funded by the heirs to a multibillion-dollar racket, advocating for unrestricted commerce in the middle of a pandemic, and enlisting as its mascot a hunched and white-haired septuagenarian who, after six decades of labor, risked personal ruin if he paused for six *weeks*. Manke, though, had no complaints about any of that. Instead, he again brought up the Jews—those pitiable Jews who "willingly got into the cattle cars"—and vowed with gusto, "I refuse to live in a police state!"

The crowd erupted in applause.

THE UNFORTUNATE PART

When quarantine advocates accused anti-lockdowners of refusing to make sacrifices during a time of national crisis, they implied a lack of patriotism. But skeptics of the scientific rationale for lockdowns rejected the premise that the nation was in a crisis. For them, what they had lost was not a sacrifice; it was a theft. Doubt about the seriousness of COVID-19 circumvented any question of selfishness. Social distancing and wearing masks didn't make you a good citizen; it made you a benighted conformist—one of the "sheeple." Such personal exoneration could be a powerful incentive for otherwise reasonable conservatives to entertain outlandish claptrap.

One of the few women I met at the barbershop was Jane, a middle-aged local from Owosso, who'd come for the company. Jane lived alone, and the forced isolation of the lockdown had been taxing for her. "I've had all-time lows," she told me in the waiting area, where she was helping to answer the phone. "The governor doesn't address mental wellness, only the virus."

"That's what they're counting on," a young man sitting near us interjected. "That people don't talk to each other." He wore a leather racing jacket. A hunting knife was sheathed on his belt and a crucifix tattooed on his hand. His name was Wyatt. "That's what the social distancing is for," he said.

"Right," responded Jane, politely.

"There's a facial-recognition company in Israel," Wyatt went on.

"They have new technology to do mass scanning of faces on the Polygon system."

"Uh-huh," Jane said.

"They need people spaced apart for it to work."

I was about to point out the benefit of masks in thwarting such technology when an older man with gray hair and orthopedic sneakers preempted me: "They have refined it to the point where all they need to see is the eyes."

Whereas Wyatt had seemed to put Jane on guard, the older man was clearly harmless. Turning toward him, she nodded eagerly. "Like what's the movie—*The Matrix*? I mean, I can relate so much of this to so many movies."

"Yes!" the older man said. "They're telling us what's going to happen."

He and Wyatt had met outside a few minutes earlier. Wyatt had driven to Owosso from Oklahoma because he viewed Manke's act of civil disobedience as a flash point in a rapidly escalating global emergency. Satan worshippers were consolidating control within the US government—and not only there. "We've had a slow roll of all these weirdos who have proliferated through academia and the media," he told Jane. "This is all online, easy to look up."

"Mm-hmm," Jane said.

"Have you heard this stuff before?"

"I've heard it. But I never really followed up on it." She sighed. "Because it all depresses me."

"That's the unfortunate part," the older man said. "We block it out because we don't want to feel that pain. But we need to feel the pain to understand."

"I agree," said Jane, sighing again. "I look at it until my anxiety gets so high, my heart starts pounding so hard I can hear it. Then I have to stop."

Wyatt seemed to have the opposite reaction. As he expounded on the Satanists, his excitement grew into a force you almost had to lean away from. It was my first brush with something that I would soon have ample opportunity to observe among Christian conspiracists: their borderline euphoric thrill at witnessing prophesy fulfilled. "I used to have more time," Wyatt told us, tense and wide-eyed. "I had weeks, and then I had days, and now it's like every couple of hours something happens somewhere in the country. If it all keeps going like this, I'm gonna push forward to D.C."

I asked what was in D.C.

"I have friends out there. They're mobilizing a task force to protect the president."

I MADE A FILE IN which I briefly summarized each theory and described the individual who'd shared it with me: age, profession, look. Apart from their near-universal acceptance of Jesus Christ as their personal savior, I discerned no obvious pattern or through line. There was the physical education teacher who thought that PCR tests were detecting exosomes, a vital component of healthy cells; the college student who ascribed the pandemic to "a depopulation agenda—they think we're flies"; the General Motors quality-control officer who believed that germ theory was "a lie implanted into the human race by Satan back in the eighteen hundreds"; and the solar-panel installer who had stockpiled an immense reserve of pennies, which, during the coming collapse, would retain their value as a raw material for electrical wire. Many people urged me to watch *Plandemic*, an online video positing that Anthony Fauci, the director of the National Institute of Allergy and Infectious Diseases, had deliberately released COVID-19, suppressed effective treatments, and falsified epidemiological data in order to enrich patent holders of lethal vaccines.

A unifying theme among the myriad and sometimes conflicting

hypotheses was that the ultimate objective of the hoax was to prevent Donald Trump from being reelected. "The Demoncrats are using every little trick in their pathetic toolbox," an elderly Tea Party stalwart named Marlene told me at Operation Haircut. She wore cheap sunglasses and a red MAGA hat with numerous pins and combs bulging underneath it. ("I was supposed to get a perm two months ago," she fumed. "I don't even recognize myself.") According to Marlene, the "Demoncrats" were desperate to neutralize Trump because he was "*the only one*" standing in the way of the New World Order.

Fear of the New World Order had fueled right-wing nativism ever since the Cold War, when antisemites like William Potter Gale leveraged widespread fears of international Communism to warn of a Jewish plot to rule the planet. After the collapse of the Soviet Union, liberal elites became the villainous puppet masters set on global totalitarianism. In 1991, the televangelist Pat Robertson published his bestselling book, *The New World Order*, which claimed that "European bankers" and the Rothschild family manipulated world events in order to preserve their economic hegemony. By 2020, George Soros had replaced the Rothschilds as the Jewish financier of elaborate schemes to subjugate white Christians (for instance, with migrant convoys from Central America). It was Soros, several anti-lockdowners told me, who had engaged Anthony Fauci to concoct the virus.

I asked Marlene what the New World Order would look like if Soros and his cohort succeeded.

"It would be a one-world government and all the people would be subject to the state," she said. "Your role in life is to work for the state. There's no pursuit of happiness. You have quotas, you have supervision, you have people telling you where to go, when to go, and with whom to go. Have you heard about contact tracing?"

Democrats in Congress had recently introduced a bill, infelicitously titled "House Resolution 6666," that would have allocated funds for hiring and training contact tracers. The legislation was crafted to support medically underserved communities with high infection rates, such as Detroit. Conservatives on social media had advanced a range of false claims, including that the bill would empower federal agents to remove people from their homes and put them in quarantine centers resembling concentration camps.

"That's not for our health," Marlene said. "That's to take away our rights."

Conspiracists projected menace onto the world—they endowed phenomena with malicious intent. At some point while I was sitting with Marlene, we stopped talking politics and lapsed into normal conversation. Her "standard drink" was tequila and tonic, which she preferred to consume with avocado potato chips. When she was younger, she'd been a green belt in judo; now she did tai chi. "I have rocks in my legs for muscles," she said. She'd grown up in Appalachia, where her father had gone to work in a coal mine when he was twelve, after her grandfather died in one. Marlene was funny, tough, and charming. When I ran out of questions, I found myself lingering with her in easy silence, the sun on our faces, admiring the cobalt sky.

"It's nice to not see chemtrails," she said.

"Chemtrails?" I asked.

"They have particles in there that when they get in your lungs it stays there. Little tiny plastic pellets."

I nodded.

"Because they're trying to kill us," Marlene said.

TOWARD THE END of the American Patriot Council rally at Rosa Parks Circle, a man with neatly coiffed white hair, pleated slacks, a

plaid button-down, and a beige windbreaker joined the militia members
onstage. He was Mike Shirkey, the Michigan Senate majority leader,
and his conventional appearance belied an ostentatious flair. Taking
the mic, the senator cleared his throat and, sans preamble, belted out
"God Bless America."

I'd heard about Shirkey's singing. On April 7, he had opened a legislative session with a stirring recital of "It Is Well with My Soul." The
pandemic was still novel, and the purpose of the session was to vote on
extending Whitmer's state of emergency, a move that would grant her
the power to issue executive orders. At the time, all American governors had invoked similar authorities. The Michigan legislature was as
riven by partisanship as the rest of the country, but that day a rare spirit
of comity prevailed. A week earlier, the virus had killed a forty-four-
year-old Democratic representative, whose empty desk was now draped
in black cloth. After Shirkey's performance, the lieutenant governor
presided over the vote in a T-shirt that read: EVERYBODY VS COVID-19.
The motion passed unanimously.

After the American Patriot Council and Michigan Liberty Militia
entered the state capitol on April 30, Shirkey released a statement condemning their use of "intimidation and the threat of physical harm to
stir up fear and feed rancor." He added, "At best, those so-called protesters are a bunch of jackasses." The political divide over COVID-19
had since yawned into an unbridgeable chasm, and Shirkey had come
to Rosa Parks Circle with hat in hand. Actually, he'd come with a Bible
and a bound copy of the Constitution in hand. "One book gives us our
rights, assigns them to us, is alienable," he declared, raising the Bible.
"The other book is supposed to *defend* our rights." The crowd liked
that. Most anti-lockdowners I had met subscribed to a version of constitutional fundamentalism that was inseparable from their Christian
faith. The only legitimate role of government, they believed, was the
protection of individual liberties vouchsafed to humanity by God. In

subordinating the Constitution to the Bible, Shirkey was accusing Governor Whitmer not only of overstepping her legal mandate, but of transgressing against Christ. "That's when these groups need to stand up and test that assertion of authority by the government," he went on. Gesturing at the same armed individuals whom, a couple of weeks before, he had called at best a bunch of jackasses, Shirkey told them, "We need you now more than ever."

The Senate majority leader's volte-face suggested that, however fringe the anti-lockdowners might seem, they were more ahead of mainstream conservatism than to the right of it. Obama had carried Michigan in 2004 and 2008, but Hillary Clinton had lost the state, by a little more than ten thousand votes. For Trump to defeat Joe Biden in November, he would need to repeat that upset. Throughout the pandemic, the president had savaged Whitmer and encouraged anti-lockdowners. ("LIBERATE MICHIGAN," he tweeted after Operation Gridlock.) He seemed to be wagering that the modest number of diehards like Marlene who showed up for protests were merely the vanguard of a much larger demographic—one that might make the difference in November. He had reason to be hopeful. On April 9, before any rallies had taken place, Garrett Soldano, a chiropractor from Onsted, had created a Facebook page called Michiganders Against Excessive Quarantine. Within a month, the group counted more than four hundred thousand members. Soldano told me that he was stunned by the response and unsure how to proceed. He soon found himself on a Zoom call with Republican state senators—"to figure out what we needed to do." The senators recommended a petition to revoke Whitmer's emergency powers. "That gave us a goal that we needed to achieve," Soldano said.

In early May, Facebook deleted several similar accounts, whose comments sections had devolved into profane, misogynistic attacks on Whitmer. On May 12, I was scrolling through Michiganders Against

Excessive Quarantine when a member of the group said of the governor, "She is literally killing people, she must be stopped." Another
wrote, "Hopefully, Nuremburg style hearings will commence to shine
the light on everyone who had a hand in this whole pandemic." That
afternoon, the page vanished.

In an email, a Facebook spokesperson said that the group had been
removed "for repeated violations of our Community Standards"; Soldano told me that he had been reprimanded for "advocating the spread
of disease" after he live-streamed a video from Karl Manke's barbershop. When he set up a new page, many of his followers joined him
there. Facebook's censorship had only quickened their sense of dispossession, proven that their unseen enemies were real, and redoubled their
determination to fight back.

"They took away our stories, our truth!"

"You just added fuel to the fire."

"THERE'S AN INFERNO BURNING."

In addition to being a chiropractor, Soldano worked as a motiva-
tional speaker. He had also authored a self-help book, *God's True Law*,
in which he explained that disease could be "caused by interferences
in the natural vibrational frequencies." In 2019, he became a national
director for Juice Plus+, a dietary-supplement company with a multilevel marketing strategy modeled on the Amway structure. Two days
after Facebook removed Michiganders Against Excessive Quarantine,
Soldano launched a website called Stand Up Michigan, whose home
page featured a video of him wearing a blue suit with a pocket square,
standing outside the capitol in Lansing. "We want to be the lantern in
the darkness of today's challenges," he proclaimed.

The website promised subscribers "dynamic content," such as "relevant and timely information on current issues" and "expert insight and
education." I became an "associate member" for ten dollars a month—
the cheapest option—but never managed to log on. The only part of

the site accessible for free was an online store, which sold backpacks ($190), yard signs ($150), and other merchandise. Products showcased the Stand Up logo: a silhouette of Paul Revere astride a galloping horse, holding a lantern.

On May 21, Soldano organized a "Freedom Festival" in Newaygo, a small town on the Muskegon River. In a park with an outdoor amphitheater, corporate-looking banners read EQUIP AND EMPOWER; tables under tents displayed Stand Up apparel. Hundreds of people spread blankets on the grass and hunkered down in camping chairs. Eventually, Soldano took the stage. He'd been a linebacker for Western Michigan University and remained solidly constructed. In his book, Soldano writes that "resonation (Law of Vibration) is an energy field you send out to God"; therefore, "whatever you focus on becomes your reality." As he led the crowd in chants of "USA," the author appeared to put this theory into practice, beaming with the spirited positivity of an ardent convert to the power of vibes. Then he issued a nonsensical series of words with such thrumming emotion that it was difficult not to be inspired by them: "Every action is a call set in motion, and its effects build on past effects, to move us in a definite direction. That direction is our destiny. That direction is the new America!" He added, "Buy some T-shirts, support the movement."

Everybody in Newaygo, not just Soldano, looked decidedly happy. Happy to be outside. Happy to be unmasked. And happy to be in like-minded company. When a woman near me asked a family at a picnic table if she could sit with them, a man told her, "If you don't mind not social-distancing."

"The only thing we're gonna spread is democracy and freedom," she replied.

The atmosphere of embattled camaraderie reminded me of a customer at Manke's barbershop who had been placing flowers on his mother's grave every Mother's Day for the past sixty years. Usually, there were so many mourners that the free cone vases for bouquets went fast. "I always keep one in the truck," the man explained. This year, the cemetery was deserted. "There were tons of cones," he said. "I was shocked." As he spoke, the other customers wagged their heads. The story illustrated for them something unspeakably grim, not about the virus but about a society that had lost its moorings.

I spent most of Freedom Festival toward the front of the audience, near the stage, beside a potbellied man in a STAND UP MICHIGAN hat and shirt. He was so profoundly in agreement with everything being said that he resembled a worshipper at a Baptist revival, punctuating the speeches with yelps of "Yes!" and "All right!" At one point, the owner of a mixed-martial-arts studio informed the crowd that he had reopened his gym after researching COVID-19 and concluding that widespread exposure to the virus would "perpetuate and move the species throughout history." My neighbor fervently applauded. When Toby Keith's "Courtesy of the Red, White and Blue" came on, he seemed momentarily overwhelmed. "I *love* this music," he told me. "I *love* this, brother." He scanned the park, taking it all in.

"*These are my people.*"

THREE

THE FIREFIGHTER

A s Sarah Anthony watched the Michigan Liberty Militia as-
semble below her office on April 30, she took to Facebook to
livestream the view from her window. One of her constituents, Michael Lynn Jr., watched the video with a rising feeling of anger
at the armed men outside. He could see that Anthony was scared—
and he took that personally. Lynn was also African American and born
and raised in Lansing. "When Black and brown people elevate someone
from our community to that level, we can't allow her to be intimidated
to speak for us," he later told me. A week after the rally, along with his
wife, Erica, and their twenty-year-old son, Michael III, Lynn escorted
Anthony from her office to an Appropriations Committee hearing. He
and Michael carried assault rifles; Erica wore a holstered Glock. Anthony, an advocate of gun-law reform, had been reluctant to accept
Lynn's offer of protection at first. But, she told me afterward, "I will
say that I felt safer."

In 1967, Huey Newton and Bobby Seale, the founders of the Black Panther Party for Self-Defense, led a group of armed African Americans into the California statehouse, in Sacramento, to protest a Republican-sponsored bill that would criminalize guns in public. Pictures of the demonstration shocked white America. After Governor Ronald Reagan signed the bill, which received the endorsement of the National Rifle Association, he declared, "There's no reason why, on the street today, a citizen should be carrying loaded weapons." Like the Panthers—and, before them, Malcolm X, who grew up in Lansing and whose home there was burned down by a white mob when he was four—Lynn viewed gun ownership as a means of empowerment and enfranchisement. He'd met Erica at a high school football game in 1998, when he was seventeen. She was sixteen and supporting the opposing team. They began talking on the phone. Lynn often mentioned his best friend, Aldric McKinstry, whom Erica was eager to meet. The weekend she was supposed to do so, Lynn and Aldric were at a party when squad cars arrived. Aldric ran, found an open storm hatch, and hid in someone's basement. The police released a German shepherd into it. They later claimed that Aldric fired on the dog. Officers shot him six times, including once in the head. Lynn is adamant that Aldric had no gun. Although he explained this to detectives at the time, Lynn told me, "They didn't want to hear it." An article in the archives of the *Lansing State Journal* features a picture of him at Aldric's funeral. "They are just trying to justify killing him," he's quoted as saying. No officers were disciplined in the affair.

After high school, Lynn married Erica, had Michael III, and started a business installing low-voltage appliances. In 2014, the Lansing Fire Department undertook to diversify its workforce with an initiative to recruit people of color. Lynn applied. "I love this community, and what better way to give back than saving lives?" he said. He excelled in his training and aced his evaluations, but when he reported to his firehouse, he was met with hostility by colleagues who resented the diversity program. "Disdain and contempt" was how Lynn described their attitude toward him. "It's a good-old-boy network, a legacy network. Minorities have had to infiltrate, but they fight it tooth and nail." Over the next three years, Lynn reported numerous incidents of harassment and discrimination to his superiors. No action was taken. Most of the white firefighters were Trump supporters, and during the 2016 election Lynn noticed a change in tone reflective of the national discourse. In early 2017, about a month after Trump took office, he was assigned to a truck with another Black firefighter. One day, they found a banana pinned beneath their windshield wiper. When their supervisor saw no reason to investigate, Lynn filed a formal complaint with human resources and, citing work-related stress, anxiety, and depression, went on administrative leave.

At the time, Michael III was a senior at Lansing Catholic High School and the star quarterback of its football team. The previous season, the San Francisco 49er Colin Kaepernick had begun kneeling during the national anthem to raise awareness of police brutality. In September, at a rally in Alabama, Trump said that any "son of a bitch" engaging in such protest should be "fired" for their "total disrespect of our heritage." A few days later, Michael and three of his Black teammates informed their coach that they, too, planned to kneel. In a letter to parents, the president of Lansing Catholic warned that "any student-athlete who chooses not to stand will receive consequences." He added, "As always, this will be handled with Christian Charity, with the goal of growth in virtue." At the next game, Michael and his teammates followed through on their word. The coach benched them—but then, with the team falling behind, Michael was put in. He threw a touchdown and ran for two more, winning the game. After the final whistle, Lynn noticed that his son was having trouble speaking and brought him to the hospital. A rough tackle had bruised Michael's heart and torn his chest wall, causing a tension pneumothorax. With every inhalation, air escaped into the pleural cavity, inflicting sharp pain. He remained in the ICU for two days.

"It was like this heroic story," Lynn recalled. "This kid stands up for his nation, wins the game, damn near dies. . . ." But the story didn't end there. Throughout the year, scouts from multiple Michigan colleges with Division 1 football teams had been courting Michael. After he took a knee, the calls stopped. He ultimately accepted an offer from Concordia University, a Division 2 school. "At the end, it was our only option to get some sort of scholarship," Lynn said. He could see how disillusioning the experience had been for Michael. "He'd put a lot into being a recruitable kid. He'd stayed out of trouble, avoided Facebook. So I think he was bitter."

Lynn was also bitter. In 2018, he'd gone back to work. Despite the fire department's much-vaunted diversity program, its new class was all white men. Lynn found himself the target of a sustained retaliation campaign, with his supervisors issuing him five disciplinary actions in as many months. According to Lynn, the infractions—of inconsistently enforced rules related to "insubordination" and "personal conduct"— were all "ramped up" and unwarranted. Lansing's Democratic mayor, meanwhile, continued to tout the diversity program by publishing pictures of smiling Black firefighters on social media. In April 2019, Lynn vented his frustration on Facebook. "White liberals want diversity and inclusion until the black man walks in the room," he wrote. "Then it's back to the same old shit." Some days later, an assistant fire chief summoned him. The reason for the meeting was not Lynn's allegations of harassment and endemic racism in the department. It was his Facebook post. Due to his failure to "maintain the highest standards of integrity," as mandated in the Lansing Fire Department operating guidelines, he was told that he'd been suspended for two weeks without pay.

. . .

I FIRST MET LYNN in a Lansing parking lot while he was en route to a shooting range for target practice. He looked exactly like an off-duty firefighter: clean-cut and in shape, with an easy confidence to his gait and posture. He also exuded a kind of hyperalertness that was typical of concealed carriers. When a sedan with tinted windows passed us, Lynn stopped talking mid-sentence and watched it until it was gone. He said that when he first applied for his concealed pistol license, in 2010, he was denied. Although he had no criminal record, state authorities cited past "police contacts," which is not a valid justification, as a reason to refuse him the permit. According to Lynn, people of color often faced unusual bureaucratic obstacles to legally arming themselves. In 2014, he successfully appealed the decision, and now he administered a Facebook page, Black and Brown 2a Advocates, which he'd created to expand minority gun ownership in Lansing. "You see these white groups, they're stockpiling ammunition while everybody else is stockpiling toilet paper," he said. "They're preparing for a war that we ain't prepared for."

The day before, there'd been another anti-lockdown rally at the capitol. In anticipation of the event, the legislature had adjourned, forestalling the possibility of an armed mob again accosting lawmakers. I had attended the protest and had come away thinking that the decision had been shrewd. Without anyone to yell at or threaten, the gathering felt directionless. The most exciting moment was when a deranged man showed up with a hatchet, causing militia members with assault rifles to shriek, "This guy has a fucking axe! He's got a weapon!" When it started to rain, everyone went home.

Lynn considered the adjournment a grave mistake. "What happened at the capitol that's not being talked about is that they shut down session because they were scared," he said. "That sets a precedent. That shows people that 'Damn, we can go down there and get whatever we want if we bring guns.'"

By then I had learned that many anti-lockdowners were already following precedent. Several had cited the Bundy family as their impetus for taking up arms. In 2014, Cliven Bundy, an elderly rancher in Nevada, had declared war against the government when the Bureau of Land Management impounded his cattle over his refusal to pay more than a million dollars in outstanding grazing fees. Hundreds rallied to his cause. After a tense standoff in which Bundy supporters surrounded law enforcement agents and trained rifles on them from a hilltop, the Bureau of Land Management released the livestock and withdrew from the area. A year later, Bundy's sons, Ryan and Ammon, fomented opposition to a federal arson case against fellow ranchers in Oregon. Dozens of right-wingers again answered the call. Some of them seized the headquarters of the Malheur National Wildlife Refuge. Their grievance was the same age-old grievance that had animated white militancy since Reconstruction: a belief that something rightfully belonging to them had been usurped or stolen. The founder of the Constitutional Sheriffs and Peace Officers Association, Richard Mack, had joined the Bundys in Nevada. "This was Rosa Parks refusing to get to the back of the bus," he later said.

The emboldening success of the Nevada showdown had led to the armed occupation in Oregon, which had inspired the storming of the capitol in Lansing. What would the emboldening success of the American Patriot Council and the Michigan Liberty Militia lead to? Lynn wasn't sure—he only knew that it would not be good for citizens who looked like him. "That's why I'm arming my people," he said. "This shit is coming. It's coming. And we need to protect our own."

MEMORIAL DAY

In 2011, while on assignment for *The New York Times Magazine*, I embedded with US Marines at a remote outpost in southern Afghanistan. A staff sergeant I befriended there, Vincent Bell, was from Detroit. Though we were the same age—twenty-eight—Vincent seemed much older to me. He'd enlisted in the Marines while he was still in high school, shipped to Parris Island, South Carolina, on his eighteenth birthday, and participated in the invasion of Baghdad two years later. He'd gone on to fight in Fallujah and Mosul; when we met in Afghanistan, he was on his fifth deployment. The outpost was called the Shrine, and it was the northernmost American position in Helmand, the deadliest province in the country. Everything beyond the Shrine—vast desert, river valleys, and canyon land—belonged to the Taliban. I had joined the previous unit at the end of its tour and was there when Vincent's battalion took over. During his first night at the Shrine, insurgents attacked the outpost with machine guns until dawn. Vincent seemed to relish the action. Crouching behind sandbags with a local police officer, who wildly showered rounds into the dark, he cried, "You boys are raw! I mean raw, raw, raw!" When the Afghan looked up with a quizzical expression, Vincent smiled. "Don't get me wrong—I like it!"

The next day, I accompanied a squad on its first foot patrol of the area. After a short distance, we were pinned down in a heavy, complex ambush. In addition to their rifles and automatic weapons, the Marines had to use grenades, smoke, and a rocket launcher to battle their way back to the Shrine, covering each other while they sprinted across dry creek beds and open fields littered with improvised explosive devices, or IEDs. It was close. As bullets whizzed and cracked into the rocks around us, Vincent displayed preternatural calm. I stayed with the unit a few more days, and then caught a helicopter to another district. A week and a half later, near the Shrine, Vincent stepped on an IED and died.

I often thought of him while I was in Michigan. The Marine Corps has long been the whitest branch of the military, and Vincent was one of a very small number of Black noncommissioned officers I had encountered during two months with various units in Helmand. What would he have made of the Michigan Liberty Militia? What would he have made of Donald Trump? Shortly after coming to Lansing I had contacted Vincent's older sister London. To my relief, she was happy to hear from me. A week before Memorial Day, London invited me to spend the holiday afternoon with her; her sister, Andrea; and their mother, Pamela, at a monument in Mount Clemens, a couple of hours east of Lansing.

I arrived early at a county administrative building outside of which a marble column, about eight feet tall, was mounted with a model of the World Trade Center. Twenty names, including Vincent's, were engraved below the words GLOBAL WAR ON TERROR. When the Bells showed up, I had to check an impulse to embrace them. Unlike most of the people I'd been spending time with, London, Andrea, and Pamela all wore masks. We sat on granite benches, and Pamela explained that this was the first year since Vincent's death that they had not visited his grave in Arlington National Cemetery. It wasn't easy, but they had decided that it would be irresponsible to travel.

For the next two hours, we talked about Vincent. September 11th had happened while he was in boot camp. His entire adult life had been defined by conflict. Yet, Pamela and her daughters emphasized, he had remained the same person he'd been while growing up in Detroit: playful, humble, gregarious, and kind. "He never lost his humanity," London said. "He was always himself." Though many of the Marines in Vincent's unit had struggled with post-traumatic stress disorder, alcoholism, or depression, Vincent had shown no signs of these. At restaurants, his self-imposed beverage allowance was two Coronas and a lemonade, served at the same time. According to Pamela, his service had been a deep and consistent source of contentment for him. The last time that Vincent had come home, in October 2011—one month before we met at the Shrine—Pamela cooked him dinner. "When are you getting out of the Marines?" she asked over the meal.

"When are *you* retiring?" Vincent replied. Pamela, who worked as a substance-abuse counselor for homeless youth, made a deal with her son: in 2021, when Vincent had completed a full twenty years in the military, they would both quit their jobs.

As she recounted this story, Pamela smiled at the memory. So far as I could tell, she harbored no resentment. She bore no grudge. Her uncanny serenity was so strikingly incongruous with the magnitude of her loss that I began to worry that she must be putting on a brave face for my sake. Finally, I asked her whether she'd ever felt any anger toward the government.

"I was angry that I had lost my son," Pamela said. "I wasn't angry at the government. I wasn't angry at the Marines. The reason is: If you only knew how much Vincent loved being a Marine. From day one, even just putting on his uniform . . . the time he would take to lay out the straps . . ."

The building in front of us was the bureaucratic headquarters for Macomb County, a collection of lakeside townships some thirty minutes north of Detroit. Months later, after we had gotten to know each other better, Pamela would tell me that her parents had moved there from Georgia in the forties, during the Great Migration of African Americans fleeing racial terrorism in the South. While she was growing up, Macomb was mostly home to middle-class automotive workers and their families. De facto segregation "was built in real clear—you knew where you should not be after a certain time in the evening."

Many whites in Macomb belonged to unions and voted Democrat. Obama, pledging to revitalize America's foundering car industry, won the county twice. The federal bailout of Chrysler and General Motors was a lifeline for blue-collar Michigan; the state added fifty-seven thousand manufacturing jobs during Obama's administration. All the same, whites in Macomb, embracing the message that they had been ignored and abused, contributed more than any other county to flipping Michigan and delivering Trump the presidency. (Three days before the inauguration, an audiotape was leaked of Jim Fouts, the mayor of Warren, Macomb's most populous city, using the N-word and musing that "Blacks do look like chimpanzees." He went on to be reelected by a wide margin.) Even before the pandemic, factory employment throughout Michigan had stagnated and then declined under Trump. But that hardly mattered. Macomb had been converted. One of the cofounders of the American Patriot Council was from the county, and I'd met numerous Macomb residents at anti-lockdown rallies.

The Bell family felt like a living rebuke to the brash and frivolous pageantry of jingoism often found at those events. The pomp and bluster of it all. I could not imagine Pamela, London, or Andrea ever chanting "USA," or adorning themselves in red, white, and blue. They didn't complain about their sacrifice or allow it to engender spite. They never even used that word: *sacrifice.* Before we parted ways, Andrea gave me a rubber bracelet printed with Vincent's name and the date of his death. Only then did I see that she wore one as well. If you hadn't been paying attention, you would never have noticed it.

BY THE TIME I GOT BACK to Lansing from Mount Clemens, a video was circulating online. It showed a white police officer killing an unarmed Black man in Minneapolis.

FOUR

ENOUGH

Within a week, the largest protest movement in American history would convulse major cities, activate the National Guard, and send the president into a subterranean bunker underneath the White House. The video, recorded by a teenage bystander, showed forty-six-year-old George Floyd lying facedown beside a squad car after being arrested for using a counterfeit twenty-dollar bill to buy a pack of cigarettes. His wrists are handcuffed behind his back. An officer, later identified as Derek Chauvin, kneels on his neck. "Please, I can't breathe," Floyd begs. Over the next eight minutes and forty-six seconds, he repeats the appeal more than twenty times, calls for his mother over and over, and tells Chauvin, "You're going to kill me, man." Chauvin never moves his knee. When Floyd's eyes close and his body goes limp, onlookers desperately scream that he is unresponsive. Chauvin withdraws a can of mace and brandishes it at them.

An ambulance arrives. For almost a minute and a half, two EMTs check Floyd's pulse and ready a stretcher. Chauvin continues to kneel on his neck.

The next day, hundreds of mourners gathered at the scene of the crime. From there, some marched two and a half miles across town to the Third Precinct police station, where Chauvin had been assigned. Confrontations between demonstrators and officers escalated over the next two days. On the afternoon of May 28, I was in a laundromat in Lansing when news came over the radio that a large mob had besieged the Third Precinct and city officials were concerned that it might have to be evacuated. I put my wet clothes in a garbage bag and went to my car.

It was a nine-hour drive to Minneapolis. I arrived around two in the morning. The highway into the city was completely empty, downtown deserted. As I neared the Third Precinct, the night sky pulsed with a dusky orange glow. I parked a few blocks from the station and continued on foot. Large buildings were on fire, slowly folding in on themselves. I came to an intersection where hundreds of people stood around two burning US Postal Service trucks. One of the trucks was upside down. A man waved frantically. "Get back! Get back!" Everyone ignored him.

Officers had surrendered the station several hours earlier, fleeing through a side exit while protesters hurled rocks at them. Smoke billowed from the ground floor, and silhouettes roamed the hazy second floor, tossing through the windows anything not bolted down: documents, folders, furniture, phones. There was an electric atmosphere of triumph and abandon. Cars spun doughnuts, motorcycles popped wheelies, fireworks and gunshots punctuated the mayhem. Men in ski masks wielded hammers and bats.

A liquor store had been broken into. Someone wearing earbuds and colorful shorts, walking a bicycle, approached me to announce, "They keep giving me booze!" Like at least half the people there, he was white and in his twenties. In a strip mall opposite the station, looters pushed shopping carts heaped with merchandise out of a Target. Ceiling-mounted sprinklers rained on empty shelves, and a fast-flowing stream carried debris into the parking lot. A group of teenagers, pant cuffs rolled up, emerged lugging mannequins under their arms.

At some point I found myself standing beside a young man silently watching the burning police station as if it were a campfire. "Do you think it's worth it?" he asked.

Having no answer to his question, I offered him the standard cop-out: I was a journalist and would be curious to know what *he* thought. "It doesn't feel right," he said. "I'm not judging anybody here, but I don't agree with all this." Then he asked me again. The fact that I was a reporter only made him more interested in my opinion. The fact that he was Black and from Minneapolis only made me more reluctant to pretend to have one.

"I don't know," I said.

He nodded. "Hopefully, they hear us."

At around four thirty a.m., SUVs from the fire department pulled up outside a roaring conflagration that had consumed several contiguous structures. "Fix this!" a man screamed at them. As we looked on, the entire third floor of one of the buildings thunderously crashed into the street like a downed aircraft.

The SUVs turned around and drove away.

Several young people who knew the Japanese owners of a café that had been trashed were salvaging potted plants from amid the wreckage. "They didn't deserve this," one of them kept saying. An immigrant from Mexico who asked to be identified as Juan pointed at a nearby building that was also engulfed in flames. It had been a Latino-managed restaurant, where his mother had worked. A man in a balaclava stood in front of the inferno, arms spread wide, posing for pictures.

Down the block, a white woman in a tank top and cutoff jeans used the butt of a fire extinguisher to smash the front windows of an independent barbershop.

"These are not the real protesters," Juan said. "These are opportunists."

As we spoke, a car stopped in front of us and a man got out to film the chaos with his phone. When someone objected, the man wheeled on him. "This is my hood! I fucking live here!"

"I live here too! Why you mad?"

"*Everybody's* mad!" the man responded, incredulous. "We're *supposed* to be mad."

I wondered what he meant—mad about Floyd's murder, or mad about the anarchy that it had unleashed? Only later did it occur to me that he'd probably meant both.

JUAN WAS CONVINCED that most of the looters had come from outside Minneapolis for reasons having nothing to do with Floyd. In the following days, local politicians also seized on this idea. Minnesota's Democratic governor, Tim Walz, speculated that 80 percent of the people destroying property were not residents of the state. He attributed the rioting to "ideological extremists" pursuing a campaign of "international destabilization." Among the protesters, rumors spread of white-supremacist infiltrators aiming to delegitimize the demonstrations and instigate a race war.

Cell phone video captured the first known instance of vandalism in the city: a white man in a gas mask holding an umbrella in one hand and using his other to break every window of an AutoZone with a hammer. The AutoZone was located in the same strip mall as the Target opposite the Third Precinct. By the time I arrived, it was a charred shell. Police would identify the man with the hammer as Mitchell Carlson, a "known associate" of the Aryan Cowboy Brotherhood, a neo-Nazi prison gang. A state investigator would write that "the protests had been relatively peaceful" prior to Carlson's actions, which "created an atmosphere of hostility and tension." The AutoZone was set ablaze shortly after Carlson broke its windows; according to the investigator, "this was the first fire that set off a string of fires and looting throughout the precinct and the rest of the city."

Blaming the ugly parts of what happened in Minneapolis on white supremacists, however, had the same effect as Governor Walz's cryptic allusions to external agitators: it elided the real grievances of the city's Black residents. The day after the Third Precinct fell, Leslie Redmond, the president of the NAACP in Minneapolis, told National Public Radio, "What you're witnessing in Minnesota is something that's been a long time coming. I can't tell you how many governors I've sat down with, how many mayors we've sat down with—and we've warned them that, if you keep murdering Black people, this city will burn."

The relationship between Minneapolis's law enforcement and its communities of color had deteriorated during the five years before Floyd's death. In 2015, after a white officer shot and killed a twenty-four-year-old unarmed Black man, Jamar Clark, activists from Black Lives Matter camped outside the officer's precinct house for eighteen days, in snow and frigid temperatures. One night a white man, whose trial would reveal a history of racist comments, opened fire on them, wounding five. The police went on to tear down the encampment and arrest a number of protesters; no charges were brought against the officer who killed Clark. A year later, in a suburb of Saint Paul, a thirty-two-year-old Black man named Philando Castile was shot by a police officer during a traffic stop for a broken taillight. Castile, who had the same concealed pistol license as Michael Lynn Jr., had informed the officer that he was in possession of a legal firearm. His girlfriend, Diamond Reynolds, and her infant daughter were in the car. Reynolds livestreamed the aftermath of the shooting on Facebook. In the video, Castile sits at the wheel, blood spreading through his T-shirt, while Reynolds pleads, "Stay with me," and the officer continues to aim his gun through the window. Castile died. Reynolds was handcuffed and detained. The officer, Jeronimo Yanez, was prosecuted for manslaughter but acquitted.

In 2018, Thurman Blevins, a Black father of three, was killed by two white officers. One of their body cameras captured Blevins running away, with a gun, while calling over his shoulder, "Please, don't shoot me!" He was shot multiple times. Prosecutors found "no basis to issue criminal charges against either officer."

George Floyd was killed on the corner of Thirty-Eighth Street and Chicago Avenue, on the Southside of Minneapolis. African Americans had been concentrated there and across town, on the Northside, ever since anti-Black housing covenants, in the early twentieth century, prohibited them from buying homes elsewhere in the city. Subsequent infrastructure projects and redlining policies diverted resources away from the Northside and Southside while inhibiting African Americans from obtaining mortgages and business loans. At the same time, white neighborhoods grew more affluent. Minneapolis often appeared on lists of the "best places to live" even as its racial disparities ranked among the worst in the country. The median annual income of Black residents in the Twin Cities was less than half that of whites, and while about 75 percent of white families owned their homes, only a quarter of Black families did. Unemployment was more than twice as high for Black residents as it was for white residents.

Many people I met in Minneapolis felt that the police both reflected and enforced these inequalities. In 1999, a law requiring officers to live within the city limits was repealed, allowing suburbanites to join the force; twenty years later, most officers were white, and few came from the neighborhoods that they policed. (Chauvin lived in Oakdale, twenty miles from where he killed Floyd.) African Americans made up about a fifth of the city's population, but when officers physically subdued people—for instance, by hitting or tasing them—60 percent of the time the subjects were Black. A 2015 investigation by the American Civil Liberties Union found that Black people in Minneapolis were nearly nine times more likely than whites to be arrested for low-level offenses such as trespassing or public consumption. That year, the city finally did away with ordinances against "lurking" and "spitting" that had been disproportionately applied against Black residents. In 2007, five high-ranking Black officers sued their employer, alleging pervasive institutional racism, including death threats signed "KKK," sent to them through the departmental mail system. The city settled the lawsuit out of court.

A culture of impunity accompanied patterns of bias. An analysis by Reuters of almost a decade of officer-misconduct claims found that 90 percent of them resulted in no consequences whatsoever. Chauvin, the subject of seventeen complaints, had been disciplined just once; another officer involved in Floyd's death, Tou Thao, had been sued after he allegedly beat up a Black man in handcuffs. (The city paid twenty-five thousand dollars to avoid a trial.) The only officer in recent memory to go to jail for killing someone was Mohamed Noor, a Black Muslim, who'd shot Justine Damond, a white woman.

In the weeks after Floyd's death, city officials would cite the Minneapolis police union as an insurmountable obstacle to accountability. The union's president, Lieutenant Bob Kroll, had been named in the 2007 discrimination suit, which claimed that he wore "a motorcycle jacket with a 'White Power' badge sewn onto it." Since the early nineties, Kroll had been repeatedly accused of racism and excessive force. "I've been involved in three shootings myself, and not one of them has bothered me," he'd said in April. "Maybe I'm different."

I SLEPT FOR A FEW HOURS in my car, then drove to Thirty-Eighth and Chicago. A block away, vehicles spanned the street. Teenage girls were hanging up a banner that announced SACRED SPACE. Messages in chalk—FIGHT BACK, STAY WOKE—covered the asphalt. Notes, cards, mementos, placards, bouquets, and candles lined the sidewalk. So did jugs of milk, used to alleviate the effects of tear gas. People congregated in the intersection. Some had known Floyd. Others had known Jamar Clark or Philando Castile. Several had had encounters with Derek Chauvin. "The cops have written so many false reports on people just because they wanted to whup somebody's ass," said one local. Another, who had grown up nearby, added that any infraction, no matter how minor, risked inciting police brutality. "The way that they conduct themselves for very insignificant situations is way, way beyond what's necessary. At what point do the citizens of a community say 'enough'?"

The community in question was the Southside of Minneapolis. But it was also the United States. Protests against police slayings had been erupting across the country with increasing frequency for the past several years—in New York, after a white officer choked to death Eric Garner, a forty-three-year-old father, on a Staten Island sidewalk; in Ferguson, Missouri, after a white officer shot dead Michael Brown, an unarmed eighteen-year-old; in Baltimore, after twenty-five-year-old Freddie Gray suffered a fatally severed spine while shackled in the back of a police transport van; and in Louisville, Kentucky, after a plainclothes unit forced its way into the apartment of Breonna Taylor, a twenty-six-year-old emergency medical technician, and killed her in her hallway. The names Garner, Brown, Gray, and Taylor, along with two dozen others, surrounded a vibrant portrait of George Floyd already painted over the brick wall of the bodega where he'd bought his last pack of cigarettes. But their stories were not all that had nationalized what might have otherwise remained a local tragedy. The night before, the president had tweeted that the protesters in Minneapolis were "THUGS," threatened to deploy the military to "get the job done right," and warned, "When the looting starts, the shooting starts." One young woman at the intersection compared this threat to Trump's goading of the anti-lockdowners in Michigan. "That clown in office is calling us thugs?" she demanded. "But white people can parade around with AK-47s in the name of a fucking haircut?"

In 1989, Trump had paid for a full-page ad in *The New York Times* advocating the death penalty for five Black and Latino teenagers accused of raping a white woman. "I want to hate these muggers and murderers," he wrote. "I want them to understand our anger. I want them to be afraid." After DNA evidence exonerated the suspects, he stood by his call for their executions. "The police doing the original investigation say they were guilty," he said. Such unconditional allegiance had won him broad support from law enforcement. In October, Lieutenant Bob Kroll had appeared with Trump at a campaign rally in Minneapolis. Wearing a COPS FOR TRUMP T-shirt, Kroll had lamented "the handcuffing and oppression of police" under the Obama administration, and praised Trump for "letting cops do their jobs."

What had disturbed me most about the video of Floyd's death was Derek Chauvin's apparent stoicism as he patiently extinguished the life under his knee. His gaze was blank. He did not bully, taunt, or curse at Floyd. He barely looked at him. The impression I had was indeed of a man doing his job, like a butcher or a barber. But where I had detected only sociopathic apathy—emptiness—the people at Thirty-Eighth and Chicago seemed to see something much more lurid and alive.

"It's pure hate," a man said of the officers who policed the neighbor-hood. Chauvin was not an aberration; he was a reminder. "Sometimes they don't even take you to jail," the man explained. "They'll take you to an alley and beat the hell out of you." He shook his head. "It's insane here, and people are sick of it."

THAT EVENING THRONGS OF PROTESTERS filled the road between the still-smoking Third Precinct house and the gutted Target. Some were equipped with helmets, goggles, and sheet metal; others wore plywood shields strapped onto their forearms. A rusty van marked with a cross of red tape served as an ambulance. Two teenagers stood on its roof, making out. Ramparts had been built with tables from the Japa-nese café. In the distance, the blue and red lights of squad cars flashed. They were parked on Lake Street, a main commercial artery that led directly to the next-closest station, in the Fifth Precinct. The protest-ers faced them, crying out Floyd's name. When the squad cars re-treated, exultation gripped the crowd.

Teenagers piled onto the hoods of slow-moving cars; people danced; residents waved from porches and lawn chairs, as if watching a parade. Night was falling as we neared the Fifth Precinct. Two perimeters made of concrete barriers topped with tall fencing surrounded the building. Officers in helmets and gas masks, armed with rubber-bullet guns, stood on the roof. At a Stop-N-Shop, men with crowbars had removed sheets of plywood from the entrance, and a stream of looters filed out with goods. A young woman in Doc Martens and a hooded sweat-shirt chastised them: "Y'all are stupid! This is about the police!" A middle-aged white man, wearing a motorcycle helmet with the face shield pulled down, ducked out carrying bulk boxes of Advil and

Tylenol. The girl pointed at the Fifth Precinct. "*That's* where we should be!"

In a strip mall behind the Stop-N-Shop, people systematically smashed storefronts with bats and shovels while others emptied a Kmart and an Office Depot. A teenager staggered across the parking lot with a large box of printing paper. "Yo, I got paper!" he joyfully announced. A white man carrying a sign that read PRAY FOR GEORGE watched the looting of a Subway with a bemused expression; when someone inside yelled, "Free cookies!" he dropped the sign and entered through a broken window. The next time I spotted the girl in Doc Martens, she was outside a burning Dollar Tree, collecting loose bottles of Crystal Geyser and stacking them in a neat pile. "People are probably going to need water," she said.

Her name was Chantaveia. She was eighteen years old and lived with her parents, a few blocks away. When I asked her the same question the young man had asked me the night before—"Do you think it's worth it?"—I was surprised by her response. "It's potentially the only way we're gonna get heard." She paused to reflect, and then added with more certitude, "I feel like rioting is the only way."

Across the strip mall, on a second-story balcony, a woman cradling an infant watched a group of men hurl rocks through the glass front of an optometrist's office below her apartment. People behind the Stop-N-Shop launched bottles, bricks, and commercial-grade fireworks at the officers on the precinct roof. Just opposite the station, a US post office was on fire. The heat was so intense that bricks were popping off its walls. A Latino man in blue jeans and polished leather boots approached as near as possible, wincing against the repulsive power of the flames. What was he doing? When he could get no closer, he leaned over, picked up a piece of concrete, and hurled it into the pyre. "Fuck you!" he yelled before walking on. The gesture felt like pure catharsis—as emotionally momentous as it was practically futile.

A Wells Fargo stood a block away. Something under the hood of a burning sedan abandoned at the drive-through ATM exploded. By midnight a mob had broken into the bank. In a room with overturned filing cabinets, computers, and money-counting machines, two men stood before a safe, arguing over a set of keys. Through a teller window, people handed out random items: iPads, documents, zippered cash-register bags. Smoke billowed. When it became clear that there was nothing to steal—or nothing left—a chant rose in volume and vehemence: "Burn it down!" As if on cue, a dreadlocked man with a bottle of Seagram's 7 in the side pouch of his backpack appeared, holding up a can of gasoline. To rhapsodic cheers, he vanished into the bank. When he reemerged, the can was gone.

"We don't need money anymore!" someone yelled.

"We are the police now!"

A kid in wraparound sunglasses with the price tag still attached stumbled past me. "Is this shit real?" I heard him mutter to himself. "Am I fucking dreaming?"

Soon the Wells Fargo was consumed by cracking flames that were big and bright enough to throw into detailed relief the officers still standing on the precinct roof.

A helicopter idled overhead. Eventually, police units reinforced by soldiers from the National Guard began pushing the crowds back with a barrage of tear gas, stun grenades, pepper balls, and rubber bullets. The rioters withdrew into the strip mall, where they improvised a series of barricades with signs, barrels, drainpipes, and other materials from a nearby construction site. A core element of these remaining protesters—most of whom, once again, were young and white—shouted orders: "Pull back! . . . Hold here! . . . Regroup!" Their tactics reminded me of the *gilets jaunes* demonstrations in 2018, in Paris, where I'd seen black-clad youth physically keep at bay a unit of gendarmerie, or military police, with paving stones pried loose from the Avenue Marceau. Many of them had identified as antifascists and belonged to a long tradition of leftist organizing that viewed law enforcement and far-right politicians as equal and allied adversaries. Though I didn't know it at the time—the gas and projectiles precluded my interrogating any-one about their ideology—this was likely my first encounter with the American version of those European activists.

After a few hours of pitched confrontation, most people had vacated the zone; those who remained were forced to withdraw several blocks. At around two in the morning I found Chantaveia again. She was sit-ting on a curb with one of her Doc Martens off, holding her foot. A rubber bullet had struck her toe; blood oozed through her sock. A friend from her high school sat beside her—his head had been grazed and his left eye was swollen shut. The police line was advancing steadily toward us, deploying more munitions. Chantaveia struggled to rise and limp away. I walked with her for a while, to the neighborhood where she lived. At some point one of her teachers picked her up and brought her home. As we said goodbye, Chantaveia assured me that she did not regret coming out. "It'll continue," she predicted. "People will be back tomorrow."

They were.

MAKE THE WORLD STOP

In the 1800s, Wachovia, a subsidiary of Wells Fargo, regularly accepted slaves as collateral for mortgages and loans. Long after slavery was abolished, Wells Fargo continued issuing mortgages and loans to whites only. As recently as 2012, the Justice Department had sued Wells Fargo for saddling Hispanic and Black borrowers with higher interest rates, fees, penalties, and payment hikes than it did its white customers. Such predatory lending significantly contributed to the financial crisis. A top sales manager from the bank testified in a lawsuit filed by the city of Baltimore that Wells Fargo had steered African Americans toward default-prone subprime loans even when they qualified for prime loans. According to the manager, Black churches in poor neighborhoods were often targeted, prompting loan officers to "morbidly joke" that they were "riding the stagecoach from hell." In a separate affidavit, a Wells Fargo mortgage consultant described his colleagues referring "to sub-prime loans made in minority communities as 'ghetto loans,'" and to minority customers as "mud people." Two months after its Minneapolis branch was incinerated, Wells Fargo would pay a multimillion-dollar settlement to the Department of Labor, for discriminating against its own employees. The CEO would explain the lack of diversity in his workforce this way: "The unfortunate reality is that there is a very limited pool of black talent to recruit from."

The sacking of the Wells Fargo felt like a concrete enactment of something that I'd sensed more diffusely behind much of the rioting in Minneapolis: disgust with American capitalism, and a general awareness that the economic inequalities it preserved aligned with a racial hierarchy kept in place by officers like Derek Chauvin. Burning down banks and precinct houses both fulfilled the same desire for revenge; "We don't need money anymore!" was another way of saying "We are the police now!" The man with the gas can and those who cheered him on wanted to destroy what the Kochs and the DeVoses were so determined to defend.

Just as the history of leftist labor organizing was bound up with that of Black and Chicano liberation movements, the legacy of free-market enterprise could not be untangled from that of white supremacy. It was no accident that the Christian American Association, whose 1940s right-to-work campaign the Michigan Freedom Fund had reprised in 2012, condemned the New Deal as a Jewish plot and organized labor as a threat to Jim Crow segregation. Or that its founder, Vance Muse, warned that unions would force white workers into alliance "with black African apes whom they will have to call 'brother' or lose their jobs." Or that Henry Ford, among the staunchest opponents of the United Auto Workers union, published a pamphlet titled *The International Jew: The World's Foremost Problem.* (For this and other contributions, Hitler awarded Ford the Grand Cross of the Supreme Order of the German Eagle.) Or that Martin Luther King cautioned his followers to "guard against being fooled by false slogans, such as 'right to work.'" Or that King was assassinated while supporting striking garbage collectors who wanted the mayor of Memphis, Tennessee, to recognize their union. Or that George Floyd's last words—"I can't breathe"—reverberated so loudly through a world racked by a respiratory virus more lethal for some than for others, a world in which air had become a commodity, breath a privilege with a dollar value. His was the same anguished appeal that impoverished Brazilians would later make from an overwhelmed hospital in Amazonia, where patients were asphyxiating. "Please," one woman would beg on social media in January, "if you have the means: *oxygen.*"

The Kmart behind the Stop-N-Shop had opened in 1978, in the middle of a major thoroughfare that connected South Minneapolis to downtown. For more than four decades, the drab monolith had stood as a partition severing minority neighborhoods from the rest of the city and its resources. Before Floyd was killed, one protester I got to know, Simone Hunter, a nineteen-year-old with red-rinsed hair and a modest stature that obscured her explosive pugnacity, had worked at a Target distribution center, packaging merchandise on a conveyor belt. Though she did not participate in any vandalism herself, Simone had been at the Third Precinct when the Target across the street was pillaged—and had found it "very satisfying." When I asked what it had felt like when the police were overrun, she said, "Like fucking therapy. Like victory." The next day, Simone quit her job. "There's no way I can come out here and be OK with burning shit down," she explained, "and also be like, 'I'm cool with accepting money from these people.' No, I can't be cool with that."

We were at Thirty-Eighth and Chicago, a week into the protests. At once a site of solemn mourning and festive commemoration, the intersection had drawn larger and larger crowds each day. The police had kept their distance: buses and barriers sealed off a portion of the neighborhood, which was patrolled by locals, some armed. A medical tent had been erected. Couches and lounge chairs were arranged under the canopy of a Speedway, between the gas pumps. Musicians shared a stage. A towering portrait of Floyd was mounted on a bus stop. Like an evolving art installation, the crossroads had become increasingly populated with statues and paintings. Fresh bouquets piled up on top of dead ones. Pastors, priests, and imams gave sermons from the sidewalk. The unprecedented extent to which Floyd's murder had unsettled white America was on display. Soccer moms wept openly, old hippies burned sage, white parents and their kids kneeled where Floyd had died. The juxtaposition of white and Black fathers who brought their adolescent sons to the memorial raised the prospect of their respective conversations on their respective trips home.

Since quitting her job, Simone had become a fixture at the intersection. Removed from a difficult family situation when she was a baby, separated from siblings, and brought up in a foster home, she'd felt buffeted by an invisible, malign system her entire life. She knew that what was happening at Thirty-Eighth and Chicago was historic, and she was determined not to miss a minute of it. At almost any hour that I swung by the memorial, Simone was there—bleary-eyed but ebullient—engaged in some task or other with missionary dedication. After a few days, she began working security at the barricades, supervising a team and enforcing rules. One afternoon, I noticed a thirty-round magazine tucked into the waistband of her yoga pants. Its conspicuousness—and her lack of a rifle—made clear it was a statement. She was ready for the revolution.

Simone's once insular social world had also opened wide. Among the city's various communities of color, she told me, "there was always friction. But this has broken all that down." Solidarity between Somali Americans and African Americans, in particular, had been forged by an urgent sense of common struggle. About seventy-five thousand Somalis lived in Minnesota, more than anywhere else in the country. Many had resettled there in the nineties, during the civil war that devastated Mogadishu. On June 6, Ilhan Omar, the Somali-born US congresswoman who represented Minneapolis, spoke at a demonstration in the city. "I might not have inherited the trauma and the tragedy that Black Americans have who come from enslaved ancestry," she acknowledged—but the ordeal of American racism had initiated her into their experience. The previous summer, Trump had tweeted that Omar and three other women of color in Congress should "go back" to "the places from which they came." In Minneapolis, Omar said, "I have lived as a Black person in this country."

Beyond a locus of camaraderie, Thirty-Eighth and Chicago had also become the hub of a massive mutual-aid effort. Most businesses that had not been shuttered by the lockdown had closed during the rioting. With the bus and light-rail lines also suspended, traveling outside the city was impossible without a vehicle. At the intersection, rows of folding tables were loaded with canned food, fresh produce, diapers, toilet paper, kitchen supplies, homemade face masks, and other provisions. Signs read: FREE and TAKE WHAT YOU NEED. Near the Speedway, the headquarters of a labor rights organization had been converted into a food pantry, its offices swamped with donated groceries. A line of people snaked out the door, below the words COMIDA GRATIS.

Lake Street—the long boulevard that connected the Third and Fifth Precincts—was a principal corridor for immigrant markets, shops, and restaurants, many of which had been ransacked or damaged by looters. In contrast to the frenzied plundering of the city's big-box retailers, it was difficult to assign any coherent political intent to such crimes. While I was walking with Chantaveia down Lake Street after she'd been shot in the foot, we'd passed a dentist's office whose front door was smashed. When I'd peered inside, a white man had hurried out, towing a wheeled tank of nitrous oxide behind him.

"I feel terrible for those people," Simone said. "I *know* a lot of those people." Ultimately, though, she had made the same calculus as Chantaveia: human life mattered more than material wealth, whose loss could never undermine the social compact as egregiously as the murder, by state agents, of Black people. Property destruction was thus acceptable, if it helped prevent such murders in the future. "If we need to make the world stop for people to pay attention to what's going on?" Simone said. "Then we're gonna make the world stop."

THE MORNING AFTER the Fifth Precinct march, cleanup crews flooded Lake Street. Like a colony of worker ants, thousands of volunteers in shorts and T-shirts, armed with shovels and rakes, filed along the sidewalks, formed ad hoc details, and busily contributed to the urgent communal task of making the world start again. The Wells Fargo was a scorched husk; in the lobby, a broken pipe spewed a roaring cascade. Dozens of affable young women used push brooms to usher the ankle-deep water out the front door. Affable young men rescued office furniture, arranging desks, chairs, and filing cabinets on the lawn, like a corporate yard sale. Many belonged to an evangelical church in Saint Paul. "We're trying to help in any way we can," one congregant told me a little breathlessly. The pastor, an agile and intrepid zoomer with shoulder-length golden hair, crawled through downed beams and dangling wires, up a rubble-strewn staircase, and into the still extremely hot second floor, searching for a shutoff valve. The only Black person bailing out the bank was much older than everybody else. I asked if he, too, was with the church.

"What church?" he said. He was from Somalia. A safe-deposit box in the flooded basement contained the passports and birth certificates of his eleven children.

WHILE THE CLEANUP OPERATION was underway, Governor Walz fully mobilized the Minnesota National Guard—"an action that has never before been taken," he noted. An eight p.m. curfew had been put in place, and at 7:55, every cell phone in the city received an emergency alert: "Go home or to safe inside location. Avoid the outdoors. The curfew is enforceable by law."

I was sitting in the road between the Wells Fargo and the Fifth Precinct house, amid a sea of protesters. As the alert triggered a ripple of apprehension, a man in a long T-shirt with golden fringes grabbed a microphone connected to a public-address system and asked everyone to remain calm. "We gotta have some order, and we have to have decorum," he urged. Assuming he was a community organizer, I was eager to speak with him. I knew there was a robust network of activists in Minneapolis, but so far the demonstrations had all been organic and leaderless. The man in the fringed T-shirt was one of the first people I'd seen giving directions. Later, he would tell me that he was not an organizer at all. His name was Cornell Griffin, and for the past year and a half he had lived as a "recluse," seldom leaving his basement and spending most of his time reading Facebook or the Bible. "I ain't gonna lie," he said. "When Trayvon Martin happened, Freddie Gray, I didn't do shit. Like, nothing." For the first three days after Floyd was killed, Cornell refused to leave the house. Then, a few hours before I saw him, he'd told himself, "Either I'm gonna live my life in fear, or I'm gonna try this one dang thing and see what comes of it."

Upon arriving at the station, Cornell had scaled a streetlight and draped from it an enormous cloth tapestry bearing Floyd's image. People started handing him the microphone, and he found he had a lot to say. After the emergency alert, a man on roller skates coasted up to him and said that soldiers were mustering nearby. The crackdown was likely to be violent and the ensuing panic might cause a stampede. The man proposed that Cornell lead away as many people as he could. Cornell announced that a march was departing, and several hundred protesters began following him downtown.

Minutes later, a phalanx of state troopers in riot gear discharged a withering fusillade of rubber bullets, marking pellets, stun grenades, and tear gas at the thousand-odd people who had stayed behind. Officers then rushed them with batons, indiscriminately hacking through the mass of bodies, which included senior citizens and children. An armored tactical vehicle followed; from a hatch, a trooper in a Kevlar helmet aimed an assault rifle with a silencer into the crowd. Dazed and bloodied protesters staggered through the clouds of gas. Cornell hurried back. Near the Wells Fargo, he came upon a woman immobilized with terror. He was getting her to walk when he saw an officer leveling a gun at them. A rubber bullet struck him in the neck.

When we met again, a few days later, Cornell's throat was still scabbed and bruised. The round had injured his vocal cords, making his voice light and raspy. Nonetheless, he was in high spirits. The experience had shifted something into focus for him. We were standing in the parking lot of the boarded-up Target, where, the morning after being shot, Cornell had constructed a plywood stage. The platform was already covered with hundreds of signatures from people who had come to hear him speak—about racism, about love, about fear. When I pointed out that this was not typical recluse behavior, Cornell laughed and said, "I'd been feeling like there's something wrong with me. And then this happened. And, all of a sudden, it all made sense. It wasn't me. *My city* is hurting. *My city* is depressed. *My city* is on fire."

FIVE

BATTLE SPACE

While no police are known to have been wounded during the protests in Minneapolis, many protesters were severely hurt by the police. A study conducted by researchers from the University of Minnesota found that eighty-nine people, ranging in age from fifteen to seventy-seven, were hospitalized. Some suffered skull fractures and traumatic brain injuries. Others, including a reporter, were partially blinded. One man lost an eye. The rioting lasted a couple of days; from then on, the only crime that most protesters committed was being out past curfew. Every demonstration I attended after May 29 was peaceful. The state troopers with nightsticks did not brutalize the demonstrators calmly sitting outside the Fifth Precinct in order to stop them from what they were doing but to punish them for what others had done. Body cam footage from later that night would capture one sergeant ordering his men to fire high-caliber rubber bullets at "the first fuckers we see." Another commander told officers, "You see a fucking group? Call it out. Fuck them up. Gas them." Such retaliatory violence marked a fateful shift in the national ferment that would lead to millions of Americans turning not only against the movement sparked by George Floyd's death but also against the very prospect of reform or redress.

Two days after the assault at the Fifth Precinct, Trump convened a conference call with state governors. Protests and riots had roiled dozens of cities, including Washington, D.C., where the president had briefly taken refuge in an underground shelter. "You have to dominate," he told the governors. "If you don't dominate, you're wasting your time—they're going to run over you." Attorney General William Barr and Acting Secretary of Defense Mark Esper were also on the call. "Law enforcement response is not going to work unless we dominate the streets," Barr said. Esper concurred: "We need to dominate the battle space." George Floyd had been dead a week. Already, what much of the country welcomed as a messy but imperative reckoning with racial injustice was being framed by the White House, the Justice Department, and the Pentagon as a threat to national security.

Trump sent the same message to his supporters some hours later. As dusk fell, hundreds of law enforcement officers, Secret Service agents, and National Guard soldiers surged into Lafayette Square, north of the White House, where protesters were peacefully assembled. Pepper balls, tear gas, stun grenades, and rubber bullets were deployed. When the square was empty, Trump walked across it to St. John's Church, accompanied by Barr, Esper, and General Mark Milley, the chairman of the Joint Chiefs of Staff, who wore his combat fatigues. At St. John's, Trump delivered no remarks and answered few questions. Instead, he posed in front of the church while holding up a Bible. Behind him, a door and windows were covered with plywood—the night before, someone had lit a fire in the nursery. Liberal pundits mocked the stunt as a clumsy attempt at projecting strength amid turmoil. But

Trump was not talking to liberal America. Far from an impromptu
gimmick, the symbolically freighted St. John's visit felt to me carefully
choreographed. It reminded me of Mike Shirkey, the Michigan Senate
majority leader, who had raised a Bible in precisely the same manner
to signal his allegiance with the American Patriot Council and the
Michigan Liberty Militia at Rosa Parks Circle. Trump's gesture, like
Shirkey's, appealed to and redirected the mutable sense of dispossession that had galvanized armed anti-lockdowners, the members of Garrett Soldano's Facebook group, and the men in Karl Manke's barbershop.
Whereas the nationwide protest movement cast white Christians as the
entitled profiteers of the historical status quo, Trump reassured them that
they were its unacknowledged casualties. (No pandemic measure galled
anti-lockdowners more than state bans on indoor worship services; now,
in addition to Democratic politicians, racial-justice demonstrators were
shuttering their churches.) Even the removal of the protesters conveyed
a legible message: the sanctioning of preemptive violence as a form of
self-defense.

In the months to come, this message would be internalized by both
law enforcement and right-wing groups claiming to follow a principle
of "no first use of force." Many of the insurrectionists on January 6
would believe that they were acting in self-defense. At the base of the
Capitol steps, while the mob swarmed over officers, I would glimpse
above the tumult a hand held high, clutching a Bible.

THE DAY AFTER CORNELL GRIFFIN led hundreds of people to
safety, large crowds gathered downtown at the U.S. Bank Stadium.
The curfew remained in place, and as eight o'clock approached, a man
announced, "If you continue to stay in this area, just know that they
have been ordered to shoot to kill us." The claim set off confusion and
debate. Could the police really use lethal rounds on protesters? Hadn't

the president threatened as much? One man asked his friends, "Did you not understand what Trump said? He said, 'We're at war now.'"

I'd met him before. A twenty-eight-year-old construction worker from the Southside, Tony Clark had been a consistent and vibrant presence on the front lines, both vocally and sartorially. He sported a camouflage-print down vest, no shirt, and a quarter-size earring gauge emblazoned with the words NOT TODAY SATAN. A small cross was tattooed under his right eye, and a diamond under his left. The night before, I had walked alongside his car as he'd driven slowly away from the Fifth Precinct, amid fleeing protesters, through a residential neighborhood of wood-framed houses with wide front porches and fenced-in lawns. Pointing a bullhorn out his window, Tony had held his phone to the mouthpiece while it played the video of Floyd's death. "Y'all hear George crying?" he'd shouted. "This is why we're out here!" Stopping his car in the middle of the street and climbing onto its roof, he had faced the police officers firing tear gas and projectiles at us. "*They* the gangsters," he'd told the protesters. "*They* the mob."

Tony had known Floyd. They'd met at a barbershop near Thirty-Eighth and Chicago, and hung out at El Nuevo Rodeo, a nightclub where Floyd worked security. Floyd was almost ten years older than Tony and had been a sort of mentor to him. "He used to tell me to use my voice," Tony had recalled. "That's what he always said. Having tattoos on my face, people get the wrong impression. That's what I loved about George. He told me, 'As soon as you start talking—that's when they're gonna see you.'" The protests were personal for Tony in another way, as well: in 2016, his brother Travis died in a car crash after being pursued by police. "I'm also doing this for him," Tony said. When I asked if his brother would have joined the protests, he answered, "Travis would've led the city."

As Tony debated whether to violate the curfew, a long procession of marchers arrived at the stadium. They had walked all the way from

Thirty-Eighth and Chicago, three miles across town. Several California activists, including Joe Collins, a congressional candidate from South Los Angeles, asked the combined groups to follow them toward Interstate 35, which was closed to traffic. As we left the stadium, I saw Tony step into the march.

Downtown was eerily silent. The protesters filled a wide four-lane avenue, their chants resonating between tall office towers and high-end apartment complexes. At the front, a man with a scarf tied around his face, headphones in his ears, and his hat brim pulled low bobbed his head while privately singing to The-Dream: "I'm feeling real Black right now, real Black right now . . ."

Reaching an on-ramp, the marchers continued down onto the empty interstate. There was nowhere else to go. A couple hundred feet away, in each direction, a wall of police spanned the highway. People were nervous. It wasn't only the cordons: the rumors of lethal ammunition and the uncertainty about what Trump's bellicose rhetoric meant had created a palpable atmosphere of fear and tension. One of the organizers from California, an older man anomalously clad in a pin-striped suit with gold cuff links, assured the marchers that as long as they remained peaceful, no harm would come to them. "You do not have to worry," he said. "We are not here for violence. They're not gonna touch you."

Tony shook his head. "It's about to get dangerous," he told the man. "Y'all are playin' with fire."

No sooner had the protesters linked arms than the officers began firing tear gas, forcing them up a dirt embankment and toward a Mobil gas station.

"Everybody remain calm!" Tony yelled, his face dripping with milk. Troopers and deputies with long batons encircled the Mobil. Joe Collins, the congressional candidate, was on his knees, being detained.

Men in camouflage, with flak jackets, gas masks, and assault rifles, paced the ranks. They resembled Special Forces operators. The marcher who'd been singing to himself raised his voice: "'Cause everywhere there's a Chicago / The only way we're getting out of here is if we hit the Lotto . . . "

I spotted Simone Hunter, the nineteen-year-old who'd quit her job at Target. She wore an ill-fitting sweatshirt and pants that looked borrowed. I recognized her backpack: since the burning of the Third Precinct, she'd kept it stocked with saline for treating tear gas, tampons for packing flesh wounds. She walked up to the troopers and started yelling at them. I had trouble hearing what she was saying—after five days, her voice was almost gone. The man in the pin-striped suit did not approve. "Ma'am, please, can you back up?" he asked Simone. "Ma'am, please. Please. Please. Please."

Simone was crying. "This is our home—this is our *home* right here," she said. "We have enemies on all sides, not just on the streets. I'm tired. I'm fucking tired. I've dealt with racist shit my whole fucking life, and I am tired."

She looked it. She had bruises from being hit with a baton; her fingers were blistered from grabbing tear-gas canisters; she had not slept more than a few consecutive hours since George Floyd was killed. Clutching the front of her sweatshirt, she said that she was wearing a stranger's clothes and had spent the night in a stranger's house. Later, she told me that she'd been walking through a neighborhood near the Fifth Precinct when an SUV pulled alongside her. A white man with an assault rifle shouted, "Go home!" Simone sprinted down alleys and side streets until she came upon two white women. They invited her to their place, where she slept on an air mattress in their living room. "I had never experienced anything like that before," she said. "This is the kind of stuff that gives you hope. It was shocking."

At the Mobil, Simone told her fellow protesters, "Your neighbors got your back!" And, pointing at the troopers: "*These* people don't got your back!"

Though no one had threatened them, the officers began firing rubber bullets and stun grenades into the crowd. National Guard units arrived in armored Humvees. Most of the protesters who had stuck around up to this point were Black. They were surrounded by more than a hundred officers and soldiers, almost all of them white. Some people screamed. Others wept. A young man beside me raised his arms. His name was Deondre Moore, and he had traveled all the way from Houston, Texas, George Floyd's hometown. "Don't shoot!" Moore pleaded. "Let us leave!" A rubber bullet struck him squarely in the chest. He fell to the pavement, gasping for breath and writhing in pain. When I crouched down to check his injury, I saw that his T-shirt bore the words I AM A MAN, the declaration printed on signs carried by the garbage collectors with whom Martin Luther King had marched in Memphis. The day before he was assassinated, King had assured the demonstrators, "Somewhere I read that the greatness of America is the right to protest for right."

Later, Deondre Moore would tell me, "I thought it was a real bullet." That was the difference between his experience and mine: I did not believe that the police could kill me. I remember feeling at the time that both the rumors of lethal rounds and the panic at the Mobil were unreasonable, excessively dramatic, maybe even a bit affected. But when I think back to Deondre Moore, hands in the air, begging the officers not to shoot him—and the crack of the gun, and Moore collapsing to the street—it looks, in retrospect, like a murder. Of course it does. That was the point.

While Moore was still catching his breath, the protesters were commanded to lie on their stomachs with their hands behind their backs—the same position Floyd had been in when he died. Simone refused. Bringing out a Sharpie from her bag of supplies, she started writing the phone number for a local bail fund on people's arms. A young officer trained his gun on her and held it there. Simone proceeded calmly with what she was doing as if she were oblivious to him. She was not oblivious to him. The scene is seared in my memory. Half-hidden behind his body armor and his helmet and his face visor, the young officer is almost not a person—almost a generic uniform, another badge. But as he points the gun at Simone, there is also something definitely human in his posture and his eyes. What makes him so frightening is that he is so frightened.

I think another reason that this moment has stayed with me is the guilty feeling of complicity with which it is imbued. Most of the journalists had left the area; among those of us who remained all but one of us were white. A few minutes later, we were separated from the protesters and told to sit on a curb while the troopers zip-tied everybody else, loaded them onto buses, and brought them to jail. It was the first time that we'd been treated any differently, but the recognition of our status only highlighted a distinction that had been there all along. The irony of white journalists covering Black protests against white prejudice had glowed brighter by the day. On social media, white photographers were facing criticism for documenting what some deemed an essentially Black story, and I was aware that just my being there implied a rejection of this view. I did reject it. Much like in Iraq or Afghanistan, whose cultures I was even less qualified to speak for, the story in Minneapolis, it seemed to me, was also about the weaponization of US power against vulnerable people—a story that I'd felt less entitled than obliged to cover. However, that didn't make my segregation from Simone Hunter, Deondre Moore, and the rest of the protesters at the Mobil any less mortifying.

After the troopers had arrested everyone, I walked back to my hotel. The protesters were issued citations for breaking the curfew and released the next morning. When she got home, Simone brought her citation outside, held it to a lighter, and watched it burn.

OTHER WAYS

By the time Minnesota achieved statehood in 1858, settlers had exterminated nearly all its bison, logged its forests, and turned its prairie into farmland. The government had restricted most of its Indigenous inhabitants—predominantly Sioux and Ojibwe people—to reservations, where missionaries endeavored to convert them to Christianity before they died from starvation or disease. In 1862, a Sioux rebellion was violently suppressed by the military, and thirty-eight Sioux warriors were hanged in what remains the largest mass execution in US history. Most of the surviving tribal members were imprisoned or expelled from the state, regardless of whether they had participated in the uprising. A century later, the Indian Relocation Act offered a variety of incentives to lure Native Americans into cities and thereby expedite their assimilation. Many Sioux and Ojibwe moved to Minneapolis, where they were met with antagonism, discrimination, poverty, and neglect.

The community was concentrated within a mile-long corridor on the Southside, not far from Lake Street. In 1968, activists from the neighborhood launched the American Indian Movement, or AIM. In the same vein as the Black Panther Party and its "cop-watchers," AIM organized patrols to monitor and document law enforcement conduct. Nationally, Native Americans have consistently suffered from police brutality at higher rates than any other race or ethnic group, including African Americans, and in those days Minneapolis officers were known to haul young Indigenous men to remote locations for vicious beatings, stuff them into the trunks of squad cars, and handcuff them to lampposts on frigid winter nights.

During my third evening in Minneapolis, I was following protesters down Lake Street when we came upon a building belonging to the Division of Indian Work, a nonprofit that provided a range of services for the city's Native population. Half a dozen armed men and women stood outside, wearing T-shirts that read: NATIVE AMERICANS WERE NEVER HOMELESS BEFORE 1492. A middle-aged man had a revolver on his hip, a machete in a leather sheath, and a shotgun balanced over his shoulder. "There's a food shelf and a youth program and a daycare center here," he told the protesters. "We're on the same team, but we can't allow what little we have left to go." I didn't know it at the time, but the enormous structural fire I had witnessed near the Third Precinct station, at four thirty in the morning after the first day of riots, was the offices of Migizi, a radio broadcast started by AIM members that later became an after-school program for Indigenous youth. (*Migizi* is Ojibwe for "bald eagle.") After old AIM activists and other leaders put out a call for help on social media, some two hundred Natives from Minneapolis and nearby reservations had assembled in the parking lot of a coffee shop called Pow Wow Grounds, which became their makeshift headquarters over the next week. The man with the shotgun and his compatriots were Ho-Chunks from a reservation on the Mississippi River, about an hour south of the city.

They were adhering to a principle that AIM had helped establish fifty years ago: given that law enforcement was complicit in their oppression, oppressed communities must protect themselves. On the surface, such armed neighborhood patrols bore a strong resemblance to vigilante groups like the Michigan Liberty Militia. But a crucial difference lay in the legitimacy of their respective grievances. Just as anti-lockdowners had attempted to appropriate the legacy of the civil rights movement ("Owosso has their little version of Rosa Parks, don't they?"), their abhorrence of the federal government was rooted in a kind of revanchism that both copied and whitewashed Indigenous reclamation campaigns. In many respects, the Bundy-led seizure of the Malheur National Wildlife Refuge was a ham-fisted imitation of the 1973 occupation by AIM activists of Wounded Knee in South Dakota. In 1890, the US Army had massacred hundreds of Sioux men, women, and children at Wounded Knee, clearing the way for the acquisition of their homeland. Like contemporary proponents of that crime, those who rallied to the Bundy cause believed that God had entrusted them with proprietorship of the physical United States. The Malheur refuge had originally belonged to the Paiute people; during their occupation, the Bundys and their supporters excavated a road through sacred Paiute burial grounds and released a video of themselves rifling through Paiute artifacts. At the earlier confrontation, in Nevada, Cliven Bundy had often cited his settler ancestors to support his claim of sovereignty over the vast public desert where he illegally grazed his cattle. Ancient sandstone petroglyphs, however, attested to the Paiute who'd lived there long before any Bundys came. After Cliven and his followers dislodged the Bureau of Land Management, some of these carvings were vandalized with bullets and spray paint.

A number of the Sioux who were slaughtered at Wounded Knee in 1890 had already been confined to a reservation, which they had fled two weeks earlier, after Indian police gunned down their leader, Sitting Bull. That reservation was called Standing Rock, and in 2016— the same year that the Bundys seized the Malheur refuge—it had become the site of another standoff. When an energy company undertook to install a pipeline that would traverse the Mississippi River half a mile upstream from Standing Rock, in an area that the Sioux had never ceded and still claimed as rightfully theirs, Indigenous activists attempted to impede its construction. Security guards assaulted and sicced attack dogs on them; law enforcement in armored Humvees cleared a protest camp using bean bag rounds, batons, tear gas, and Tasers. Two weeks after Trump won the election, officers blasted peaceful demonstrators with water cannons in below-freezing weather, causing widespread hypothermia. A concussion grenade nearly severed a woman's arm. Undercover employees of TigerSwan, a private military contractor hired by the energy company, infiltrated and spied on the protesters. Although the Sioux practiced nonviolence with extraordinary discipline, TigerSwan documents obtained by *The Intercept* compared them to "an ideologically driven insurgency with a strong religious component" that followed a "jihadist" model.

Some of the activists likened themselves to modern-day Ghost Dancers. The Ghost Dance had originated in Nevada in 1889, when a Paiute healer prophesied that it would stop the American colonization of Indigenous lands. Within a year, the Sioux of Standing Rock were practicing the ritual. Alarmed government agents, misinterpreting the Ghost Dance as a prelude to rebellion, deployed thousands of Army troops to the reservation and ordered Sitting Bull to forbid his followers from participating in the ceremony. He was killed after refusing to do so. The TigerSwan mercenaries and militarized deputy sheriffs outside of Standing Rock in 2016 treated the Sioux much as their nineteenth-century antecedents had (as a dangerous enemy), and for the same reason: because they feared what they did not understand.

On June 1, the day after Simone Hunter was arrested at the Mobil, a group of Ojibwe women visited the memorial at Thirty-Eighth Street and Chicago Avenue. One sported a red beret and an AIM patch: REMEMBER WOUNDED KNEE/1890–1973. Their colorfully embroidered outfits, adorned with feathers, beads, and abundant little metal cones, were jingle dresses: they chimed like tambourines as the women danced to a drum beat within a ring of candles and flowers circumscribing the intersection. The jingle-dress dance was an Ojibwe healing ritual conceived during the influenza pandemic of 1918. It was later relied on for soothing other maladies, including grief. At Thirty-Eighth and Chicago, the women danced clockwise in a circle. "You only go forward, and you don't turn around," one of them later told me. "You don't want disease to follow you." They also weaved their steps, snaking from side to side. "The zigzag way is the way to Heaven, it's a spiritual way," the dancer explained. "It's not human to walk in a straight line."

Earlier that afternoon, Terrence Floyd, George's younger brother, had come to the intersection. After stopping to admire the mural with George's portrait surrounded by the names of Eric Garner, Michael Brown, Freddie Gray, and Breonna Taylor, he sat down on the curb where someone had painted the silhouette of a prostrate body with its hands manacled behind its back and angelic wings spreading from its shoulders. Overcome, Terrence bowed his head and sobbed. "I understand y'all upset," he told the crowd through a megaphone. "But I doubt y'all half as upset as I am." He admonished those who had looted and rioted. "If I'm not out here wilding out, if I'm not over here blowing up stuff, if I'm not over here messing up my community, then what are y'all doing? Let's do this another way," he said. "Let's stop thinking that our voice don't matter, and *vote*. That's how we're gonna hit 'em. Because it's a lot of us. It's a lot of us. *It's a lot of us!*"

Terrence fell silent. Or almost silent. The megaphone amplified his exhalations. A reverend stood at his side. Leaning over, he whispered in Terrence's ear. It was so quiet you could hear him: "Breathe. . . . Breathe. . . . Breathe. . . . Breathe."

SUMMER

SIX

———

TERRORISTS

While I was in Minneapolis, large demonstrations had also taken place across Michigan. In Grand Rapids, a gathering at Rosa Parks Circle gave way to rioting at night. Businesses were looted and cars were burned. Similar acts occurred in Lansing. The brief lawlessness had dispirited Michael Lynn Jr., who'd kept his distance from the protests. "We'd been making progress, and that went against all our work," he told me when I returned to Lansing in mid-June. We were at a bar in the neighborhood where Lynn had grown up with Aldric McKinstry, his high school best friend who was killed by the police while hiding in a basement. "We were out here protesting and trying to get people interested back *then*," Lynn said. "But we couldn't get nobody to stand up." The shooting had been swept under the rug. Every year, on the anniversary of Aldric's death, the Lansing Police Department published an online tribute to the German shepherd that died when officers opened fire on Aldric. In a summary of the dog's heroism, Aldric was identified solely—and, according to Lynn, falsely—as "an armed subject."

The apathy that Lynn had faced while struggling to bring aware-ness to Aldric's death, to the climate of racism in the Lansing Fire Department, and to his son's experience after he kneeled during the national anthem at a high school football game had left Lynn wary of the sudden enthusiasm among white liberals for racial justice. He sus-pected that much of it was posturing and doubted it would last. Mean-while, the right-wing reaction was just beginning. Anti-lockdown groups in Michigan had gone quiet for three weeks after Memorial Day, but the American Patriot Council was set to hold another rally at the capitol—its first since George Floyd was killed—on June 18. This time, rather than protesting Governor Whitmer's pandemic policies, it would be showing support for armed militias. Attendees were encouraged to bring weapons and flags. The event was scheduled for the eve of June-teenth, when African Americans celebrated the end of slavery.

"Why would they do something like that?" Lynn asked.

It seemed obvious to him that the timing was deliberate, intended as a provocation. The organizers must have also known that since late May, protesters had been rendezvousing every evening at the capitol and marching through downtown. The marchers were led by a thirty-four-year-old named Paul Birdsong. Birdsong's father had been one of the founders of the West Side Piru, a Los Angeles street gang that had evolved into the Bloods. The impetus for the West Side Piru had been to defend poor Black communities against the Crips, an older and larger Los Angeles gang. Although many Bloods came to engage in the same rapacious activities as their rivals—including in the neighborhood around Thirty-Eighth and Chicago, in Minneapolis—Birdsong claimed to uphold the original Piru code: "To live, love, and learn, and to keep each other off strong drugs, out of jail, and from dying." During his marches, he often carried a handgun; other protesters brought assault rifles. When we spoke on the phone, the night before the June 18 rally, Birdsong told me that he made no distinction between fighting Crips, demonstrating against police brutality, and confronting right-wing militias. "We will stand up to any destructive forces that attempt to invade and pollute our communities," he said.

When I arrived at the capitol a little before six p.m., hundreds of armed white citizens were already milling around the base of the steps. A man and a woman with clipboards, in Stand Up Michigan T-shirts, collected signatures. It was the petition to revoke Governor Whitmer's emergency powers that Garrett Soldano—the chiropractor, former Juice Plus+ director, and author of *God's True Law*—had launched on the advice of Republican senators. The demands had grown considerably more ambitious and now included extensive amendments to the state constitution, such as abolishing Michigan's civil rights commission.

I spotted Michelle Gregoire, the school bus driver who, in April, had been dragged out of the legislature by chief sergeant at arms David Dickson. She was talking to Phil Robinson, the founder of the Michigan Liberty Militia. With his shaved head and long beard spliced into three tight braids, Robinson lived up to his nom de guerre and Facebook handle, "Odin Heathen." Both he and Michelle carried semiautomatic rifles. A tactical tomahawk also dangled from Robinson's belt; a Glock was holstered on his thigh. I went over and said hello. I'd spoken with Robinson on several occasions and found him thoroughly mystifying. The mystery was this: How had he come to wield such influence in the world? He was not charismatic, intelligent, rich, or attractive. No past deeds commanded esteem. He struggled to articulate himself. Why did people follow Robinson? Why did they respect him? Yes, he had a gun—a big one—but in Michigan so did everybody.

I'd eventually decided that some conservatives were drawn to Robinson because he was a special kind of zealot: a true believer not in the toxic ethos at the core of right-wing militarism but in the euphemism and innuendo that made up its facade. Norse traditions had long been popular with white supremacists, some of whom embraced them as a more ethnically pure alternative to Christianity. Paganism was widely practiced in the Aryan Brotherhood—and the perpetrator of the 2019 New Zealand mosque massacre had ended his manifesto with "See you in Valhalla!" But when I'd broached the subject with Robinson, he'd become surprisingly emotional and said that it infuriated him to see others "using my religion for hate." I don't think he was being disingenuous. More than a purveyor of the Kool-Aid, Robinson had drunk it. His earnestness was his appeal: it reassured others of their own moral rectitude.

The first Michigan militia was formed in 1994, during a national wave of white paramilitary mobilization prompted by the government's botched attempt to arrest the right-wing conspiracist Randy Weaver at his cabin on Ruby Ridge, in northern Idaho. Two months after federal agents killed Weaver's wife and son, neo-Nazis and Klansmen from around the country congregated at a YMCA in Estes Park, Colorado. The confab brought together Christian Identity elders like Richard Butler, the founder of the Aryan Nations—whose Idaho compound the Weavers had frequented—and Beltway lobbyists for the firearms industry. The anti-government movement that emerged fatefully wedded white nationalism to gun-rights advocacy and apocalyptic survivalism. For more than a century and a half, antipathy toward the federal government had been virtually synonymous with the subjugation of Black people; after Ruby Ridge, militia members began enlisting the Second Amendment to cast themselves as victims of persecution. The deadly siege, less than a year later, of the Branch Davidian compound in Waco, Texas, and the Clinton administration's ban on assault weapons in 1994, reinforced the right-wing narrative that white Christians were under attack. The Michigan Militia ballooned after Waco, to an estimated seven thousand members, making it the largest in the country. A year later, Timothy McVeigh, a white supremacist who'd attended several Michigan Militia meetings, detonated a massive truck bomb in Oklahoma City on the anniversary of the Waco massacre, killing 168 people, many of them children. The leaders of the Michigan Militia decamped to Alaska, and the organization collapsed. Not until Barack Obama became president did rural Michiganders again feel called upon to muster. By the end of Obama's second term, the state had more than a dozen militias, some with only a handful of men, others with thousands.

Nationally, Obama's election spurred what came to be known as the Patriot Movement: a loose federation of hundreds of armed groups organized on the pretext of gun rights but often hostile to Muslims, immigrants, and the LGBTQ community. Although Patriots were seldom overtly racist or antisemitic, they depicted the administration as corrupted by un-American forces inimical to Christian values and interests. In the heady aftermath of his victory over the Bureau of Land Management, in 2014, Cliven Bundy hinted with unscrupulous candor at the underlying source of Patriot loathing for Obama. "I want to tell you one more thing I know about the Negro," the plain-speaking rancher confided to reporters. "They abort their young children, they put their young men in jail, because they never learned how to pick cotton. And I've often wondered: Are they better off as slaves?"

Phil Robinson had told me that he'd created his militia in 2015, "after seeing what happened with the Bundys." Yet every time we spoke, he was exceedingly anxious to impress on me that he and his men were not racist. "We're here for everybody," he said in Lansing. I nodded and duly recorded in my notebook, "Not racist. . . . Here for everybody." Of course, during eight years of the Bush administration's extraordinary infringements on personal privacy, due process, speech, and religious freedom, the Patriots had been dormant. What had brought them roaring out of hibernation was the ascension to the White House of a Black man with a foreign-sounding name whom many on the right believed to be a Muslim. The first event to which Robinson deployed his militia was an anti-Islam rally at a mosque in Dearborn, Michigan. The armed protest was one of several across the country promoted by the Oath Keepers, a Patriot outfit whose members had stood with the Bundys in Oregon and Nevada. "As this invasion of Muslim colonization continues unchecked on American soil," the Oath Keepers had declared on Facebook, "now is the time to save our Republic." I don't doubt this is what Robinson believed he was doing.

When I mentioned to Robinson and Michelle Gregoire that Paul Birdsong might be showing up, they both laughed. "That would be awesome," Robinson said. I asked whether he was worried about potential conflict. "Have you looked around?" he scoffed. "You'd be a fool to come here and start shit."

The cofounders of the American Patriot Council, Jason Howland and Ryan Kelley, greeted attendees. They were both relatively normal looking. (Relative to Odin Heathen, at any rate.) Howland was overweight, goateed, bespectacled. He ran the Jason Howland Corporation, based in Macomb County, which, as far as I could ascertain, was named for its sole employee and mainly offered workshops on an innovative sales technique called "the Action-Closer System." I'd watched dozens of videos of Howland feverishly extolling the revolutionary benefits of action closing. I still had no idea what it was. Stylistically, his mix of high-octane panache and substantive inscrutability reminded me of Garrett Soldano. "When you become an action closer, you're gonna see your life change, the lives of everyone around you," Howland effused in one clip. "You're gonna expand economies, you're gonna blow up your own economy, you're gonna *be* your own economy—because you're gonna be able to get things done."

Despite such lofty promises, most of the clips had attracted fewer than a hundred views. Then, on March 29, the Jason Howland Corporation published a different kind of content. In a cell phone recording of a triage tent for COVID-19 patients, Howland asked a security guard, "Is that where all the virus people are?" A caption declared, "We can tell the truth from lies!" It was watched more than fifteen hundred times. A couple of weeks later, Howland and Kelley created the American Patriot Council.

Ryan Kelley was a rail-thin real estate agent from Grand Rapids who sported the same tinted aviator sunglasses, white denim jeans, and untucked purple dress shirt every time I saw him. He and his wife had accrued a modest following on YouTube posting elaborate gender-reveal stunts for their abundant children and at least one semi-graphic video of a home birth in an inflatable pool. When I asked him in Lansing why he had decided to hold the pro-militia rally, Kelley replied, "Chaos across the United States. Antifa taking over areas of the country. People not feeling safe." On May 31, the day Simone Hunter, the congressional candidate Joe Collins, and more than a hundred other peaceful protesters were detained at the Mobil gas station in Minneapolis, Attorney General Barr had released a statement claiming that the George Floyd movement had been "hijacked by violent radical elements." Trump— who stood beside Kelley in Kelley's Facebook profile picture, giving a thumbs-up—had simultaneously announced his intention to designate "Antifa" as a terrorist organization.

In casting the civil disobedience of people like Simone as the work of state enemies, the administration echoed such segregationists as William Potter Gale, the Posse Comitatus leader, who had ascribed the civil rights movement to a communist plot to divide the country. (Gale's analysis was shared by FBI director J. Edgar Hoover and many other establishment figures.) In the 1960s, the point was not merely to negate Black appeals for justice; it was also to render such appeals sinister and dangerous—part of a larger, darker threat to white Christians. Trump had achieved the same effect by invoking Antifa as the vanguard of a vast left-wing menace bent on sowing discord in America, which was what had prompted the American Patriot Council to shift its attention from public-health policies to domestic security. When I asked Kelley about the rather abrupt evolution, he told me, "COVID is nonsense, and so the evolution of that is the Democratic Party continuing to do anything they can to get Trump out of office, including hiring people to riot and loot in the streets."

A few minutes later, Howland climbed the steps. He wore a baseball hat embroidered with the acronym "TAT." In one of his early videos, he had explained that the letters stood for "Take Action Today," and that indeed appeared to be what he was doing. With the same fervent aplomb he'd once channeled to pitch the Jason Howland Corporation's economy-exploding sales tool kit, he boomed, "We the people of the United States of America are the strongest force in the world under God! And so, as we hold close to our hearts all the events that have happened recently, we must ask ourselves: Why? Why is this happening?"

I felt my stomach sink. I had spent the past three weeks listening to residents of Minneapolis talk about almost nothing else. Simone Hunter had literally lost her voice shouting to anyone who would listen her many specific answers to this question. "Hopefully, they hear us," the first person I'd met in the city had told me. But Jason Howland hadn't heard them. He'd heard Barr. He'd heard Trump. "Our enemies are the operatives of fear and dissent," he went on, "and they have created both an invisible monster and a very visible hate."

When it was Kelley's turn at the mic, he pointed to the officers monitoring the scene. "We say thank you for being here," he told them. "Thank you for standing up for our communities." This was another pivot. Before Floyd's death, much of the anti-lockdown anger had been directed at law enforcement. David Dickson, the state police who served Manke with a cease-and-desist order, Attorney General Nessel—they'd all been denounced as jackbooted Nazis, or worse. When officers issued citations to some of the stylists at Operation Haircut, protesters had likened them to the gestapo. "People like me used to fucking back you!" one Iraq War veteran had yelled at them. "But you are trash!" I recognized several of the officers whom Kelley now praised as the same ones who'd been castigated that day.

"There's a lot of chaos right now," Kelley continued. "There's rioters coming in and burning down cities . . ."

Suddenly, a large group of young people appeared on the lawn, led by Paul Birdsong. Notably taller than those around him, Birdsong had the thick but softened build of a former athlete. He wore red Chuck Taylors, black shorts, and a red bandanna tied around his wrist. Walking into the middle of the demonstrators, he lay facedown and crossed his hands behind his back, reenacting Floyd's final minutes. The rest of the counterprotesters did the same. None had weapons, though some wore empty holsters.

"What are we gonna do here, guys?" Kelley asked the crowd. "What are we gonna do?"

The militia members, it would be fair to say, were triggered. Leaning over the counterprotesters, they called them "faggots," "pieces of shit," "pussies," and "fucking inbreds." A man with American flag suspenders held up a Bible, as if to exorcise the evil before him. Someone in a Michigan Home Guard hat barked, "Your grandfathers and your uncles and your brothers—every one of them that fought for our country is ashamed of you!"

Birdsong calmly told those lying around him, "Don't say anything." Kelley, meanwhile, yelled into the microphone, "We will not stand for the destruction of our state, of our country, of our citizens! You will not terrorize us!" Howland walked through the prostate bodies, filming with his phone. Pointing at a white man clothed in black, he announced, "This is Antifa!"

Eventually, Birdsong rose to his feet.

"This is our state!" a woman shouted at him.

"This is our city," he said. "We live here. In my city, you don't threaten anybody."

"A mouth, that's all you are," said a man with an assault rifle, an ammo vest, and a Hawaiian shirt. Tourniquets were attached to his shoulder straps, and he wore a radio earpiece. On his chest was a patch with the Latin adage SI VIS PACEM, PARA BELLUM: "If you want peace, prepare for war." He glared at Birdsong. "I can look at you and tell you're a weak fucking man," he said.

Birdsong silently held his stare, then turned his back. Later, when I asked about this moment, he told me, "That's the Piru training. I refuse to be provoked."

The man in the Hawaiian shirt was Adam Fox. In October, the FBI would accuse him and five members of a militia called the Wolverine Watchmen of plotting to kidnap Governor Whitmer. Charging documents would cite a recorded phone call between Fox and an informant on June 24, a week after I saw him confront Paul Birdsong. "In all honesty, right now, I just wanna make the world glow," Fox is quoted as saying. "I'm just so sick of it. That's what it's gonna take for us to take it back. . . . Everything's gonna have to be annihilated. . . . We're gonna topple it all."

The Michigan Liberty Militia member with the Mohawk whom Dayna Polehanki had photographed in the Senate chamber on April 30 would also be implicated in the affair. His name was William Null, and he and his twin brother, Michael, would be charged with providing material support to Fox and the Wolverine Watchmen while they scouted Whitmer's vacation home and worked out the logistics of abducting her. I was standing next to William Null when some of the counterprotesters in Lansing raised their fists. "If they want to stand there with their fists up, let them," Null told Phil Robinson, who was becoming upset. "They look like Hitler. Don't fucking worry about it, brother, this fucking shit ain't nothing."

"If these motherfuckers wanna go up a caliber, I am ready," Robinson said. "I am *ready*."

Null nodded. "So am I."

Jason Howland pulled Robinson and Birdsong aside. "We're all Americans," he told them.

"Am I?" asked Birdsong. He pointed out that the Constitution whose foundational intent they were so eager to restore had not considered him one. And he added: "Slavery is only abolished as long as I'm not incarcerated. I'm just saying—you guys weren't slaves."

Robinson looked baffled. "So Irish people were never slaves?" he demanded. Rather than be further insulted, he threw up his hands and stalked off.

Howland was also upset. "Don't ever call me a slave owner," he said. "That's something I won't tolerate. I'm not guilty of you being a slave. So why do we have to have that fight?"

"Because this country was built by my people's enslavement," Birdsong replied with equanimity. "And this country labels me as three-fifths a human."

"It's been a hundred and fifty years," Howland said.

Like Robinson—who'd been told and I think sincerely believed that chattel slavery and Irish indentured servitude were identical—Howland was not so much disinterested in the past as he was attached to his own version of it. Historical nostalgia was fundamental to the

Patriot mindset. Confederate and Betsy Ross flags were often flown at anti-lockdown events; Three Percenters honored the colonists; "Seventeen seventy-six!" was a staple rallying cry; and I had met many militia members with "We the People" tattooed across their forearms in the ornamental font of the Constitution's original preamble (as it was penned before the Fourteenth Amendment superseded article 1, section 2, clause 3—popularly remembered as the "Three-Fifths Compromise"). The lost American greatness that Patriots yearned to make again extended ever further back in time, from the childhood of Karl Manke's generation, to the Civil War, to the settling of the frontier, to the Revolution, and beyond. On January 6, I would come face-to-face with the extreme limit of this atavistic fetish, in the form of an insurrectionist dressed up as Captain Moroni, the military hero who Mormons believe vanquished enemies in North America, noted for their "skin of blackness," in the first century BC. "Unfortunately, they don't have any costumes for ancient American warriors," he would tell me, indicating his Roman greaves and tunic. Then he would explain that Captain Moroni had fought against the distant ancestors of Native Americans, and that those people had descended from the Jews.

"I'm still three-fifths a human," Paul Birdsong insisted.

"Not true," someone interjected. We all turned to find Ryan Kelley frowning with disapproval.

"Yes, it is true," Birdsong said.

"No, it's not true," Kelley said.

"Yes, it is true," Birdsong said.

"No, it's not true. It's not true. It's not true."

The discussion appeared to have reached an impasse. Eventually, the counterprotesters left to conduct their nightly march through downtown. Three days later, the American Patriot Council published an article on its website that described Birdsong as a "local thug" and "an ongoing problem in the community." Black Lives Matter was a

"Democrat-run hate group." For some reason, the article also mentioned Michael Lynn Jr. Though Lynn had nothing to do with Birdsong or his marches, the Lansing firefighter was denounced as a "gang banger." The anonymous author signed their byline with a nom de plume: "A Closer."

DO SOMETHING

When he called Paul Birdsong "a weak fucking man," Adam Fox was thirty-seven years old, divorced, broke, and living with his dogs in the basement of a friend's vacuum cleaner repair shop. His ex-wife had filed for a protective order in 2015, alleging abuse and alcoholism. Nothing about Fox indicated "ringleader" or "mastermind"—descriptors used for him by the media. The owner of the vacuum shop told the *Detroit Free Press*, "He's not a leader, he's a follower. He couldn't lead a mouse to cheese."

It appears likely that Fox, the Null brothers, and the Wolverine Watchmen would never have gotten as far as they did without the aggressive encouragement of undercover FBI informants, and after Fox's lawyer argued that he had been a victim of entrapment, his trial would end with a hung jury. (Ironically, the FBI honed this technique in the wake of 9/11, when agents infiltrated mosques and federal prosecutors accused hapless Muslim Americans of plotting against the country, exacerbating the rampant Islamophobia that helped give rise to the Patriot Movement in the first place.) But the FBI had not been alone in motivating Fox. In a Facebook livestream, he had ranted about Governor Whitmer's executive orders, called her a "tyrant bitch," and insisted, "We gotta do something." From where did this sense of urgency come, if not from the likes of Mike Shirkey, the Michigan Senate leader, who'd stood on a stage with the Null brothers in Grand Rapids and told the armed men arrayed before him that they must "stand up and test" what he called an unconstitutional and un-Christian "assertion of authority by the government"?

After Fox and the Nulls were charged with terrorism, Shirkey condemned them as "criminals and traitors." Dar Leaf, the Barry County sheriff who spoke in Grand Rapids before Shirkey, responded somewhat differently. "A lot of people are angry with the governor," Leaf explained during an interview on a local news channel, "and they want her arrested. So were they trying to arrest her, or was it a kidnapping attempt?" The sheriff went on, in his didactic way, "It doesn't say if you're in elected office you're exempt from that arrest. So I have to look at it from that angle, and I'm hoping that's more what it is."

The idea that patriotic citizens could "arrest" politicians whom they deemed corrupt was vintage Posse Comitatus. It went hand in hand with the notion of common-law grand juries, for which Leaf had also advocated in Grand Rapids. "It's amazing when you start looking into this stuff," he'd marveled, the Nulls standing at his side. "They don't teach this stuff to us anymore."

"Thank you for teaching us!" a woman had called out.

According to the government, after the Wolverine Watchmen captured Whitmer, they intended to "remove her to a secure location in Wisconsin for a 'trial.'"

Fox, the Nulls, and the Wolverine Watchmen all identified as Boogaloo Bois. In 2012, users on the website 4Chan had appropriated the title of *Breakin' 2: Electric Boogaloo*—a 1984 movie about break dancing—to sardonically dub their anticipated insurrection "Civil War 2: Electric Boogaloo." White supremacists, envisaging the boogaloo as a race war, popularized the meme online. Since then, the concept had been adopted and modified by Second Amendment advocates, preppers, survivalists, and others. An alternative name for the boogaloo was the "big luau," which accounted for the Hawaiian shirts worn by its enthu-

siasts. Many Boogaloo Bois believed violent revolution was necessary
and inevitable, and that it was their civic responsibility to help bring it
about. After a Boogaloo Boi killed a security guard and a deputy sheriff in California, Facebook banned proponents of the ideology from its
platform, erasing over a hundred groups. I'd been following several of
them. The discussions had tended to revolve around defining boogaloo priorities, a debate often reduced to who should be "yeeted." The
general tone of trollish misanthropy was distinct from the often shrill
self-seriousness of other Patriots. Many Boogaloo Bois were also viru-
lently racist and antisemitic. Jews lay behind all manner of diabolism
that the boogaloo would remedy, from the media to child pornogra-
phy. Because of their desire to precipitate the country's descent into
open conflict, Boogaloo Bois were often categorized by extremism experts as "accelerationists." The Boogaloo Bois I had met in Michigan
and followed on Facebook, however, all seemed to feel that things were
accelerating already, with or without them. And this vertiginous sen-
sibility was shared by most Patriots, whether or not they wore Hawaiian shirts. As Wyatt, the customer at Manke's barbershop who'd driven
all the way from Oklahoma, told me, "I used to have more time." Even
before the uprising in Minneapolis, the looming election had sufficed
to foster a climate of gathering crescendo. "Soros, Pelosi, the whole
gang—they're old and this has to happen in their lifetime," one anti-
lockdowner had explained to me. "If they'd gotten Hillary, they'd be
right on schedule. But they got Trump, so they have to accelerate."
Ryan Kelley's belief that Democrats were "hiring people to riot and
loot in the streets" suggested how the George Floyd protests had become both part of that acceleration and proof of it.

Such was the disquieted attitude of millions of right-wing and conservative Americans when, on July 3, Donald Trump addressed them
from Mount Rushmore.

A WARTIME PRESIDENT

The Black Hills of South Dakota, or Pahá Sápa, are a sacred homeland for the Sioux, whose ancestors called them "the heart of everything that is." In 1868, the US signed a treaty guaranteeing the Sioux "absolute and undisturbed" dominion over the area. Then gold was discovered there. General Philip Sheridan—whom historians credit with first uttering some approximation of the words "the only good Indian is a dead Indian"—charged Lieutenant Colonel George Armstrong Custer with evicting or exterminating Pahá Sápa's legal wardens. At the Battle of the Little Bighorn, in 1876, warriors led by Chiefs Sitting Bull and Crazy Horse defeated Custer and his Seventh Cavalry Regiment. But a quarter century later, the military put a grisly end to Sioux resistance with the murder of Sitting Bull at Standing Rock and the atrocity at Wounded Knee. The dynamiting of four white men's faces into a hallowed mountainside was another violation—not least because one of them, Abraham Lincoln, had authorized the hanging of thirty-eight Sioux men in neighboring Minnesota. In 1980, the Supreme Court found the seizure of the Black Hills to have been a "ripe and rank case of dishonorable dealings," and ordered the government to pay the region's remaining Sioux more than $100 million. The Sioux refused the compensation, which still sits in an account at the Bureau of Indian Affairs, accruing interest, and is now worth over a billion and a half dollars. They do not want the money. They want Mount Rushmore closed and the Black Hills returned to them.

Given that gold had driven Americans to annex the Black Hills, it was, in a way, appropriate that Trump—a man who'd once sold bottles of vodka with twenty-four-karat gold-leaf labels bearing his initial, and who had descended on a golden escalator into the lobby of his own gilded hotel to announce his candidacy for president—went there, on the eve of Independence Day, to celebrate that crime and the righteousness of its beneficiaries. "Mount Rushmore will stand forever as an eternal tribute to our forefathers and to our freedom," he told South Dakotans assembled at the foot of the monument, eliciting chants of "USA." He did not mention the Sioux. His fourth day in office, Trump had issued an executive order for construction to resume on the oil pipeline near Standing Rock (which Obama had suspended in response to the protests in 2016). Now, Trump exalted "Western civilization" and, citing the same divine entitlement asserted by Christian Identity, characterized the possibility of restitution as a threat of dispossession: "That which God has given us we will allow no one to take away."

At the beginning of the pandemic, when Trump proclaimed, "We must sacrifice together, because we are all in this together," what had made his speech so atypical was less its conciliatory words than their intended audience. For once, he spoke to the entire country. Calling COVID-19 "the invisible enemy" of all Americans, he readily assumed the mantle of "a wartime president." Four months later, Trump had largely dismissed the peril of COVID-19 and had set his sights on a different enemy. "Our nation is witnessing a merciless campaign to wipe out our history, defame our heroes, erase our values, and indoctrinate our children," he warned. Agents of "far-left fascism" and "totalitarianism" were determined to "unleash a wave of violent crime in our cities," "demolish both justice and society," and impose widespread "repression, domination, and exclusion." The end goal of these subversives? To "overthrow the American Revolution."

Even Lincoln, at the height of the Civil War, had avoided vilifying Confederate soldiers, in the interest of promoting reconciliation. At Mount Rushmore, Trump not only labeled half of the country irredeemably depraved; he exhorted the other half to *do something* about it. "It is time, it is time," he told his supporters, conjuring a familiar sense of acceleration. "For the sake of our honor, for the sake of our children, for the sake of our nation, we must protect and preserve our history, our heritage." Alluding to 1776, he issued what any Three Percenter would have recognized as a call to arms: "Here tonight, before the eyes of our forefathers, Americans declare again, as we did 244 years ago, that we will not be tyrannized, we will not be demeaned, and we will not be intimidated by bad, evil people."

I'd heard this language before. It was the language Ryan Kelley had used. It was the fearful, fearsome language that had come to Kelley when Paul Birdsong lay down at his feet.

It was the language of the boogaloo.

THE CURIOUS THING ABOUT TRUMP declaring himself a wartime president was that he already was one. As a candidate, he had said of ISIS, "I would bomb the shit out of 'em," and five months after he took office, the US led a devastating aerial offensive against the Syrian city of Raqqa, which ISIS had made its capital. While embedded with Arab and Kurdish ground troops that summer, I'd been shocked by what appeared to be a strategy of total annihilation applied against an urban landscape that still harbored a significant civilian population. Over four months, the US deployed thousands of munitions, ranging from laser-guided Hellfire missiles to one-ton unguided bombs. Marine artillery battalions complemented the barrage with more than thirty thousand shells. The most distinguishing characteristic of the Global War on Terrorism had always been its asymmetry, but in Raqqa the dissonance between the impact of American arms and the absence of US service members was unlike anything I'd ever seen. Each day, all day, explosives whistled out of the sky, sending up tall plumes of dust and smoke. Yet I encountered almost no Americans on the front. While ten thousand Syrian allies of the US died in the campaign, only one

US soldier did. This meant that few people stateside ever heard about the battle. During the three weeks that I spent there, the entire foreign press corps never numbered more than two or three reporters.

I returned to the city in early 2020. Although most of the streets had been excavated from beneath vast mountains of rubble seeded with bodies and unexploded ordnance, the destruction remained so profoundly comprehensive as to be visually disorienting. It was as if the cumulative energy of the American bombardment had scrambled the normal order of things, leaving behind an Escher-like reality to which the mind could not immediately adjust. Staircases dangled vertically from twisted rebar; cars teetered upside down; roofs jutted at weird angles; slabs of concrete undulated like rumpled cloth; trees cowered from old blasts. Whole blocks were missing several stories, as if truncated by the level swing of a giant's scythe. Some buildings appeared to defy physics, frozen mid-fall. Others had been trucked away, the only trace of them a square of dirt. Not a single structure—not a house, not a fence, not a school—had escaped the Americans unscathed.

Around a hundred thousand people lived amid the ruins, occupying every habitable pocket of half-collapsed apartment towers, crowded into rooms with bowed ceilings and bulging walls, masses of cement literally pressing in on them. Many had lost loved ones, limbs, or both. The only public hospital had been obliterated. When the director brought me to his once state-of-the-art facility, we had to scrabble through downed pipes and caved-in floors, every surface scorched black by fire. The remnants of medical supplies lay scattered like debris: white piles of cast plaster, contorted gurneys, smashed exam tables. All of the X-ray machines, CAT scanners, and MRI devices were irreparably damaged. According to the director, American commanders had visited the hospital on several occasions, taken pictures, and promised support. None had ever been given, and now even the visits had stopped. Trump had ordered a rapid withdrawal from the area;

the military had abandoned its bases; the future of Raqqa and its residents was no longer our concern. None of the diplomats, entrepreneurs, opportunists, and humanitarians who, for nineteen years, had reliably populated such zones remained. I never saw an American. In this sense, Raqqa was a fitting denouement to the tragic saga of US force at the start of the twenty-first century: an unprecedented spectacle of violence followed by unprecedented indifference to the wasteland of human and physical wreckage left in its wake.

Because it had barely registered with the electorate, Raqqa had not made Trump, in his own estimation, a wartime president. Neither, for the same reason, had Afghanistan, where I'd last reported in 2019. At the time, the conflict was the deadliest in the world. During the first half of that year, US and Afghan forces killed more civilians than the Taliban and ISIS did—over a hundred a month. US air strikes pummeled isolated areas where casualties were impossible to confirm, and CIA-sponsored militias conducted relentless deadly night raids. In Nangarhar province, a middle-aged laborer brought me to his former house, where one such unit had murdered fourteen of his relatives. He showed me where he'd found the corpses of his father, three brothers, and brother-in-law, an Afghan soldier home on leave. His mother had also been shot. "I swear to God the only weapons in our house were kitchen knives," she said. A nine-month-old girl had been killed. The family appeared to have been targeted because it had recently escaped to the village from a district that was under the control of ISIS. "We bought this house because we dreamed of living in a place where we could sleep peacefully," the laborer said.

In a nearby valley, on the mountainous border with Pakistan, I visited the ravine where, three months into Trump's term, the US had deployed the largest nonnuclear weapon in its arsenal: a twenty-thousand-pound Massive Ordnance Air Blast, or MOAB, colloquially known as the Mother of All Bombs. It had killed more than ninety people. Up a rutted dirt road that paralleled a swiftly flowing river, Black Hawk helicopters lifted off from a US Special Forces base. American soldiers lobbed mortars into distant hills. They wouldn't speak with me. Neither, of course, would the CIA or its local proxies. Journalistic access to combat units had become almost nonexistent. But then, so had public interest. While air strikes and night raids had made the war even more hellish and destructive for Afghans, they'd also made it more abstract for Americans. The rise in the number of Afghan dead and wounded had corresponded with a decline in the number of US dead and wounded. "We're not fighting a war," Trump told reporters while I was in Kabul. "If we wanted to fight a war in Afghanistan— and win it—I could win that war in a week." He added, "Afghanistan would be wiped off the face of the earth."

For Trump, a war hidden from the American people—however many other communities and lives it claimed—was not a real war. A real war would be felt at home. Perhaps, like the campaign for the Black Hills, during which the Sioux were nearly wiped off the face of the earth, it would be *waged* at home.

SEVEN

THE HARDEST CITY

On June 18, the same day the American Patriot Council held its pro-militia rally in Michigan, protesters in Portland, Oregon, marched to the German American Society, outside of which a bronze statue of George Washington stood atop a marble plinth. After spray-painting GENOCIDAL COLONIST on the plinth, they lashed nylon straps around the statue and toppled it. YOU'RE ON NATIVE LAND was added to the graffiti. Two weeks later, under Washington's gaze at Mount Rushmore, Trump declared, "They are determined to tear down every statue, symbol, and memory of our national heritage."

"Not on my watch!" someone in the audience called out.

"That is why I'm deploying federal law enforcement to protect our monuments, arrest the rioters, and prosecute offenders to the fullest extent of the law," Trump said.

Over the next month, Portland became the site of large-scale confrontations between leftist demonstrators and militarized federal agents. In late August, I rented an efficiency in an extended-stay motel downtown. A couple of days after I arrived, while driving to a friend's house, I pulled onto a street full of honking pickup trucks bedecked with American flags and TRUMP 2020 banners. I followed the convoy onto an interstate and out of the city. Without realizing that dozens of vehicles had broken off from the caravan and headed downtown, I continued on my way.

At some point I checked my phone and found reports online of local residents shouting obscenities and throwing water bottles at the Trump supporters who'd diverged from the highway. Some Trump supporters had fired paintball guns and pepper spray from their vehicles, others had gotten out and assaulted bystanders. It was dark when I reached a wide avenue in the shopping district. People sprinted by my car as I parked. Walking in the opposite direction, I soon came upon a small crowd facing a police cordon. Behind the officers, a dead body lay in a pool of light.

The victim was an affiliate of Patriot Prayer, a pro-Trump evangelical movement started in Vancouver, Washington, during the lead-up to the 2016 election. The group's founder, Joey Gibson, was a thirty-six-year-old house flipper and former high school football coach. Muscular, brash, and partial to form-fitting T-shirts that exhibited his many tattoos—including one of a Spartan helmet and the words WARRIORS FOR FREEDOM—Gibson had created Patriot Prayer after coming to feel that his political views and religious beliefs were taboo in liberal enclaves. Over the phone, he'd told me that his objective had been to venture into "the hardest cities to voice your opinion in as a conservative": cities like Berkeley, San Francisco, and—just across the Columbia River from Vancouver—Portland.

Gibson had held his first Portland rally, billed as the March for Free Speech, in 2017. During the march, a man named Jeremy Christian

was filmed barking racial slurs and wielding a baseball bat. The next
month, Christian boarded a Portland train and accosted two Black teenage girls, one of whom was Muslim and wore a hijab. When three men
intervened, Christian fatally stabbed two of them. In the courtroom,
during his arraignment, he screamed, "Get out if you don't like free
speech! You call it terrorism, I call it patriotism!" The murders took
place amid a historic surge in anti-Muslim hate crimes, which Trump's
critics linked to his pattern of Islamophobic rhetoric (such as when he
called for "a total and complete shutdown of Muslims entering the
United States"). Nine days later, Gibson led another free-speech rally
in Portland. After presiding over a moment of silence for Christian's
victims, he introduced a speaker who recounted having recently "cracked
the skulls of some commies" in Berkeley. The man, Kyle Chapman, was
a known white nationalist who would later write on social media about
the need to "confront the Zionist criminals who wish to destroy our
civilization," and to defend "the right for White men and women to
have their own countries."

Over the next two years, Patriot Prayer continued to regularly
gather in Portland, and chaotic brawls with counterprotesters became
recurrent events downtown. Then, in 2019, Gibson was charged with
inciting a riot at a local bar popular with leftists, after he brought a
gang of followers there and one of them was filmed striking a young
woman on the head with a baton, knocking her unconscious and fracturing her vertebra. Since his arrest, he'd stayed away from the
city. The pandemic had also redirected his sense of purpose. Four
days after Operation Gridlock—the first anti-lockdown protest in
Michigan—Gibson joined Three Percenters, Oath Keepers, and Boogaloo Bois for a similar demonstration in Olympia. Patriot Prayer went
on to become a major anti-lockdown force in Washington. According
to Gibson, one of his most committed supporters during this period

was thirty-nine-year-old Aaron Danielson. After Gibson learned about the Trump convoy—which had been organized online by a different network—he and Danielson had decided to participate together, riding into Portland in the same truck. They had accompanied the main body of vehicles out of town, but then received messages about the ongoing skirmishes and returned to the city separately.

Danielson had been shot a few minutes before I arrived. Michael Reinoehl, a forty-eight-year-old counterprotester, would later admit responsibility, claiming self-defense. A canister of bear spray and a telescopic truncheon would be found on Danielson. At the time, however, nobody in the crowd knew what had happened or who was involved. I asked a few people whether they'd seen anything. The prevailing assumption seemed to have it backward: the Trump supporters had killed a local activist.

"What are you doing here?" a voice beside me asked.

A man in a balaclava was addressing a man with wraparound sunglasses and a baseball hat bearing the name of the Republican gubernatorial candidate for Washington, Loren Culp.

"It's Joey Gibson," someone said. They sounded somewhat uncertain, and for several moments, people seemed to doubt that it was true. Gibson had not been seen in Portland for over a year. Later, he'd tell me that he had happened on the crime scene accidentally and had no idea that the corpse lying thirty feet away from us was Danielson.

When someone told him that the victim was a protester, Gibson waved dismissively. "That's what they always be yelling and screaming about—'Some white supremacist killed someone tonight.' They say that shit all the time."

"Because you bring white supremacists to town all the time," a woman said.

"I'm brown," Gibson, whose mother was Japanese, replied. He rolled up his sleeve and showed his skin tone. People shouted at him to leave. "Why don't *you* guys stop acting like Nazis?" Gibson asked. A man holding a tall can of beer, wearing a sweatshirt with the logo of the progressive political web show *The Young Turks*, pitched forward and spat in his face.

The weaponization—and criminalization—of spit had become a peculiar motif of the pandemic in America. In Flint, Michigan, a man had been charged with two felonies for spitting on a police officer. In Pontiac, Michigan, a man had announced that he was infected with COVID-19 before spitting on a doctor. In a hospital in Aurora, Pennsylvania, a woman in respiratory distress spat on a nurse who wanted her to sign some paperwork. In Hanover, Pennsylvania, a woman was arrested after spitting on meat and produce in a supermarket. The charges ranged from battery assault to "terrorist threats." Each time I read another article about a belligerent spitter, I imagined a certain kind of citizen. The citizen I imagined did not wear a *Young Turks* sweatshirt or hang out with leftists in Portland.

"Can we stop with the hate?" said Gibson, making no move to wipe the saliva clinging to his brow.

Protesters continued to arrive. As the ferocity of their insults grew, Gibson turned to a blond woman who'd been standing at his side. "Let's go," he told her.

At least fifty young people followed them. Gibson's hat and sunglasses were snatched away. Objects were hurled at him, drinks were emptied on him. Someone smashed an egg on his head. He was punched and pepper-sprayed. With the blond woman's help, he staggered forward blindly while a man rattled a cowbell in his ears and others strobed flashlights in his eyes.

"Kill the Nazi!"

As far as I could see, all of Gibson's assailants were white. I began to feel ashamed about documenting what was happening to him. I had filmed a mob kill somebody in Iraq once, and I did not wish to repeat the experience. That the man had belonged to ISIS was as irrelevant as the question of whether Joey Gibson was a white supremacist.

After a few blocks, several people pushed their way to Gibson and his friend and escorted them down the street. "Let him leave, goddammit!" a short Asian man with glasses, long hair, and a bicycle helmet yelled. "Everyone back the fuck off!"

Gibson and the woman ducked into a gas station, and an employee locked the door behind them. The man in the bicycle helmet blocked the entrance, but people smashed the windows and kicked open a side door. One protester pleaded, "He's a fucking Nazi, but are you gonna *lynch* him?"

Eventually, the police arrived. Inside the gas station, Gibson vomited and rinsed the pepper spray from his eyes. He called a friend to pick him up. As soon as he got into the car, his phone rang. It was a reporter trying to identify the shooting victim. He texted Gibson a picture of Danielson being treated by medics. "I recognized him right away," Gibson later told me.

I found the man in the bicycle helmet at a nearby 7-Eleven. His name was Rico De Vera, and he was a twenty-seven-year-old Filipino American who studied engineering at Portland Community College. Earlier, a Trump supporter had shot him in the face with a paintball gun; the flesh around his left eye was stained neon pink. Rico had been protesting almost every day since George Floyd was killed. He remained enthusiastic about the movement but had little tolerance for the sort of behavior we'd just witnessed. "It pisses me off," he said. "People are going to use tonight to say that Black Lives Matter is a bunch of thugs."

We walked a few blocks to a park outside the Multnomah County Justice Center, where people had congregated by a perimeter of concrete barriers and metal fencing. This was where most of the Patriot

Prayer rallies and counterprotests had taken place. More recently, it had become a rally point for Black Lives Matter demonstrations. In June, huge crowds had lobbed fireworks, bottles, and other projectiles at the Justice Center, a fortress-like monolith that contained the municipal police headquarters and the county jail. The Justice Center stood beside a US district courthouse, and after Trump called for the deployment of federal agents to protect government property, more than a hundred members of the Department of Homeland Security and the US Marshals Service arrived in Portland, ostensibly to defend the building. Cell phone video showed men in military fatigues snatching people off the street and bundling them into unmarked vans, without explanation. A marshal shot a twenty-six-year-old protester in the head with an impact munition, fracturing his skull. The protester, who had been holding up a boom box with both hands, suffered severe and lasting cognitive damage. Such excessive force drew larger and larger crowds until the feds began relinquishing responsibility for the courthouse to the Oregon State Police. Most of the protesters went home. Many dedicated activists did not.

Around a hundred of them now stood outside the Justice Center, amped up from the day's events, chanting loudly, "Whose streets? *Our* streets!" A shirtless, shoeless man with yellow hair hanging halfway down his back punctuated the call-and-response with a trumpet. After a while, a young Black woman made an announcement. "I just got word that the person who died was a Patriot Prayer person," she said. "I don't know about y'all, but I am not sad about a Nazi dying!"

"Hell no!"

The woman seemed to recognize that a line had been crossed—and she wanted us to know that she had no regrets. "Our community held its own and took out the trash!" she yelled. "I am not sad that a fucking fascist died tonight!"

The trumpet blared. The mob cheered.

WE GO WHERE THEY GO

Two months before he killed Aaron Danielson, Michael Reinoehl wrote on Instagram, "We truly have an opportunity right now to fix everything. But it will be a fight like no other! It will be a war and like all wars there will be casualties!" Reinoehl also claimed that he was "100% ANTIFA all the way!"

What did it mean to be Antifa? One of the originators of American antifascism, a fifty-one-year-old hip-hop artist named Mic Crenshaw, happened to live in Portland; when I visited him to ask this question, I was surprised to learn that he had grown up in Minneapolis, not far from Thirty-Eighth Street and Chicago Avenue. In high school, Crenshaw, who is Black, had joined with one Ojibwe and five white students to organize a punk crew called the Baldies. "We were trying to become the Minneapolis version of what the kids in England had been doing for years," he recounted. They shaved their heads, found bomber jackets at an Army-surplus store, and bought Doc Martens from mail-order catalogs. The British punks whom the Baldies emulated had been influenced by Jamaican immigrant culture and believed in multiethnic working-class solidarity. Punk music also appealed to neo-Nazis, however, and shortly after the Baldies formed, a local gang called the White Knights began harassing people of color throughout Minneapolis. When Crenshaw learned where the leader of the White Knights lived, he threw a chunk of concrete through his window. "That was the jump-off," he recalled. "A protracted period of street violence" followed. Soon the Baldies and the White Knights were brawling in alleys and at concert venues several times a week. Bats, chains, pipes, knives, brass knuckles, and pepper spray were standard implements. "Luckily, no one died," said Crenshaw. "People were definitely going to the hospital, though."

During their campaign against the White Knights, the Baldies made pacts with militant leftists and gravitated toward anarchist tenets of mutual aid and community defense. Crenshaw was drawn to communism. "From that survival-based organizing our politics began to emerge," he explained. Another former Baldie later told me, "Although many of us were interested in reading theory, what was driving our action wasn't adherence to a particular ideology—it was meeting the threat as it needed to be met. It was very practical." For Crenshaw, it was existential: "As a Black kid, I was fighting against people who wanted to kill me."

One hub for young radicals in Minneapolis was Back Room Anarchist Books, which sold revolutionary newspapers from Europe. In publications like *Class War*, the Baldies read about Anti-Fascist Action, a British group dedicated to physically confronting racists and anti-semites. Anti-Fascist Action had revived a legacy in England stretching back to the 1930s, when Londoners prevented Oswald Mosley and his British Union of Fascists from publicly assembling. It belonged to a pan-European tradition, which, in countries that had endured the horrors of fascism in the mid-twentieth century, remained a deeply relevant component of left-wing politics. The demonstrators I had seen in Paris, on the Avenue Marceau, traced their struggle directly to the French resistance against Nazi occupiers and their collaborators.

Inspired by these movements, the Baldies resolved to expand their crusade against white supremacy beyond the skinhead subculture. In 1987, after effectively chasing the White Knights out of Minneapolis, they established Anti-Racist Action, or ARA, and began recruiting skaters, college students, and Black and Latino gang members. Explaining their decision to tweak the British name, Crenshaw said, "To us, the word *fascist* sounded too academic. But everybody knew what a racist was."

After high school, Crenshaw and his friends went on the road, following punk tours around the country and setting up ARA chapters in other cities. In 1991, the group convened its first national conference, in Portland. Portland had been central to the white power movement since the seventies, when William Potter Gale launched the Posse Comitatus there. The Aryan Nations, in neighboring Idaho, sponsored neo-Nazis throughout the Pacific Northwest who talked of turning the region into an all-white ethno-state. Prior to the ARA conference, an Ethiopian immigrant in Portland named Mulugeta Seraw had been beaten to death by three acolytes of White Aryan Resistance, or WAR. A week before Seraw's murder, WAR leaders had appeared on the daytime talk show *Geraldo*. One of them had called a Jewish audience member a "kike" and a Black guest an "Uncle Tom," instigating a violent free-for-all on live television, during which a neo-Nazi broke the host Geraldo Rivera's nose. "Portland was in the national spotlight as a hotbed of racism," Crenshaw said. "We wanted to let our presence be felt and to say, 'We're not gonna stand for that.'"

After Mulugeta Seraw was killed, ARA members, collaborating with Skin Heads Against Racial Prejudice, or SHARP, mobilized to expel neo-Nazis from Portland. A running conflict resembling the one in Minneapolis between the Baldies and the White Knights yielded a similar result. Within a couple of years, white power skins had all but vanished from the city. WAR and the Aryan Nations were crippled by civil lawsuits. As the neo-Nazi threat appeared to recede, so did ARA membership.

Then, in 2007, white supremacists attempting to reinvigorate the vestiges of WAR planned to hold a white power music festival near Portland. Former ARA members helped pressure the host venue to pull out. Half a dozen of these activists, sensing a need for renewed vigilance, created a group called Rose City Antifa—the first antifascist organization in America.

. . .

ONE AFTERNOON IN EARLY SEPTEMBER, I sat across from two
members of Rose City Antifa, Sophie and Morgan, at a picnic table in
a Portland park. As much as anyone, these were the "bad, evil people"
who Trump had claimed would "overthrow the American Revolution." (Asking for anonymity, they used pseudonyms.) Sophie was transgender, and Morgan identified as a butch lesbian. A number of Rose
City's founders, they told me, were women. Whereas "some of the ARA
groups were in a world of toxic masculinity," said Sophie, Rose City
Antifa had "a strong feminist and queer component." This had led
to different priorities. "ARA was street-level confrontation with white
supremacist gangs," Morgan said. "We wanted to broaden the scope to
encompass more activities." Rose City dedicated most of its energy to
online research: identifying and tracking violent promoters of bigotry,
compiling dossiers, mapping their relationships, and sometimes publicly exposing—or "doxing"—them. Though they wouldn't disclose total
membership, Sophie and Morgan estimated that such investigations
took up around a hundred hours per week.

Notwithstanding this intelligence-focused approach, Morgan also
acknowledged that "research and action go hand in hand." Whenever
people deemed worthy of doxing held gatherings in public spaces, antifascists undertook to shut them down. After the Second World War,
Jewish veterans in England had created the 43 Group, which stormed
fascist assemblies with the aim of knocking over the speaker's platform. In *Antifa: The Anti-Fascist Handbook*, the scholar Mark Bray writes
that, while conservatives and liberals alike criticize "no-platforming"
as repugnant to free speech, antifascists take the 43 Group's view that
incipient fascism tends to metastasize if left unchecked. Given that
fascist movements aspire to mass oppression and even genocide, they
must be stifled early, while they still can be.

THE STORM IS HERE

Despite the foreboding militarization of the Patriot Movement during the Obama administration, most liberals tended to concentrate instead on the swelling momentum of its political analog, the Tea Party. That changed with Trump, whose rise was buoyed by a wave of strident white nationalism calling itself the alt-right. Unapologetic neo-Nazis, much like those the ARA had battled in the eighties—and in some cases the very same—were as enchanted by Trump as were the militias and Three Percenters. Michael Peinovich, also known as Mike Enoch, who advocated for a white ethno-state on his podcast *The Daily Shoah*, boarded the Trump train early on. So did Richard Spencer, the director of the National Policy Institute, which sought to "elevate the consciousness of whites, ensure our biological and cultural continuity, and protect our civil rights." After the 2016 election, Spencer—who had befriended Stephen Miller, the policy director of Trump's transition team, when they belonged to the same conservative student group at Duke University—was filmed proclaiming to a roomful of brethren in D.C., "Hail Trump! Hail our people!" A number of men stood and raised their arms in Nazi salutes.

In 2017, Enoch and Spencer both spoke at the Unite the Right rally, in Charlottesville, Virginia, where throngs of white supremacists paraded through downtown, carrying torches and Nazi flags. While many Americans were nonplussed by the rally, antifascists were prepared. Hundreds of them showed up, in fidelity to a credo espoused by Mic Crenshaw and the original ARA: "We go where they go." The author Cornel West, who accompanied a group of clergy members to Charlottesville, recalled on *Democracy Now!*, "We would have been crushed like cockroaches if it were not for the anarchists and the antifascists." Clashes culminated in a neo-Nazi plowing his car through a crowd of counterprotesters, killing a woman. An audio recording captured Richard Spencer, later that same day, ranting about the "kikes" and "octoroons" who had disrupted the event. "My ancestors fucking enslaved those little pieces of fucking shit!" Spencer screamed. "They look up and see a face like mine looking down at them! That's how the fucking world works!"

Another notable attendee was the former KKK grand wizard David Duke. "We are determined to take our country back," Duke told a reporter. "We're going to fulfill the promises of Donald Trump." After Trump famously maintained that there had been "very fine people on both sides" in Charlottesville, Duke praised the president's "honesty" and "courage."

While equivocating about the neo-Nazis, Trump was more categorical when it came to the antifascists, denouncing them as "troublemakers" who were "very, very violent." This marked the first occasion that the president deflected criticism of himself and his most extreme supporters by demonizing Antifa. After George Floyd was killed, he revived the tactic—and ever since Mount Rushmore, his reelection strategy had seemed to hinge increasingly on making Americans more afraid of Antifa than of the deadly pandemic raging out of control under his scattershot management. The week before I met Sophie and Morgan, the Trump campaign had sent out a series of texts soliciting donations. "BIDEN WOULD LET ANTIFA DESTROY OUR NATION," read one. And: "ANTIFA THUGS WILL RUIN SUBURBS." And: "Do you stand AGAINST Biden & Antifa?" And: "ANTIFA ALERT: They'll attack your homes if Joe's elected."

A review by the Center for Strategic and International Studies had found that right-wing terrorists had carried out 140 attacks since Trump's inauguration; left-wing terrorists, a dozen. Aaron Danielson was the sole American ever to be killed by someone professing an antifascist agenda; right-wing extremists, by comparison, were responsible for more than 320 deaths in the past quarter century. These, however, were mere facts. According to Trump and his allies, to appreciate the singular threat that Antifa presented to the country, all you had to do was look at Portland.

UTOPIANS

Since the federal drawdown from the Multnomah County Justice Center in July, the protests had transitioned to targeting the Portland Police Bureau with nightly "direct actions." Despite Trump's portrayal of the city as a "beehive of terrorists" that was "ablaze all the time," many actions attracted fewer than a hundred people, and their impact was rarely detectable beyond a couple square blocks. Still, property destruction did occur, and because most protesters were white, this had become a source of tension with some residents of color. In June, after rioting damaged several businesses along Martin Luther King Jr. Boulevard, in a storied African American neighborhood, a consortium of Black community leaders held a press conference to condemn the vandalism. J. W. Matt Hennessee, the pastor of Vancouver Avenue First Baptist Church, told the protesters, "Get your knee off our neck. That is what you are doing when you do stuff like this."

Two days after Aaron Danielson was killed, I attended an action outside a building where Ted Wheeler, the city's Democratic mayor, owned an apartment. In Portland, the mayor serves as the commissioner of the police bureau, which the protesters were determined to see defunded. Most of the people there were clad in black bloc, a style of dress that rendered them indistinguishable from one another by obscuring their identities with similar dark clothing. It was Wheeler's fifty-eighth birthday, and some protesters wore festive party hats strapped over their helmets and ski masks.

A picnic table from a nearby restaurant was dragged into the street and set on fire. A man in a tank top and peacoat led the crowd in chants of "Fuck Ted Wheeler!" He was a twenty-three-year-old nurse named Najee Gow. I'd met him the previous week, when several young women had staged a sit-in in Wheeler's lobby. Najee had been incensed that no African Americans were included in the demonstration. "It's what they've always done," he'd told me. "Hijack Black people's movements. This is disgusting." Now, as we greeted each other by the burning table, we were interrupted by the sound of shattering glass. A white man was swinging a baseball bat into the window of a dentist's office on the ground floor of Wheeler's building. "That makes me want to beat *them* up," Najee said. Like Rico De Vera, he feared that such antics only aided Trump and others who wanted to malign Black Lives Matter, and that they bred animosity toward Black people generally. "They're putting Black lives at risk," Najee said. "African Americans are constantly out here telling them to stop, but they won't. So, at the end of the day, it's like, 'Are *you* racist?'"

A white man with a hammer had joined the one with the bat. Soon, a loud explosion echoed from inside the dentist's office, followed by smoke and flames. Najee walked over to confront the vandals. While they argued, a white woman spray-painted an arrow on the wall, pointing to the broken window. She then shook the can and scrawled, THIS IS THE LANGUAGE OF THE UNHEARD.

WITH A POPULATION that was only 6 percent Black, Portland was the whitest big city in America. Historians traced the origin of these demographics to the founding of Oregon, which settlers envisaged as a white utopia. When Oregon joined the union in 1859, it became the only state with an outright ban on Black people. In the 1920s, Portland had more Klansmen per capita than any other city. Later, redlining policies and urban renewal projects displaced many African Americans—

a process reprised by more recent waves of gentrification. When Mic Crenshaw moved from Minneapolis to Portland not long after the ARA conference, he stepped away from activism, in part because the struggle there consisted largely of white people combating white racism in white spaces. "I couldn't do that anymore," he said. "I would be the only Black person in the room, and fighting white supremacy is different when you're white."

While Black activists and ad hoc collectives had organized the first massive demonstrations in Portland after the killing of George Floyd, by the time I got there it was hard to say who, if anyone, was in charge. The nightly direct actions were resolutely nonhierarchical. Every day, a message circulated on social media announcing a rendezvous point (usually a park), from which protesters would march to a proximate destination (usually a precinct house). As a rule, white protesters did seem to defer to their Black and brown peers—who, though far less numerous, were generally the only people to use megaphones, deliver speeches, and lead marches. I had the sense, however, that a more complicated dynamic played out behind the scenes. A diffuse, opaque network, communicating on encrypted messaging apps, planned the actions and chose their locations. One of the groups that seemed to wield outsize influence was the Pacific Northwest Youth Liberation Front, or YLF, a crew of bombastically radical high schoolers who described themselves as "a bunch of teenagers armed with ADHD and yerba mate." Although the YLF carefully guarded their anonymity and abhorred the press, they had acknowledged on social media that they were "majority white."

Nearly all of the protesters I met in Portland situated their mobilization against racism within the context of a more ambitious political agenda. One night in September, as people mustered in a park to march on a sheriff's station, I sat on the grass with a group of twenty-somethings called the Comrade Collective. They all had on black bloc and carried small rubber pigs that squealed when squeezed. Each had adopted a nickname. Firefly, a self-proclaimed Marxist-Leninist, told me, "It's more than just Black Lives Matter. That's why a lot of people out here have extremist ideologies. We believe that racism is built into capitalism, and we want to destroy the system of oppression."

Spinch, who was transgender and wore a blue bandanna over their mouth, said, "It often gets boiled down to: 'capitalism is the problem.' Which, like, yes. But also: colonialism." Spinch had been protesting since May. "I'm objectively very young and haven't been an autonomous adult for very long—so this is my first real foray into dedicated activism," they admitted. The experience had been eye-opening. "I got tear-gassed my first night out here. If that doesn't radicalize you, I don't know what will."

Brat, another transgender Comrade, agreed. "Before COVID, I was trying to get more involved in local politics," they said. "Now I sort of feel like that's a dead end."

"I was gonna run for city council!" said Spinch. It was as if they were confessing an embarrassing former vice. "But there's no point. The system is fucked."

I asked what the alternative was.

"Anarchism," said Spinch.

Brat nodded. "And one simple way to get us closer to that is defunding the police."

The animating consensus that America's economic, governmental, and judicial institutions were irremediable set Portland protesters apart from others around the country. Firefly, Spinch, and Brat viewed inequality not as a failure of the system but as the status quo that the system was designed to sustain; accordingly, the only way forward was to dismantle it and build something new. The evening after Supreme Court justice Ruth Bader Ginsburg died, I accompanied a march to the Gus J. Solomon US Courthouse, where protesters smashed the glass doors and cut down an American flag that had been lowered to half-mast. The flag was brought to the police headquarters, doused with hand sanitizer, and set on fire. On a boarded-up window, a white man in black bloc spray-painted: THE ONLY WAR IS CLASS WAR.

Portland demonstrators were also unique in the extent to which their damning appraisal of America was ecological. With its old-growth forests and powerful timber industry, the Pacific Northwest had long been a battleground for militant environmentalism. The YLF, whose green-and-black emblem features a cedar tree, was formed in 2018, the year Greta Thunberg installed herself outside the Swedish Parliament with a sign that read SCHOOL STRIKE FOR CLIMATE. One of the first actions that the YLF organized was a walkout from Portland schools, to raise awareness of global warming. In Oregon, the matter of environmental stewardship was inseparable from that of Indigenous rights. Before Lewis and Clark's expedition to the mouth of the Columbia River, before Christian missionaries blazed the Oregon Trail, and before a deluge of pioneers and homesteaders undertook to fulfill the manifest destiny of the Anglo-Saxon race, the Pacific Northwest had been the bounteous domain of the Chinook, Umpqua, Klamath, and Nez Percé. In 1850, when federal legislation allowed white settlers to freely stake claims throughout the Oregon Territory, millions of acres were appropriated. Multnomah County, which includes Portland, is named after a river people who were displaced from the banks of the Columbia and forced onto an arid reservation across the Cascades. The Paiute, whose burial grounds the Bundys had bulldozed, were decimated by the US Army and civilian militias, which opened their land to ranchers and prospectors. For many leftists in Oregon, this history undergirded the ecological critique of capitalism. Not only had the US exploited and despoiled the natural world; its rationale had been one of racial superiority. A direct consequence of that original sin was a heating planet that threatened the species as a whole.

The Native American struggle seemed to offer a crucial link between the climate activism that had preoccupied young white radicals
in Portland before George Floyd was killed and the racial-justice movement that followed. Black victims of slavery and Indigenous victims
of settler colonialism were recognized in the same breath with the
chant "Stolen bodies, stolen land." The gravity of the impending peril
that capitalism and white supremacy were understood to present—
human extinction—made extreme action all the more permissible.
"Right now, for youth, it feels like the Titanic is sinking and our politicians are the band still playing like everything is fine," Gregory Mc-
Kelvey, the vice chairman of Oregon's Democratic Black Caucus, wrote
on Twitter. "Don't be shocked when they smash your violin."

But would smashing violins, as opposed to playing them, rescue
anyone from drowning? On the weekend of Columbus Day, which
Portland recognized as Indigenous Peoples' Day, around two hundred
protesters rampaged through downtown. Outside the Portland Art
Museum, a statue of Theodore Roosevelt was toppled. Abraham Lincoln went next. On the plinth, someone spray-painted DAKOTA 38, in
reference to the mass execution of Sioux warriors in Minnesota in
1862. Bullets shattered the windows of a restaurant owned by a Black
veteran, and people broke into the Oregon Historical Society, where
they stole a quilt commemorating African American heritage, stitched
by fifteen Black women in the 1970s. Police found the quilt lying in
the rain a few blocks away. After the action, the YLF tweeted: "now
THAT is how we fucking do it. Didn't that feel wonderful?" The next
day, representatives from thirty Native American groups published a
statement denouncing the protesters and discouraging them from "mim-
icking the brutish ways of our colonizers."

EIGHT

LESS LETHAL

When Mic Crenshaw was a teenager, the punks in Minneapolis used a code word to alert one another to the presence of law enforcement: "ACAB," or All Cops Are Bastards. Many of the kids who hung out at Back Room Anarchist Books believed in a world without police. For years, however, few people even in the radical left considered this a realistic possibility. Not until George Floyd was killed, and vehement chants of "A-C-A-B!" rang out from protests across Minneapolis, were local activists able to channel the groundswell of anti-police sentiment roiling their city toward support for the proposition. As the organic uprising of late May transitioned to coordinated events with scheduled speakers, calls to eliminate the police grew louder and more common.

On June 6, protesters had marched to the mayor's apartment. Jacob Frey, a thirty-eight-year-old Democrat and former civil rights lawyer, had emerged from his home and navigated a dense crowd to where

Kandace Montgomery, the director of the group Black Visions Collective, stood in a truck bed. Looming over the mayor, Montgomery asked, "Yes or no—will you commit to defunding the Minneapolis Police Department?" After some vacillation, Frey responded, "I do not support the full abolition of the police department." Montgomery yelled at him to "get the fuck out of here," and the mayor returned to his building though a gauntlet of middle fingers, shouted insults, and chants of "Shame!"

The following afternoon, nine of thirteen city council members, a veto-proof majority, publicly vowed to "begin the process of ending the Minneapolis Police Department." The president of the city council declared, "Our efforts at incremental reform have failed. Period." All at once, what had long been regarded as a revolutionary pipe dream was official city policy. Beyond thrusting Minneapolis into uncharted territory, the move had far-reaching ramifications for the country. Abolitionists nationwide soon steered the popular energy of the George Floyd protests away from more modest objectives that enjoyed broad support and toward a vision for society that was as divisive as it was uncompromising. I was at Thirty-Eighth and Chicago, sitting with Floyd's old friend Tony Clark, when reports of the council's pledge appeared on my phone. Tony looked taken aback. "Like, no police?" he asked. It was the first he'd heard of the concept. He turned to another protester, a twenty-seven-year-old named Lavish James. "Bro, you want the cops to go home?" Tony asked.

Lavish, who had grown up three blocks away from the intersection and who'd been arrested at the Mobil with Simone Hunter and Deondre Moore, was unreserved about his loathing for law enforcement. All the same, he replied without hesitation, "No. If the cops go home, we're fucking turning into Hamas."

There had been no referendum on the city council's decision, and little community input whatsoever. Polls conducted after the pledge showed that a large majority of residents disagreed with it. The same was true nationally. Seventy-eight percent of Black Americans surveyed by Gallup opposed abolishing their local police departments. Activists I met in Portland could be remarkably dismissive of these people. One antifascist organizer I interviewed—a white medical resident—suggested that African Americans who did not want to get rid of law enforcement must not be poor. "I feel like that has to do with class," the organizer said when I mentioned the resistance to decreasing the police in communities with high rates of gun crime, such as Chicago. "People who can see the police as something that is a sign of safety—that has to come from a place of privilege."

Months of bitter and traumatic confrontations had left many Portland protesters with a venomous grudge against the police in their city specifically, which seemed to have hardened their attitude toward law enforcement generally. The result was a progressive radicalization of the movement as accumulated grievances bolstered abolitionists while sidelining—or converting—more moderate voices. Because the Portland Police Bureau used a specialized rapid-response team for crowd control, the same sixty-odd officers were invariably tasked with breaking up every direct action. At most protests, the same incident commander would announce over a loudspeaker that the gathering had been declared a "riot" or an "unlawful assembly," after which the rapid-response team would attempt to disperse the demonstrators with a combination of arrests, tear gas, stun grenades, and "less lethal" munitions. Some of the munitions were solid foam, others consisted of a plastic casing that released a chemical irritant. A volunteer medic named Izzy told me that the casing shards tended to cause nasty lacerations. "We had someone with a full-thickness neck injury," she said. "They were gargling blood out of their neck." Izzy had converted her camper into an ambulance. Since June, her team had treated "everything from twisted ankles to traumatic brain injuries."

Arrests by the rapid-response team often looked vindictive and gratuitously violent. I saw many officers tackle protesters, shove them down, and jab them with batons. They kneeled on necks and backs, stepped on heads, and sprayed mace into the eyes of compliant or restrained people. One evening I watched an officer chase after an apparently random man, throw him to the ground, straddle his chest, and repeatedly punch him in the face. Oregon Public Broadcasting later reported that the man was a volunteer medic; after he was arrested, for "assaulting an officer," he was admitted to the hospital where he worked as a nurse.

There was a striking incongruity between the prominence of the Portland protests in the national discourse and their distinctive smallness. I don't mean small in the sense of scale, although there was that, too. Rather, they were so *intimate.* The police had taken to concealing their name tags—"to reduce the risk of being doxed," according to a spokesperson—but the protesters knew who many of them were, and the animus on both sides was incredibly personal. Before demonstrations were declared unlawful, the rapid-response team would stand in tight formation, surveilling the crowds, and during this interlude, without fail, the protesters would unleash an effusive, acid torrent of verbal harassment.

"Fuck you, piggies!"

"Eat shit and die!"

"Did you beat your wife last night?"

"Stick it in your mouth and pull the trigger!"

Once, a young white woman in a red tank top walked up and down a line of officers, pointing at each of them while shouting piercingly, "Bitch!" The officers—some of their riot gear colorfully splattered from previous volleys of paint-filled water balloons—gazed sullenly through their face shields. The scene felt like a duplicate of the viral image of the anti-lockdowner with the shaved head and blond beard screaming at David Dickson, the chief sergeant at arms, in the capitol in Lansing.

It didn't matter that Joe Biden adamantly opposed defunding the police, or that he had helped author the 1994 federal crime bill, which provided for a hundred thousand additional officers, allocated billions for prisons, expanded the use of the death penalty, and exacerbated mass incarceration for decades: the intransigence of abolitionists was campaign fodder for Republican political candidates, from the president on down. It also reinforced a conviction among armed right-wingers that law enforcement could no longer be depended on to keep the enemy at bay. It would fall to Patriots to hold the line.

ACROSS THE RIVER

A memorial for Aaron Danielson took place on September 5 in the small Vancouver park where Joey Gibson had first gathered local Trump supporters in 2016. Several hundred people attended. Near a line for hot dogs and hamburgers, I struck up a conversation with a middle-aged man wearing a Patriot Prayer T-shirt and a holstered pistol. A self-described "meme creator" and "info warrior," he wanted me to know that Antifa answered to George Soros, who collaborated with China, which controlled the United Nations, which was using COVID-19 to guide Americans "lockstep into a one-world global medical tyranny." Of Aaron Danielson, he said, "We're a hornet's nest and we've been kicked. We need to be feared. A central message that we've portrayed over and over again is: they must respect us."

While we were talking, another man glided up to us on an electric longboard. He gave his name as Tim and claimed to have been with

Danielson when he was shot. "He was like a brother to me," Tim said. "You never heard a negative thing from his mouth. The world lost an amazing man."

I asked Tim whether he felt that justice had been served. Five days after killing Danielson, Michael Reinoehl had appeared on Vice News, from an undisclosed location, and recounted his version of the shooting. Trump had tweeted, "Everybody knows who this thug is," and commanded law enforcement to "do your job, and do it fast." Hours later, near Olympia, a fugitive task force led by US Marshals gunned down Reinoehl while he sat in a parked car. Roughly thirty rounds were fired. A gun was found in Reinoehl's pocket. Multiple witnesses later told *The New York Times* that the officers neither identified themselves nor attempted to detain him. Still, Tim said, "He got off easy. He's just lucky the police got him before some other people got to him." He added, "It's not done."

"There are already some conspiracies," the info warrior said. "Like: Why was there no blood? Was this a setup? We believe there were about twelve people involved."

"There were two shooters, I'll tell you that much," Tim said. "I was two feet behind them. They cut right in front of me. One was a Black guy. He fired a round."

A pair of cell phone videos had captured the shooting from different angles. In the footage, Tim can be seen skateboarding toward Danielson and another Patriot Prayer supporter when Reinoehl walks between them. Someone, presumably Reinoehl, shouts, "We got a couple right here!" As Reinoehl approaches Danielson, Danielson lunges at him, spraying a can of bear mace. Reinoehl fires two shots, one of which hits the can, making it explode in a thick mist. Then he runs. Tim also flees. Danielson takes several steps before collapsing. No Black man is shown firing a round.

Many people at the memorial wore T-shirts that read JUSTICE FOR J (the letter was Danielson's middle initial and nickname), and as friends delivered eulogies from a covered stage, they all seemed to share Tim's dissatisfaction with the death of Michael Reinoehl. I was reminded of the afternoon when Derek Chauvin was arrested for third-degree murder. I'd been at Thirty-Eighth and Chicago when the news broke, and the reaction there was twofold: disappointment about the charge, and indignation that the other officers involved in the slaying remained free. In both Minneapolis and Vancouver, the belief that guilty parties were eluding punishment inflamed a sense of injury, fueling a movement. But here again, the difference was one of authenticity. Whereas Chauvin's accomplices were made of flesh and blood, Reinoehl's were paranoid projections.

When Joey Gibson took the stage, he talked about resisting hate, and the importance of forgiveness. Though he made no mention of what he had endured in Portland, he pointedly extolled the courageous faith of Jesus, who "walked straight into death." As he paced back and forth, at times referring to notes on his phone, you could see how the preceding chapters of his life had prepared him for this one. Leading a violent evangelical movement was not so different from praising the kitchen layout of a remodeled condo to prospective home buyers or giving a pep talk to football players in the locker room at halftime. Even more than Jason Howland of the American Patriot Council or Garrett Soldano of Stand Up Michigan, Joey Gibson required a public. While he might have genuinely disliked being associated with white supremacists, he also genuinely liked attention, from whomever it was offered. During our interview, he spoke with strange ardor about "working on my speeches," as if they were sculptures or paintings whose aesthetic value transcended their content. At Danielson's memorial, I couldn't shake the suspicion that the pleasure Gibson derived from addressing such a large and sympathetic audience more than counterbalanced whatever grief he was expressing.

Rose City Antifa would later publish a photograph from the park of Gibson with his arm around Chester Doles, a former imperial wizard in the KKK. Doles had spent much of the nineties behind bars in Maryland after he and another Klansman pulled a Black man from his truck and beat him with an axe handle. He went on to become a leader in the National Alliance, a violent neo-Nazi organization, and was returned to prison on federal weapons charges. In 2016, he was arrested again, for his involvement in a bar fight between skinheads and an interracial couple. Before accepting a plea, Doles marched at the Unite the Right rally in Charlottesville with members of Hammerskin Nation, a white supremacist gang. More recently, he had created a pro-Trump political organization, American Patriots USA, which promoted "constitutionalism." Even so, he'd told a Georgia news channel in 2019, his old hood and robe still hung in his closet.

In an email, Gibson said of Doles, "I took pictures with over 50 people that day. I have no idea who he is."

AFTER THE SERVICE, a few dozen men lingered on the edge of the park, away from the other mourners. Most of them wore black-and-yellow Fred Perry polos, a throwback to the skinhead fashion of the 1980s. Mic Crenshaw and the Baldies had sported Fred Perry polos— as had their nemeses, the White Knights. When I walked over, I was greeted by a man with long graying hair and a thick white goatee, who held the hand of a woman about half his height. "PROUD BOY" was tattooed on his arm, and he, too, wore a gun on his hip. He introduced himself as David Machado.

Machado was a sixty-one-year-old air force veteran, a retired flight engineer, and a founding member of the Vancouver Proud Boys. Around the same time that Gibson launched Patriot Prayer, Gavin McInnes, a cocreator of Vice Media, formed the first Proud Boys chapter, in New

York City. Unlike Gibson, McInnes openly celebrated violence against the left. The official mission of the Proud Boys was "reinstating a spirit of Western chauvinism" in America, which they set out to achieve mostly by engaging in drunken street combat. (The group's initiation ritual involved consuming large quantities of beer and starting a fistfight.) On the eve of Trump's inauguration, McInnes was filmed punching a peaceful, unsuspecting demonstrator in Washington, D.C. The same year, it was a former Proud Boy who organized the Unite the Right rally in Charlottesville. By then, David Machado and a handful of other Patriot Prayer supporters had started their own Proud Boys chapter in Vancouver. When Gibson held his first March for Free Speech, they served as "security." Machado had been hospitalized twice for injuries sustained in brawls with antifascists in Portland. Ever since posters with his image calling him a Nazi had appeared around his neighborhood, he never left his house unarmed. "I'm on their list," he told me. "They want me gone."

Machado and his wife, Carie, were children of Mexican immigrants. They had become involved with Patriot Prayer because, like Gibson, they'd felt persecuted for their values. "If you're for Trump now, you're a white supremacist," Machado said. "We have Mexican kids, Mexican families. It's just not right."

"My husband shouldn't have to tell me that if he's not with me I can't wear my Trump gear," Carie added.

While we spoke, the other Proud Boys headed to a nearby bar. Machado scanned the park. "We're gonna have to go because I don't wanna be out here all by myself," he said.

I looked around. A young couple pushed a stroller over the grass. The smell of grilled meat wafted on the summer air. I thought of Marlene, the elderly Tea Partier at Operation Haircut who, gazing at a blue sky, had told me, "They're trying to kill us." It must have been exhausting to live in such a world.

The next time I saw Machado, it would be to hear his version of what happened after he'd joined his friends at the bar. They hadn't been there long when he noticed a man filming them with his phone. "He was trying to dox us," Machado would insist. A bouncer asked the man to leave, and some of the Proud Boys followed him into the parking lot. What took place next is disputed. At some point, the man got in his vehicle and ran over one of the Proud Boys, fracturing his skull and rupturing his eardrum.

A GoFundMe page was set up to cover the victim's medical expenses. Gavin McInnes, the Proud Boys founder, gave a thousand dollars. McInnes had had little to do with the group since 2018. That winter, he'd appeared at the Metropolitan Republican Club, in Manhattan, to celebrate the fifty-eighth anniversary of the assassination of Inejirō Asanuma, a Socialist Party chairman in Japan. Outside the club, cell phone and surveillance videos captured Proud Boys assaulting antifascists in black bloc—calling them "faggots" and kicking them while they were curled on the sidewalk. Nine Proud Boys were arrested. During their trials, McInnes released a video in which he said that his legal team had advised him to disavow the group because doing so would demonstrate that the suspects did not belong to a criminal organization with a hierarchy. "I'm officially disassociating myself from the Proud Boys, in all capacities, forever," he stated.

In the comments section of the GoFundMe page, a single word appeared beside McInnes's name:

"War."

ONE HUNDRED NIGHTS

After parting ways with David Machado, I drove back across the Columbia River to Portland, where the hundredth consecutive direct action since George Floyd's death was scheduled to depart from Ventura Park. I arrived as the sun was setting. More than a thousand people had gathered on the gently sloping greens. Lines formed at tents and tables. Middle-aged supporters distributed first-aid supplies, helmets, respirators, tactical gloves, plastic goggles, earplugs, and knee and elbow pads. There were umbrellas for blocking pepper balls, and orange traffic cones for snuffing tear-gas canisters. A disabled person had bolted protective sheet metal to the front of their wheelchair, and two women pulled a wagon through the crowd loaded with tall shields constructed from fifty-five-gallon plastic drums.

While I sat under a tree with members of the Comrade Collective, a Black woman in a flak jacket announced that we would be marching to the East Precinct. In an arch tone, she reminded everyone, "We celebrate a diversity of tactics."

The maxim had first been codified by demonstrators at the 2008 Republican National Convention, in Saint Paul. To foster cohesion among sometimes fractious leftists—progressives, socialists, communists, anarchists—activists in Saint Paul had prescribed acceptance of all styles of protest. "No bad protesters in a revolution," Portland demonstrators often said. The vandalism that I'd witnessed had been perpetrated by a small minority, but even fewer people dared to intervene. Those who did were disparaged as "peace police." The result was that the most extreme behavior generally set the tone of the direct actions, a tangible marker of the movement's ideological drift.

After leaving Ventura Park to the martial beat of a snare drum, we soon encountered the rapid-response team. At the head of the march, I found Rico De Vera, the engineering student who'd shielded Joey Gibson from the mob the night that Aaron Danielson was killed. I was telling Rico about seeing Gibson in Vancouver, when a Molotov cocktail shattered a few feet away from us. Flames splashed and a protester danced off with his leg on fire. While medics tended to him, two more incendiary devices exploded nearby, brightly whooshing just shy of the rapid-response team. The officers answered with tear gas, stun grenades, and impact munitions, scattering the march. A helicopter hovered. People stumbled into side streets, coughing and retching.

I lost Rico in the melee but caught up with him a few hours later on a commercial boulevard. He was arguing with a white protester in black bloc and a gas mask. Rico was furious about the Molotov cocktails; the white protester defended their use. "If you guys keep playing war games, there's gonna be an actual war," Rico yelled at him. "They're looking for a reason. No one here is prepared for what real war is like. Everyone here will be fucked—and people of color will be especially fucked."

The white man muttered something inaudible and walked off. A friend of Rico's, who was African American and also upset about the Molotov cocktails, shook his head. "They all use the same argument: 'Oh, a Black person called for a diversity of tactics.'" He added of the protests in general, "It's become a mockery. When you have Trump using this to be reelected, it's like, 'OK, guys, wake up.' But they don't care."

Respect for a diversity of tactics had always been about strengthening militant activists, never about swaying moderate voters. The liberal position that violence and vandalism were undemocratic rang hollow to radical leftists for the same reason that appeals to free speech did: from their perspective, we did not live in a real democracy and our speech was far from free.

Later, I followed a group of protesters into a neighborhood where a man and a woman gazed down from the second-story window, backlit by a ceiling lamp.

"Get away from our cars!" the woman snapped.

Insults were exchanged. Exasperated, the woman said, "We're *Democrats*, you fucking jerks."

Mayor Ted Wheeler was also a Democrat. In January, he'd pepper spray a protester accosting him in a parking lot. Three days earlier, while Joe Biden was taking the oath of office, a crowd in black bloc had attacked the Oregon Democratic Party headquarters, smashing windows, spray-painting anarchist symbols, and lighting dumpsters on fire. Some of the antifascists carried signs and banners. One read: WE DON'T WANT BIDEN / WE WANT REVENGE!

Later, protesters would falsely accuse Rico De Vera of working for law enforcement. After "self-proclaimed antifascists" threw bottles at him and called him a "cop collaborator," he would stop attending the direct actions. The experience would sink him into a deep depression. "It was my life," he'd explain. "Getting ripped out of that was difficult. It made me feel hopeless to know that I lived in a city where, as a person of color, I'm not allowed to take part in the conversation." Even former friends of his would refuse to acknowledge him in public. The excommunication would feel like the very thing that Rico had been so inspired to see Portlanders mobilizing against in the wake of George Floyd's death.

NINE

DARK SHADOWS

A week after the Ventura Park march, wildfires burned over a million acres and four thousand homes in Oregon, forcing forty thousand people to evacuate and killing eleven. The sun was a hollow circle traced on a russet sky, and the state's air quality became the worst in the world. Fires also devastated California, Washington, and Colorado. For the first time since Floyd's death, activists suspended their nightly demonstrations and turned to relief efforts. Some protesters set up a donation point in the parking lot of a shopping mall; others delivered food supplies to rural shelters.

The prodigious scale of the conflagrations was linked to severe winds, temperatures, and drought. Because these were all predictable effects of climate change, many Americans required an alternative explanation. Just as left-wing environmentalists held up global warming as an indictment of capitalism and an argument for Indigenous land reclamation, the right-wing denial of climate science amounted to a defense of the Western exploitation of natural resources. To admit that American industry was rendering the planet uninhabitable would be to contradict basic assumptions about the special covenant between white Christians and God. The need to assign *other* causes to extreme weather events had reached its absurd apotheosis in 2018, when Trump visited Paradise, California, where eighty-six people had recently burned alive. Standing amid the charred ruins of the incinerated community, the president told journalists, "You gotta take care of the floors, you know? The floors of the forests." In Oregon, a different culprit was identified. As quickly as the flames, a rumor spread that antifascists were responsible for the catastrophe. Calls to 911 inquiring about Antifa arsonists flooded dispatch services, and civilian checkpoints slowed evacuation efforts. During a public Zoom conference, a captain in the Clackamas County Sheriff's Office related accounts of "extremist groups staging gas cans," and "suspected Antifa" members felling telephone poles with chainsaws "in the hopes of starting further fires." The sheriff soon repudiated the reports, but not before a Clackamas County deputy was caught on video telling residents, "Antifa motherfuckers are out causing hell." In a separate clip, the same deputy warned a group of people that if they killed miscreants they could be charged with murder—however, he counseled, "you throw a fucking knife in their hand *after* you shoot them, that's on you." While the FBI pleaded with citizens to stop propagating the stories, Trump, during a campaign rally, said of Antifa, "They have to pay a price for the damage and the horror that they've caused."

Two years earlier, the president had pardoned a pair of ranchers from Harney Basin convicted of igniting fires on federal land. It had been their imprisonment for arson that had inspired the Bundys to occupy the Malheur National Wildlife Refuge in 2016.

. . .

THE FABRICATIONS ABOUT Antifa arsonists had been amplified online by acolytes of QAnon. I'd first encountered such people in Michigan, where their distinctive signage had made them easy to spot at
anti-lockdown rallies: SAVE THE CHILDREN; TRUST THE PLAN; WHERE
WE GO ONE, WE GO ALL. These were all references to a baroque uni-
verse of conspiracy theories that had been evolving since 2017, when
an anonymous source claiming to be a senior government official with
Q clearance—the most restricted security access at the Department
of Energy, which manages the country's nuclear arsenal—began re-
leasing putatively classified information on right-wing message boards.
The revelations added up to a dismaying picture: an occult society
of cannibalistic Satan worshippers, including Barack Obama, George
Soros, the Clintons, and other liberal celebrities, was ritualistically raping and devouring sacrificial children. The good news was that Trump
had dedicated his presidency to ending the turpitude. This was the real
battle of consequence unfolding behind the headlines, and "Q" had
taken to the internet to alert Americans and enlist their aid.

In Michigan, I'd largely overlooked QAnon as a discrete phenomenon, for the simple reason that it had not seemed any more or less
fantastical, dangerous, or interesting than so many other risible beliefs
circulating in the anti-lockdown ether. Did Q's contention that lockdowns were an elaborate ruse orchestrated by Democratic elites to dis-
tract from their sexual enslavement of minors really merit more of my
attention than, say, the customer at Karl Manke's barbershop who told
me that the 1990s sitcom *Buffy the Vampire Slayer* was "full of factual
information," even if, he allowed judiciously, it was "presented in a cartoonish way"? Apparently yes. As the pandemic worsened and the election neared, QAnon had exploded in popularity. Social media pages
that interpreted Q's cryptic prognostications, run by fanatics called

"decoders," attracted tens of millions of views. Decoders with large followings, also known as a new type of influencer, multiplied on You-Tube. A book for QAnon initiates became an Amazon bestseller. Polls suggested that anywhere between 10 and 30 percent of Americans believed some or all of Q's claims; one survey found that 56 percent of Republicans did. Tens of millions of people, in other words, even by lowball estimates. During the Republican primaries, a five-term US congressman from Colorado was ousted by Lauren Boebert, a thirty-three-year-old bar owner who'd said of QAnon, "I hope that this is real because it only means America is getting stronger and better." In Georgia, a neurosurgeon promising Republicans "all the conservative, none of the embarrassment" was defeated by Marjorie Taylor Greene, a QAnon proponent who described the Trump administration as "a once-in-a-lifetime opportunity to take this global cabal of Satan-worshipping pedophiles out."

Trump celebrated Greene's victory and hailed her as a "future Republican star." He'd already shared dozens of tweets from QAnon influencers. When a reporter asked about QAnon at a White House press conference, Trump replied, "They like me very much, which I appreciate." The reporter pressed a little. "The crux of the theory is this belief that you are secretly saving the world from this satanic cult of pedophiles and cannibals. Does that sound like something you are behind?" Trump: "Is that supposed to be a bad thing? . . . If I can help save the world from problems, I'm willing to do it." During a Fox News interview a few days before the fires in Oregon, Trump spoke of an airplane "almost completely loaded with thugs, wearing these dark uniforms, black uniforms, with gear and this and that." He linked the plane to "people that are in the dark shadows," controlling Joe Biden. Liberals were bewildered. Many other Americans experienced something thrilling and novel: the sensation that a sitting US president was speaking to them. The enjoyment of a perceived personal connection

to Trump was part of QAnon's appeal. Decoders pored over his statements and appearances, deciphering hidden communications. The color
of his tie, the number of flags behind his podium, his pronunciation
of the word *you*—any mundane detail could become a furtive wink
directed at the chosen few. Some QAnon followers referred to Trump
as "Q+"; certain influencers maintained that Trump *was* Q. In offering a feeling of exception by virtue of complicity with an idealized
leader, the movement bore an obvious resemblance to most cults. But
its allure also transcended Trump. QAnon flattered Americans with
the same emotionally gratifying illusion as the historical myth of the
revolutionary 3 percent: a feeling of belonging to a select class, a Prae-
torian Guard, which was willing to do more for the country than were
other citizens.

But do more how, exactly? Do what? On the Hoover Dam, a QAnon
follower blockaded traffic with an armored truck full of guns and ammunition; in New York, another murdered a Mafia boss; in Arizona,
another smashed up a Catholic chapel; in Massachusetts another led
police on a high-speed chase with infants and toddlers in his vehicle;
in Canada, another rammed his truck through the front gates of the
prime minister's residence; and in Kentucky, Colorado, and Utah, others kidnapped or tried to kidnap children.

One day in Portland, I visited the protester-run donation point in
the parking lot of the shopping mall. Rows of tables were loaded with
groceries, used clothes, personal hygiene products, blankets, and toys.
Volunteer mechanics repaired bicycles and cars; nurses administered
checkups; a food truck served free meals. I recognized one of the cooks
as Gary, a middle-aged activist who was registering an official Black
Lives Matter chapter in Oregon. Gary told me that he had just returned from Mill City, about an hour south of the city, where the fires
were still raging. He had filled his car with food and water, planning
to help evacuees and thereby show them that Black Lives Matter was

nothing to be feared. A few miles outside Mill City, he parked and opened his trunk. Though Gary had been involved in activism since the Rodney King riots in Los Angeles, what he experienced next took him aback.

"I was told to get the fuck out of town and called the N-word four or five times," he said. "People were passing by and yelling out their windows at me."

ˎ THE GRAY ZONE

On October 5, 2017, three weeks before Q's first online post, Trump hosted a dinner at the White House for his top military brass. While posing for pictures with the commanders, he asked the press, "You guys know what this represents?"

"Tell us, sir," a journalist replied.

"Maybe it's the calm before the storm."

The remark would form the basis for a cardinal QAnon prophecy, according to which "the storm" was when Trump would institute martial law and preside over tribunals for all the deviants and Satanists. A "great awakening" would then permit survivors of the purge to reconcile and live in harmony.

If this sounds like a campy bastardization of New Testament eschatology—Jesus returning to earth, consigning sinners to hell, and rewarding believers with the rapture—that is because its fusion of evangelicalism and patriotism sprang naturally from the premise that the US was a Christian nation. The more I learned about QAnon, though, the more I was reminded of the millenarian theologies promoted by America's most committed foreign adversaries. Many Islamic fundamentalists anticipated a climactic battle between Muslims and infidels that would trigger Armageddon and usher in a day of judgment. There was even scripture that identified where the confrontation would occur: a small town in northern Syria called Dabiq. In 2013, I spent a month in the Syrian city of Aleppo, where poorly equipped rebels were engaged in horrific, attritional combat against a merciless dictatorship. To reduce our exposure to air strikes, my interpreter, a photographer, and I slept each night on a farm outside the city, a few miles from Dabiq. Every morning on our way back to the front lines, we passed the headquarters for the Syrian branch of Al Qaeda, where sentries with long beards and Kalashnikovs stood guard below a black standard. Many Syrians who supported the revolution fretted over the growing role that these extremists played in it. Not long after I left Aleppo, however, a new group—ISIS—routed secular and Islamist rebels alike throughout much of Syria, ruling in a manner that made Al Qaeda look humanistic by comparison.

What accounted for the meteoric rise of ISIS? The factors were manifold and complex. To a degree, though, I think it was the same thing that accounted for the meteoric rise of QAnon: a spiritual yearning of the faithful for the end of time. Beyond offering their followers the prospect of experiencing the apocalypse, QAnon and ISIS both made the extraordinary claim that it was within the power of their followers to help bring the apocalypse about. Like the Boogaloo Bois, they were accelerationists.

Not coincidentally, all three of these movements were also expert at packaging their draconian ideas in a highly produced aesthetic that appealed to internet habitués. In addition to a steady rollout of phantasmagorically macabre snuff videos, ISIS published a sleek online magazine called *Dabiq*. In 2015, an entire issue of *Dabiq* was dedicated to "the extinction of the Gray Zone." In it, jihadi writers explained that their objective was to create a world in which practicing Islam in Western democracies was untenable, thereby obliging Muslims everywhere to join the caliphate. Trumpism could be distilled into similar terms.

It strove to convince Americans that being a patriot or a Christian under Democratic governance was untenable. Just as ISIS targeted its fellow rebel factions in Syria as ferociously as it did the regime, Trump- ism attacked heretical conservatives, elevating politicians like Lauren Boebert and Marjorie Taylor Greene. A few weeks after the fires in Oregon, Trump would deride RINOs—Republicans In Name Only— as "the lowest form of human life."

This was how extremism worked. By eliminating the possibility of moderate participation, it forced people to choose between an intoler- able enemy and the radical flank of their own party, sect, or tribe. That often meant no choice at all.

TEN

PEOPLE

On September 26, Proud Boys from across the country met in Portland for a rally against "domestic terrorism." I arrived at a muddy field on the outskirts of the city at eleven a.m. to find many of them already drunk. One carried a round wooden shield spray-painted with the words MERICA, FUCK YEAH. He held it up as a behemoth in a tank top wailed at it with an aluminum bat. When the shield splintered, a circle of onlookers emitted a communal grunt of "Uhuru," the Swahili word for "freedom," which the Proud Boys had co-opted as a satirical war whoop. Other inebriated men sang "Proud of Your Boy"—from the Broadway version of *Aladdin*—for which the group was sardonically named. The scene felt less like a dream than like the shoddy reenactment of one, a low-budget renaissance fair whose disgruntled actors had got into the mead.

As I wandered around the bizarre and boozy carnival, it made sense to me that the founder of the Proud Boys, Gavin McInnes, had also been the creative force behind *Vice* magazine. Before McInnes left the company in 2008, Vice Media had marketed edgy iconoclasm, expressed mainly via debauchery and mean-spirited humor, to disaffected millennials entering adulthood during the second Bush administration. "I been following Gavin since all the way back in the *Vice* days, reading his articles, watching his videos," Shane, a thirty-seven-year-old welder from Spokane, told me. He had a bushy red beard, a bulletproof vest, and a holstered Beretta. Each front pocket of his jeans contained a loaded magazine; a rear one, a copy of the Constitution.

"We're just a fraternal organization and a drinking club," Shane insisted. Prior to 2020, there might have been some truth to this. In so grossly distorting the threat posed by antifascists, however, Trump had raised their small-scale rivalry with the Proud Boys to a matter of national security. The resulting amalgam of goofiness and militance, buffoonery and thuggery, had afforded the Proud Boys a convenient means of deniability while they aggressively expanded their operations and recruitment. Depending on their audience, they could present themselves as a besotted version of the Loyal Order of Moose or as valiant knights engaged in a civilizational crusade. Echoing Phil Robinson and the Michigan Liberty Militia, Shane said that the Proud Boys welcomed all comers. "We love everybody," he told me.

I had noticed several men wearing RWDS—"Right-Wing Death Squad"—hats and patches; others had on T-shirts with images of bodies being thrown from helicopters. Both were nods to Latin American juntas that had systematically tortured and executed civilians for alleged subversion. One Proud Boy's shirt declared PINOCHET DID NOTHING WRONG—a tribute to the Chilean dictator whose interrogators had introduced live rats, through tubes, into the vaginas and rectums of leftist dissidents.

"Do you love communists?" I asked.

"Fuck no," Shane said. "Commies aren't people."

He wasn't being glib. I'd heard other Proud Boys state the same opinion. "Under communism, you're literally just a number—you're a cog in the machine," Shane explained to me, sipping a can of Pabst Blue Ribbon. His tone was pedantic, as if this were a debate he'd had and won before. I supposed that I could see a certain kind of logic that must have felt unassailable: *communists are not human because communism is inhuman.* "When you have an ideology that is completely antithetical to Western culture and our traditions, we can't let that go on," Shane continued. "It's a cancer eating at the soul of America. We're not gonna sit back and take it."

White vigilantes had cloaked their identity-based violence in the ideological guise of anti-communism for decades. In 1979, when the Communist Workers Party held a "Death to the Klan" march in Greensboro, North Carolina, members of the KKK and the American Nazi Party opened fire on the demonstrators, wounding seven of them and killing five. An all-white jury acquitted the gunmen, inspiring white supremacists to parade through Detroit with signs that read SMASH COMMUNISM: GREENSBORO AGAIN. When federal prosecutors went on to charge nine of the Greensboro Klansmen and neo-Nazis with violating civil rights laws, another all-white jury exonerated them a second time, accepting their defense that they had been politically rather than racially motivated. This wasn't just a cunning legal gambit. In *Bring the War Home*, the historian Kathleen Belew writes that "white power activists in Greensboro understood themselves as participating in a global war against communism." Belew chronicles how thousands of Vietnam veterans viewed the domestic terrorism of the KKK and similar groups as an extension of the conflict they had fought in overseas. Beyond their white-supremacist organizing stateside, some Klansmen and neo-Nazis with combat experience traveled to Latin America and served as mercenaries for the same homicidal regimes to which the Proud Boys now paid homage.

The Reagan administration vigorously supported communist-eradication programs in the Southern Hemisphere, and white power militants often found themselves in common cause with CIA agents and American advisers abroad. In 2020, the "communist" anachronism—though wildly inaccurate for most of the individuals to whom it was applied—facilitated a similar collaboration between Patriots and the Trump administration. The more histrionically Trump exaggerated the left-wing menace, the more explicitly he endorsed extrajudicial remedies. After Michael Reinoehl was gunned down, Trump declared, "That's the way it has to be. There has to be retribution." Attorney General Barr added, "The streets of our cities are safer with this violent agitator removed." On August 25, armed conservatives traveled to Kenosha, Wisconsin, which was beset with unrest after a white officer shot a Black man seven times in the back. During altercations, seventeen-year-old Kyle Rittenhouse shot to death two people and wounded a third. Trump defended Rittenhouse's actions, and conservatives glorified them. The right-wing lionization of Rittenhouse mirrored that of the Greensboro shooters. As I was speaking with Shane, I spotted a Proud Boy whose T-shirt featured a portrait of Rittenhouse framed by the words: THE TREE OF LIBERTY MUST BE REPLENISHED FROM TIME TO TIME WITH THE BLOOD OF COMMIES. A jury would later acquit Rittenhouse of both homicide charges; once free, he would travel to Florida to visit Trump, who would praise him as a "really good" and "nice young man."

A desire to resurrect the specter of communism in order to frame right-wing violence as defensive and political, rather than offensive and racial, might have helped explain the otherwise puzzling case of Henry "Enrique" Tarrio, who had become the national chairman of the Proud Boys after Gavin McInnes's departure. Tarrio lived in Miami and was the son of Cuban immigrants. Though he'd done time in federal prison for stealing and reselling medical devices, he often cited his family history to portray himself and the Proud Boys in a noble light. "I was born a Proud Boy," Tarrio liked to say. He also identified as Black, which Proud Boys never tired of holding up as proof of their unimpeachability. I observed Tarrio at multiple events and found him to be as confounding a leader as Phil Robinson of the Michigan Liberty Militia. In an organization replete with flamboyant personalities, if Tarrio stood out at all it was for his reticence. He boasted certain far-right bona fides: he'd marched in Charlottesville, was the chief of staff for Latinos for Trump, and supported QAnon. On the conservative social media site Parler, he could be nasty and flip in a way that felt derivative of McInnes. But in person, Tarrio was so subdued and lackluster that his absence of personal gravitas often seemed to resemble a shortage of conviction. In Portland, his face was hidden behind reflective sunglasses and a baseball hat with the brim pulled low. After uttering a few perfunctory words—"We're here for Jay, we're here for Kyle"—he relinquished the microphone.

If Tarrio gave the impression of a figurehead, the contrast with his top deputy, Joe Biggs, didn't help. A thirty-six-year-old veteran of Iraq and Afghanistan, Biggs had been medically discharged from the army after receiving two Purple Hearts. He'd left at the rank of staff sergeant and still carried himself with the authority of a hard-charging NCO. Unlike Tarrio, Biggs visibly enjoyed giving commands. With his broad strip of white hair and muscular arms sleeved in tattoos—"RWDS" was inked across his right bicep—he also looked the part. It was Biggs, not Tarrio, who emceed the Portland rally, leading the Proud Boys in chants of "Fuck Antifa!" and admonishing them, in a deep rasp, to "show some fucking motivation." Then he switched gears: "We're gonna celebrate the man we love the most, which is Jesus Christ." With the exception of a couple pagans, everyone kneeled in the wet grass. "Reveal your purpose to the Proud Boys," a chaplain intoned. "Use us to lift up this city." I spotted Shane among the flock, head bowed, Pabst in hand, eyes squeezed shut in diligent worship.

Speakers blared an electric guitar solo of "The Star-Spangled Banner" while an enormous American flag ascended from the stage through green smoke. A number of Proud Boys, instead of placing their hands over their hearts, made "OK" signs. In 2017, trolls on 4Chan—the same uncensored message board where the boogaloo was conceived and where Q first appeared—contrived to persuade the media that the innocuous hand symbol had become a code signifying white power. (The three upturned fingers were said to form a *W*; the thumb, index finger, and arm a *P*.) White supremacists adopted the gesture in earnest. As with their other puerile tropes, the Proud Boys mostly seemed to revel in its suggestive ambiguity.

After the anthem, Biggs introduced Shane Moon, the man who'd been run over outside the bar after Aaron Danielson's memorial. "I tell you what," said Moon, "I feel sorry for Antifa. Because if all you guys feel like me, they're in trouble."

More details had emerged about the driver of the car. He had no connection to any antifascists or to other Portland protesters. After reviewing the evidence, prosecutors would drop the charges against him. Like Danielson's murder, however, the incident had intensified a sense of brotherhood and beleaguerment that felt less like a drinking club than like a platoon in combat.

"I will live and I will die for this fraternity," Moon vowed.

NOW WHAT

After leaving the Proud Boys, I drove across Portland to Peninsula Park, where Rose City Antifa had organized a rival event. About fifteen hundred people had shown up. A few wore black bloc, but the gathering was family friendly, and most of the attendees had dressed accordingly. Booths erected in a leafy grove offered herbal teas and tinctures, arts and crafts, condoms and morning-after pills, radical zines, and organic vegetables. A "therapy llama" stood by for restorative hugs. The Portland Socialist Rifle Association distributed firearms education literature and paper targets of a hooded Klansman. "Guns aren't just for right-wingers," one pamphlet was titled.

Mic Crenshaw, the former Baldie from Minneapolis, stepped onto a covered stage wearing sunglasses, a backward baseball cap, and a bulletproof vest over a plaid flannel shirt. He might have been conspicuously older than most of the audience, but he was also conspicuously brawnier. "I never thought, thirty years ago, I'd be standing up here with one of these things on," he said. He traced a direct line between the neo-Nazi skinheads he had battled as a teenager, during the Reagan administration, and the Proud Boys assembled on the other side of town. Their relationship with the state, from local law enforcement to the White House, hadn't changed much either. "What we're seeing is across-the-board collusion between the same elements that stood opposed to our liberation back then, still do today, and will into the foreseeable future," Crenshaw told the young inheritors of the movement he had helped to forge when he was their age.

Later, Rose City Antifa would publish a picture of an attendee at the Proud Boys rally who, like Crenshaw, was fifty-one years old. His name was Kyle Brewster, and he had once belonged to East Side White Pride, a local skinhead gang with ties to White Aryan Resistance. In 1988, Brewster and two other men had beaten to death the Ethiopian immigrant Mulugeta Seraw, causing Crenshaw and his fellow Baldies to come to Portland for the first national conference of Anti-Racist Action. Brewster served thirteen years in prison, after which he was sent back for continuing to socialize with white supremacists, a violation of the terms of his parole. Since his last release, he'd become a Trump supporter in the vein of David Duke and Chester Doles. On January 6, after the Capitol attack, Brewster would post on Facebook, "I long ago gave up hope that people had enough back bone to fight for their freedom in this country but i obviously was wrong." A week later, he would add that "no part of me is sorry, remorseful or regretful" for having killed Seraw. "So yeah," Brewster would write, "racist murderer, all that. Now what?"

FALL

ELEVEN

BAD NEWS

spent Election Day 2016 on the outskirts of Mosul, in northern Iraq. An offensive was underway to liberate the city from ISIS, which had captured it two years earlier. During the interim, the group had rigged ubiquitous booby traps, developed a formidable system of defenses, trained snipers, and stockpiled an enormous arsenal of rockets, mortars, drones, and armored suicide vehicles. Thousands of jihadists from around the world had resolved to fight to the death. A few weeks into the campaign, the Iraqi military had already endured some of the most grueling urban combat seen anywhere since the Second World War.

To cover the battle, the photographer Victor Blue and I had embedded with an elite SWAT team from Mosul's former police force. Most of the men in the unit had loved ones trapped inside the city whom they were desperate to rescue. On the eve of the US election, the Mosul SWAT was supporting an Iraqi tank division struggling to penetrate a neighborhood called Intisar. Victor and I waited in a makeshift aid station, listening to automatic gunfire and watching smoke plumes mushroom from explosions up ahead. Soon a SWAT member arrived with a partially severed hand. Then another, dead and wrapped in a blanket. Then a third, also dead, caked with white dust. Two Humvees followed, each packed with bloodied, dazed, and shaken men. Finally, at risk of annihilation, what remained of the Mosul SWAT retreated from Intisar and regrouped several miles back from the front, in a town called Hamdaniya.

The critically wounded were evacuated to Baghdad. But almost everyone had suffered injuries. In a bombed-out apartment, young officers sat around a kitchen table, feverish with exhaustion but unable to sleep. Earlier, one of them had been reported dead and later discovered half-conscious beneath a heap of rubble. He avoided eye contact with the others now, grinning sheepishly, as if equal parts relieved and embarrassed to be alive.

The major who'd led the mission had locked himself in a dark bedroom. Staring into space with the covers pulled to his chin, he resembled a child jolted by a nightmare. His head was wrapped in gauze. "In the first suicide attack, I think one whole family was killed," he told me. "Their snipers made rabbits of us."

The following afternoon, the men shuffled around the courtyard of an abandoned school, chain-smoking cigarettes, limping painfully from blast-torqued backs and knees. Four of their seven Humvees had been destroyed; mechanics worked on the remaining three, all badly damaged by RPGs.

Air strikes, mortars, and artillery had decimated Hamdaniya, and there was no running water or electricity. One of the SWAT members wired a generator to the fuse box of an empty house, and that night the commander, a middle-aged colonel with a handlebar mustache and corresponding swagger, installed himself in a salon lit by blue and purple ceiling lamps. He was gazing at a flatscreen when I joined him. I'd completely forgotten about the election; Trump and Clinton could not have felt less relevant. On the TV, a Saudi Arabian news channel played a CGI tour of the US Capitol. The race was tighter than expected. Due to the time difference, when Victor and I unrolled our sleeping bags in a shelled office strewn with debris, results were still coming in. Even if we'd had internet on our phones, I doubt that either of us would've bothered staying up.

In the morning the colonel was still watching the flatscreen.

"Bad news," he said to me in English.

I feared that the unit had been ordered to return to the meat grinder of Intisar. Or that one of the wounded had died. Or that a limb had been amputated. Or that ISIS militants had raped or kidnapped or decapitated someone's parent, spouse, or sibling. At that time, in that place, anything was possible.

Then I saw that the colonel was grinning.

ONE OF THE INTERPRETERS I worked with in Mosul was a Kurdish friend of mine named Sangar Khaleel. In early 2020, when I returned to the region for my assignment in Raqqa, Sangar and I crossed together into Syria, over the Tigris River, from Iraqi Kurdistan. It was his first visit to the city, and he was as stunned as I by how thoroughly it had been leveled. One night, while we were huddled close to a kerosene space heater in the freezing apartment we had rented, Sangar said, "It's not fair. Nothing ever happens to America."

I knew what he meant. The last thing that Sangar would have wanted was for some foreign enemy to make Americans pay. He could not understand, though, how we hadn't made *ourselves* pay. How had a people capable of such destructive fury, such madness and cruelty, continued to enjoy the strongest and most stable economy in the world, minimal civil discord, and a political system that featured the regular, uneventful transition of power? It was this that felt unfair—the disconnect between our careless belligerence abroad and peace and prosperity at home.

When we got back to the Iraqi-Syrian border, in late February, everyone was talking about the virus. Two thousand people had died in China and parts of the Lombardy region of Italy were in quarantine. As for the US, there'd been a few dozen cases and one death. To Sangar, it seemed only natural that we would be spared. "Of course," he said, "the whole world will be infected but not you."

THE BEST IS YET TO COME

As his bid for a second term approached and poll after poll showed him significantly trailing his Democratic challenger, Trump began laying the groundwork to contest the vote. "The only way we're going to lose this election is if the election is rigged," he told his supporters in August. "We can't let that happen." During his first debate with Biden, he would not commit to discouraging people from engaging in violence while mail-in ballots were counted. When Chris Wallace, the moderator and Fox News host, pressed him to ask white supremacists, specifically, to "stand down," Trump responded, "What do you want to call them? Give me a name." Biden mentioned the Proud Boys, and Trump said, "The Proud Boys? Stand back and stand by. But I'll tell you what, I'll tell you what. Somebody's gotta do something about Antifa and the left."

On Parler, Joe Biggs wrote, "Trump basically said to go fuck them up! This makes me so happy." Within hours, "standing by" had become a new Proud Boys mantra, and T-shirts emblazoned with the phrase were available online.

As COVID-19 continued to kill thousands of Americans each day, Trump spent the end of the campaign on a whirlwind tour of swing states, holding large, crowded, and mask-optional rallies in North Carolina, Pennsylvania, Wisconsin, and Michigan. His final stop was Grand Rapids, where he was scheduled to appear at a private airfield at ten thirty, the night before the election. I arrived five hours early, and the line to access the tarmac was already half a mile long. It was forty degrees, and a bitter wind lashed the open fields. I waited behind a married couple and their thirteen-year-old daughter, who had asked to attend the rally for her birthday present. Every time a plane touched down, she wondered aloud if it might be Air Force One. Three hours later, her excitement still hadn't waned. It was dark and we'd reached a part of the line that doubled back on itself over and over between metal safety barriers. My fingers and toes were numb. The foot traffic had churned the ground into sucking mud. When we came to a small lake that covered several rows of barriers, forcing us to trudge straight through the ankle-deep water, a man remarked, "The things we do for our president!" Nobody laughed, and he quickly added, "He does more for us, though."

Given the near-unanimous prediction of a decisive defeat for Trump, I had expected the mood to be somber and defiant. What I found instead was jubilant celebration of a historic victory considered all but guaranteed. No doubt this had something to do with the previous election, when pundits had derided Trump's chances much as they were doing now. But the fanciful optimism also went deeper than distrust of the polls. The people in line weren't merely confident that Trump would win—they were sure that it would be a "landslide." The word was Trump's, and it was not the only thing that his followers had borrowed from him. They all seemed to be practicing the same kind of magical thinking that had become a staple of his presidency—the belief that if you insisted something was true with adequate conviction and persistence, you could will its reality.

"We got this," one man said with easy nonchalance when I asked if he was nervous. "The only problem is, when we win the Democrats are gonna say it was fraud."

After passing through security checks, the supporters packed around an empty stage and filled the risers between twin jumbotrons that promised "THE BEST IS YET TO COME!" More hours of waiting followed. Trump did not get in until midnight, by which time some of the older attendees looked borderline hypothermic. The apparition of the man sent a bolt of adrenaline through the crowd. His speech was disjointed and hard to hear, but no one cared. A chant I didn't recognize spread across the airfield. Rhythmically, it sounded very close to "U-S-A!" As the words grew louder, however, I realized it was something else.

"We-love-you! We-love-you!"

Trump smiled. "Thank you. I love you too."

Neither he nor they would ever accept that anyone could beat them without cheating.

THE POLLS OPENED a few hours after Trump left Grand Rapids. Like the rest of the country, Michigan saw historic turnout. Also like the rest of the country, an unprecedented number of people, concerned about COVID-19, voted by mail. I headed to the TCF Center in downtown Detroit, where some eight hundred election workers had been charged with tallying nearly two hundred thousand absentee ballots. The workers sat around tables in a large exhibit hall, opening envelopes, removing ballots from sealed secrecy sleeves, and logging names in a digital poll book. The ballots were then brought to a row of high-speed tabulators, devices resembling Xerox machines, which could process up to fifty sheets per minute.

Republican and Democratic challengers—appointed party members authorized to observe—roamed the hall. The press were confined to a taped-off area, but as far as I could see, the Republicans were given free rein. They wandered from table to table, checking computer monitors that displayed the growing list of names. In the afternoon, a man's voice came over a loudspeaker, reminding the election workers to "provide for transparency and openness." Christopher Thomas, who'd served as Michigan's election director for thirty-six years and came out of retirement to advise the city clerk's office in 2020, surveyed the floor. He was very pleased with the way things were going. The few challengers who'd raised objections had mostly misunderstood technical aspects of the process. "We work through it with them," Thomas told me. "We're happy to have them here." I returned to my hotel amazed by how uneventful the day had been.

THROUGHOUT THE RACE, Trump had relentlessly denigrated absentee voting. Returns from in-person voters were therefore expected to skew his way. Because such ballots were fed directly into tabulators, these results could be made public almost instantaneously. The process of opening envelopes and secrecy sleeves was far more onerous and time-consuming. Over the summer, Democrats in Lansing had proposed legislation that would have allowed the counting of mail-in ballots to start before Election Day, reducing the otherwise inevitable lag period. Republicans had blocked the bill. Consequently, while early returns showed Trump ahead in Michigan, it was unsurprising when his lead diminished as results began arriving from Detroit and other heavily Democratic jurisdictions. Nonetheless, the appearance of a trend reversal was enough for Trump, a little after midnight, to declare on Twitter, "We are up BIG, but they are trying to STEAL the Election."

When I went back to the TCF Center the next day, I found an angry mob outside. Police guarded the doors. Most of the protesters had driven down from Macomb, the pro-Trump county where I'd met Vincent Bell's mother and sisters on Memorial Day. "We know what's going on here," one Macomb man told me. "They're stuffing the ballot box." He said that his local GOP office had sent out an email urging people to descend on the TCF Center. *Politico* later reported that Laura Cox, the chairwoman of the Michigan GOP, had personally implored Republican activists to go there. I'd seen Cox introduce Trump at the rally in Grand Rapids. "Four more years," she'd told the crowd. "Or twelve—we'll talk about that later."

Dozens of protesters had managed to enter the TCF Center before it was sealed. I showed the police my credentials and went downstairs. Republicans pressed against a glass wall of the exhibit hall, yelling at the election workers on the other side.

"Let us in!"

Each party had been allocated one challenger per table. Although the Republicans had already exceeded their limit, they were irate about being shut out. When an elderly ACLU observer was ushered past them, a Macomb man with a thin beard and receding hairline demanded to know where she was from. The woman ignored him, and the Macomb man shouted, "You're a coward, is where you're from!"

"Be civil," another woman admonished. I had met her earlier—her name was Lisa. Unlike almost everyone else there, she was Black and from Detroit. She gently asked the Macomb man, "If this place has cameras, and you've got media observing—you've got different people

from both sides looking—why do you think someone would intentionally try to cheat?"

"You would have to have a hundred thirty-four cameras to track
every ballot," the man answered.

"My point is, why would somebody intentionally try to cheat in an
open forum—"

"Why not? You know how easy it is?"

"These ballots are from Detroit," Lisa said. "Detroit is an eighty percent African American city. There's a huge percentage of Democrats.
That's just a fact."

The man agreed. "The numbers are so important in Detroit. You
can win or lose based on Detroit."

Lisa gestured at the poll workers, the vast majority of whom were
Black. "I don't think these people came here with the intention of,
'Hey, I'm gonna sway an election,'" she said. "This is my whole thing:
I have a basic level of respect for these people."

In response to this, the Macomb man said that thirty thousand illegal ballots had been smuggled into the TCF Center at three in the
morning. The source of the allegation was a cell phone video that
showed a man removing a case from the back of a van, loading it in a
wagon, and pulling the wagon into the building. I had watched the
video that morning and had recognized the man as a member of a local
TV news crew whom I'd seen in the taped-off area for press the day
before. I distinctly recalled admiring the wagon, which he'd used to
transport his camera gear.

After another protester cited the video, he told me, "There's a lot of
suspicious activity that goes on down here in Detroit. There's a million ways you can commit voter fraud, and we're afraid it was committed on a massive scale." I had seen the protester on Election Day,
working as a challenger inside the exhibit hall. Now as then, he wore

a set of army dog tags and a hooded National Guard sweatshirt with the sleeves cut off. I asked whether he had observed any fraud with his own eyes. He had not. "It wasn't committed by *these* people," he said. "But the ballots that they were given and ran through the scanners—we don't know where they came from." He repeated: "There's a million different ways."

The man didn't remember me, but we'd met in May, at Operation Haircut. "Shame on you!" he'd shouted at officers issuing citations to the stylists at the capitol. "What is this country coming to? Threats and intimidation by the police!"

A number of other Republicans at the TCF Center also looked familiar. I recognized one man from a press conference I'd attended at Karl Manke's barbershop, in Owosso. A research scientist with a doctorate in molecular biology, the man had stressed the importance of mourning the pandemic's "economic patients" and suggested lowering flags to half-mast for shuttered businesses. Now he was going around with a notepad, asking people denied access to the exhibit hall if they wished to join a lawsuit. A few days later, Karl Manke's personal attorney would sue Detroit for violating the statutory rights of Republican challengers, alleging that they had suffered "irreparable harm" from the "fraudulently manipulated" election.

I'd been chatting with the man in the National Guard sweatshirt for several minutes when he received a text message and abruptly said that he had to leave. I asked if everything was OK. No, the man replied. Everything was not OK.

"Black Lives Matter is here," he explained.

I nodded. "So, you're worried about—"

"Losing my life," the man said.

I followed him back outside to see what was happening. Apart from a few people quietly holding placards that read COUNT EVERY VOTE, I did not spot anyone who might have been mistaken for Black Lives

Matter. More Trump supporters had shown up, though. One wanted me to sign something. It was the petition that Stand Up Michigan had been circulating at the most recent American Patriot Council rally—the petition started by Garrett Soldano back in April. The proposed changes to the state government still included abolishing its civil rights commission, and I noticed a new amendment that would allow any citizen to bring criminal charges against elected officials suspected of violating the Constitution. "It shall be presumed that the defendant did so intentionally," the provision stipulated. Two convictions would be punishable with up to ten years in prison.

TWELVE

LINE IN THE SAND

After every ballot was counted, Joe Biden won Michigan by about 155,000 votes, a far wider margin than Trump's had been in 2016. Only a handful of protesters came to the TCF Center the next day. Ryan Kelley and Jason Howland, the founders of the American Patriot Council, were there. So was Michelle Gregoire, the Home Guard member I'd met on my first visit to the barbershop. She wore the same Donald Trump fleece as she had that unseasonable morning in May. The sleeves were pushed back to her elbows, exposing a "We the People" tattoo across her left forearm. Since I'd last seen Michelle, Michigan had largely reopened, but when I asked if she'd resumed working as a school bus driver, she said that she had been suspended. Prosecutors in Lansing had accused her of assaulting David Dickson, the chief sergeant at arms, when she'd refused to vacate the gallery overlooking the legislature.

"There's an attack on conservatives right now," Michelle said. In addition to facing a felony charge and losing her job, she'd been kicked off Facebook after posting content about the Michigan Home Guard. "If the left gets their way, they will silence whoever they want," she told me. She was friends with William and Michael Null, the twin brothers in the Michigan Liberty Militia who'd been arrested for their alleged role in the plot to kidnap Governor Whitmer. Michelle believed that the Democratic Party was engaged in neutralizing Patriots like the Nulls who threatened its despotic agenda. "That terrifies me. In other countries, they've said, 'That will never happen here,' and before you know it their guns are confiscated and they're living under communism." She added, "A lot of conservatives are really scared right now."

Michelle didn't look scared. She looked angry. But fear and rage seemed to grow in concert with most Patriots, and the more they grew, the harder it became to distinguish one from the other. Was the theft of a presidential election frightening or infuriating? If, after the lockdowns and the riots, you were already scared and angry, it was above all vindicating—confirmation that your feelings were not irrational. It is a lot to ask of people to reject confirmation that their feelings are not irrational. Still, when Michelle brought up the video of the man smuggling a case of ballots into the TCF Center, I told her that he was a journalist and that I had seen him unloading equipment from the case. "No," Michelle said. "Those were ballots. It's not a conspiracy when it's documented and recorded."

SEVERAL STATES HAD NOT YET finished tallying votes, the most important of which was Pennsylvania. A Biden win there would make him president. As with Michigan, in-person returns were reported first and favored Trump. But when absentee results came from Philadelphia—another Democratic stronghold with a large African

American community—Trump's lead evaporated. On November 6, I flew to Pennsylvania, where Biden was announced the victor the next morning.

I was at the state capitol—a monumental Beaux Arts complex in downtown Harrisburg that Theodore Roosevelt once called "the handsomest building I ever saw"—when every major news network declared the election over. By noon, Biden and Harris supporters had gathered to celebrate on a wide flight of granite steps sloping down from the rotunda. Volunteers from CASA in Action, a nonprofit that had worked to turn out voters of color, delivered speeches in English and Spanish. "I, along with tens of thousands of fellow Puerto Ricans and fellow Latino and Black voters in Pennsylvania, have taken back our country," a young activist declared.

"Stop the steal!" Trump supporters chanted from the sidewalk. A woman in a T-shirt with the words VOTE NO FOR JOE & THE HOE carried a sign that read HERD IMMUNITY BEATS HERD STUPIDITY. A tractor trailer drove by, horn blaring. JESUS IS MY VACCINE was painted on its cab. The day before, Trump supporters in Harrisburg had been joined by Representative Jim Jordan, of Ohio. "This election, in the end, is really about this," Jordan had told them. "The left doesn't like this country. They don't. *We* love this country."

Although I did not see Jordan now, I did notice another man wearing a blue windbreaker stitched with the seal of the US House of Representatives. He was Dan Meuser, a congressman from Pennsylvania's coal region. Meuser was listening attentively to a stone-faced biker with shoulder-length hair and a leather vest whose patches included an Iron Cross and a Confederate flag.

"This fight's not over," Meuser assured him.

"I've been leaving a bunch of messages."

"I'll be your voice," Meuser said. "I'll be in direct contact with the House and Senate leaders."

A protest was developing on the opposite side of the capitol, and I accompanied the biker and the congressman around one of the long wings. While we walked, Meuser told us that the same thing had happened in Philadelphia that had happened in Detroit: clandestine ballot deliveries in the middle of the night. "They're happening—you heard about the one up in Wisconsin," he said. Absentee votes in Milwaukee had swung Wisconsin to Biden. As in Michigan and Pennsylvania, Republican lawmakers in the state had prevented the counting of mail-in ballots prior to Election Day, ensuring a reporting delay. A *Federalist* article attributing the late results to a "mysterious all-Biden vote dump" had been widely shared online, and Trump had claimed that his lead "started to magically disappear as surprise ballot dumps were counted." Tellingly, Meuser shook his head and marveled to the biker, "It sounds so excessive it's almost unbelievable."

Behind the capitol, hundreds of Trump supporters had congregated in an open plaza with a large fountain. An elevated mezzanine curved around the space in a sweeping semicircle. More people lined the balustrade. Meuser went to the center of the arc, where someone handed him a megaphone. "I promise you we're gonna get a recount here in Pennsylvania," he vowed. On his right, a man held up a plastic tote lid with a message scrawled in Sharpie: STANDING BACK / STANDING BY / MR. PRESIDENT! On his left, an elderly woman waved a sign with the first letters of "Stop" and "Steal" stylized to resemble Nazi SS bolts.

"Do something!" a man yelled at Meuser.

"Do something!" others echoed.

"Do something! Do something! Do something!"

AWAY FROM THE CROWD, I passed someone whose face was hidden beneath a red MAGA hat that was several feet in diameter and made of foam. The giant bill lifted to reveal a woman talking on her cell phone. "Where's the other three precincts, and where are the votes?" she demanded. "I screenshotted them, so if you need me to email them to you, I can do that." Her acrylic nails were red, white, and blue, and she'd used fabric paint to write KEEP AMERICA GREAT 2020 across each of her slip-on shoes. In front of her, papers marked with yellow highlighter were held down by a pack of menthol cigarettes. When she hung up, she told me that the pages were printouts from a government website that published live election results. According to the woman, whom I'll call Stacey, they showed discrepancies in Philadelphia, which she'd just reported to a voter hotline.

"They were very interested," she said.

Stacey had taken note during the first presidential debate, when Trump had cautioned, "Bad things happen in Philadelphia." While the city posted its returns, she'd tracked them online, from her home in West Virginia. A few years ago, she had joined a pro-Trump club in the Ohio River valley that traveled to Trump rallies and "Trump trains" in a commercial-size motor coach—"the Trump bus"—owned by one of its members. Stacey and her mother had caught the Trump bus to Harrisburg early that morning. The all-day trip was a lot for her mother, who was seventy-eight, but Stacey told me, "We had to. We can't have them stealing our votes."

None of the Trump supporters I met in Harrisburg had any doubt that this is what had happened. After all, a US congressman had just told them so—and Dan Meuser was far from an outlier. Jim Jordan had been accompanied by Representative Scott Perry, and later that afternoon Pennsylvania state senator Doug Mastriano would make an appearance. The message from the Republican establishment was plain: the will of the people had been subverted in what amounted to a bloodless coup.

"If we allow the fraud to go through, you can say goodbye to a free

THE STORM IS HERE

republic," one Trump campaign surrogate said from the mezzanine. "You are no longer represented."

"Line in the sand!" a bitter voice cried out.

The sun was setting when I went to check on the Democrats. The steps were almost empty, and the volunteers from CASA in Action were packing up. They'd planned to stay longer, but a group of heavily armed Trump supporters had made them nervous. One of the volunteers had already sent her teenage daughter home. "These people aren't safe to be around," she said. While the remaining Democrats rolled up their signs and unplugged their speakers, a woman in Ray-Bans paced back and forth a few feet away, screaming at them over and over at the top of her lungs, "The only good commie is a dead commie!"

RESURRECTION

The armed men who had spooked the Biden supporters were members of the Pennsylvania Three Percent militia. Laden with assault rifles, hand guns, flak jackets, magazines, tourniquets, first-aid kits, hydration systems, tactical gloves, and fixed-blade knives, they stood in a tight circle, backs to each other, scanning their respective sectors of fire. One of them was so encumbered with weaponry and gear that when he dropped his water bottle, he had to ask a bystander to pick it up for him. Nodding toward the CASA in Action rally, he cautioned, "We got BLM-Antifa on the other side of the building with baseball bats and helmets."

His name was George, and he was the group's "combat-skills instructor" and "law enforcement liaison." A badge clipped onto his belt identified him as a retired police officer. "Law enforcement knows we're on their side," he told me. "It's like meeting someone from the same fraternity." Squad cars from the Harrisburg Police Department had escorted the militia to the statehouse. George lived in York County, where, he said, "I got the number for the sheriff. He's a Republican. If things go sideways, we'll be deputized."

I asked what the chances were of things going sideways.

"It's coming," George said.

He invited me to attend a service at his place of worship, Freedom Biker Church, the next morning. When I arrived at the low-slung brick building off the interstate, people were smoking cigarettes and sipping coffee near a row of customized Harleys leaning on their kickstands. George puffed a fat cigar. His leather vest was embroidered with BRO-KEN CHAINS, a support network for Christian bikers in recovery. He introduced me to the pastor, Jim Quoss, whom everybody called Pastor Jim.

"I'm a Trump supporter, but this church is all about Jesus," Pastor Jim assured me. His gray hair was tied back in a ponytail, and his kind, bright eyes glinted above an untamed beard. Bulky silver rings adorned his fingers. Despite the disclaimer, Pastor Jim acknowledged that he did not consider Biden's win to be legitimate. "Until now, the Democrats have been the resistance," he said. "Now, we're the resistance. It will come down to a battle of wills—is their will to succeed greater than our will to resist."

There was no animus in Pastor Jim's voice, and I had the sense that he might be looking forward to the role reversal. In general, the vibe at Freedom Biker Church was something like the opposite of the insurrectionary fervor that I'd witnessed in Harrisburg. The weather was pristine, spiked with an invigorating nip of East Coast autumn, and the congregants seemed above all stoked for such an epic day to ride. I detected none of the emotional devastation that many liberals had experienced in the wake of their 2016 defeat. Religion clearly helped. In the lead-up to the election, a belief in predestination had allowed many conservative Christians to dismiss the consistently foreboding polls; since the election, it had nourished the delusion that Trump might still somehow prevail. "I firmly believe Trump's gonna win," a man in a leather cowboy hat, with a Springfield .45 on his hip, had told me in Harrisburg. "I look at it this way. God's using Trump to expose the sins of the leaders to the people, and then it's up to us to decide if we're gonna put up with it." This idea—that Biden's fraudulent victory was a divine stratagem to pull back the curtain on Democratic malfeasance—would soon gain wide purchase among Republicans.

Yet such invincible hopefulness did not require belief in the supernatural. It also followed logically from the assumption that Donald Trump and his supporters were on the winning side of history. Americans like Trump had dominated the country since its founding. Faith in the continuation of that dominance wasn't necessarily spiritual. Sometimes it was just myopic.

At Freedom Biker Church, George greeted people at the door as they made their way inside. A rock band played Foo Fighters songs with Christian lyrics grafted on. The congregation recited the pledge of allegiance, and a leather boot was passed around for the offering. Then Pastor Jim stepped to the pulpit. "This is where the rubber meets the road," he said. "It's not the time to give up, it's the time to *get* up." He invited us to consider how the disciples of Christ must have felt while he was hanging on the cross. Like their world was over. Like they had lost. Their enemies, meanwhile, rejoiced. "The Pharisees and all the religious people who had conspired to have Jesus crucified believed that this was the end of this guy and this movement," Pastor Jim said. He took a breath. "And then Jesus walked out of the tomb."

THIRTEEN

INFO WARRIORS

When the Soviet Union and the threat of global communism vanished in 1991, so did the pretext for Christian paramilitarism that had aligned conservatives with white supremacists for decades. In his journal *The Seditionist*, the prominent Klansman Louis Beam wrote, "Who will be the enemy we all agree to hate?" A year later, in Estes Park, Beam answered his own question: "the federals" and the New World Order would replace the Bolsheviks. Conspiracy theories have always helped rationalize white grievance, and those who exploit white grievance for political or financial gain often purvey conspiracy theories. Trump began floating the idea of a presidential bid during Barack Obama's first term, when he became an evangelist for birtherism. Despite the release of Obama's official and long-form birth certificates, confirmation of his birth in Hawaii by the state's health department, and birth announcements published in two local newspapers, the burgeoning Patriot Movement—and, according to polls, roughly half of all Republicans—refused to accept that the first Black president of the United States was American. Hitting the cable news circuit, Trump claimed the documentation was a "fraud" and suggested foul play when Hawaii's health director died in a plane crash.

Whether or not he believed the slander, he had been apprised of its political utility by his friend Roger Stone. A former adviser to Richard Nixon and self-described expert at "the black arts" of political chicanery, Stone had worked as a lobbyist for Trump's casino business in the nineties. In 2000, he helped organize the Brooks Brothers riot in Florida, where the presidential contest between George W. Bush and Al Gore hung in the balance. Although Bush had won the state by fewer than two thousand votes, far more ballots than that appeared to have been improperly disqualified by tabulators. In Miami, then a Democratic bastion like Detroit or Philadelphia, election workers began manually recounting more than half a million votes. A mob of Republicans, many wearing Brooks Brothers blazers, stormed the board of elections, assaulted people, banged on windows, and yelled, "Let us in!" The recount was called off, clinching Bush's victory.

Stone often appeared on the Infowars web show hosted by conspiracy theorist Alex Jones. Jones was a native of Texas, where, as a high schooler, the Waco massacre had precipitated his political awakening. He claimed to believe that the architects of Waco had been New World Order agents running a shadow authority within the US government—"the deep state." Ruby Ridge, Oklahoma City, September 11th, and the Sandy Hook Elementary School massacre were all likewise deep-state operations. According to Jones, the bottomless depredations of the New World Order would include mass genocide, engineered starvation, and sprawling death camps in which children would be harvested for energy to fuel the decadent lifestyles of a few depraved elites in league with the devil. During the 2016 campaign,

Stone arranged for Trump to be a guest on Infowars, where Trump told Jones, "I will not let you down." Jones went on to warn his listeners that "Obama and Hillary both smell like sulfur," and that Clinton was "an abject psychopathic demon from hell."

Ahead of the vote, Stone created a website to undermine Clinton's expected victory by claiming that the election had been rigged. He named the site Stop the Steal. After Trump won the electoral college, Stone and Jones argued that fraud accounted for his deficit in the popular vote. On one Infowars episode, Jones said that Clinton had "stolen" half a dozen states from Trump; four days later, Trump tweeted, "I won the popular vote if you deduct the millions of people who voted illegally." This compact with the conspiracist right only strengthened over the next four years, as Trump characterized his impeachment and the special counsel Robert Mueller's report on Russian election meddling as deep-state "hoaxes" designed to "overthrow" him. (Stone was convicted of seven felonies related to the Mueller investigation, including making false statements and witness tampering.) In 2020, when Trump reprised the allegation of a plot to steal the election, it made instinctive sense to Americans who'd already come to see him as an adversary of the deep state. Like all good conspiracy theories, it affirmed and elaborated preexisting ones. Conversely, rejecting the allegation could mean renouncing an entire worldview.

The day after the election, a new page had appeared on Facebook called Stop the Steal. Its description read, "Democrats are scheming to disenfranchise and nullify Republican votes. It's up to us, the American People, to fight and to put a stop to it." One of the first posts on the page was a cell phone video of the Republican challengers at the TCF Center, chanting to be let in. Overnight the page gained more than 320,000 followers, making it among the fastest-growing in Facebook history. Its creator was a thirty-year-old Republican activist from

Georgia named Kylie Jane Kremer. Kremer's mother, Amy, was a former flight attendant who had helped launch the Tea Party movement
in 2009. Facebook promptly deleted the Stop the Steal page, and a few
days later the Kremers announced that they would be holding a rally
in Washington, D.C., on November 14. Online, the event became known
as the Million MAGA March. Alex Jones organized a "Stop the Steal
caravan" to travel from Texas to the Capitol, and Enrique Tarrio, the
Proud Boys chairman, wrote on Parler, "Standby order has been re-
scinded." The head of the Indiana Proud Boys, a former neo-Nazi gang
leader, posted a video promoting the march, set to the "Mannerbund
Anthem," a fascist paean.

On November 11, the founder of the Oath Keepers appeared on
Infowars. An army veteran and graduate of Yale Law School, Stewart
Rhodes had started the organization in 2009 as a network of retired
and active-duty members of the military and law enforcement who
viewed Obama and other liberal politicians as enemies of the Constitution that they had sworn to defend. Wearing his signature black pi-
rate patch over his left eye—he accidentally shot himself in the face
in 1992—Rhodes told Jones, "We have men stationed outside D.C. already, as a nuclear option, in case of an attempt to remove the president illegally."

"This is an insane time to be alive," said Jones.

UPON A HILL

In early June, after Trump's walk to St. John's Church, the security
perimeter around the White House had been expanded, subsuming
large green spaces previously open to the public. On the north side of
the premises, a tall metal fence sealed off Lafayette Square. Protesters

had decorated the fence with cardboard signs, converting it into a living memorial to victims of police violence. Muriel Bowser, the Democratic mayor of D.C., renamed the two blocks leading to the fence Black Lives Matter Plaza, and had BLACK LIVES MATTER painted across the pavement in thirty-five-foot-tall yellow letters.

On the morning of November 14, thousands of Trump supporters filed through Black Lives Matter Plaza on their way from their hotels to Freedom Plaza, the rally point for the Million MAGA March. When I arrived a little before ten a.m., a small group of activists was patrolling the fence. Behind them, Lafayette Square featured a bronze statue of President Andrew Jackson astride a horse standing on its hind legs. Green stains discolored the plinth; over the summer, demonstrators had poured acid around the horse's hooves, lashed ropes around the statue, and nearly toppled Jackson, an unrepentant enslaver who signed the Indian Removal Act, which resulted in the Trail of Tears. I'd been at the fence a couple of minutes when a young man in camouflage pants and a DON'T TREAD ON ME tank top, carrying a TRUMP 2020 flag over his shoulder, walked up and began methodically ripping down signs, one after the other. Two Black women inserted themselves in front of him. The man stood there, mutely staring at them, and then moved on.

"Fuck these cracker-ass motherfuckers!" one of the women yelled. Her long braids hung out the bottom of a sweatshirt that read BLACK LIVES MATTER D.C. Her name was Toni Sanders, and she'd been at Lafayette Square every day since George Floyd was killed. Toni, her wife, and her nine-year-old stepson were among the peaceful protesters dispersed by the police with tear gas and rubber bullets ahead of Trump's visit to St. John's Church. "Here we were thinking we were going to teach him about nonviolent civil disobedience," she said of her stepson. "And the lesson he came away with was, the government hates Black people."

As more Trump supporters approached us, I recognized several of them from the memorial in Vancouver for Aaron "J" Danielson. They were led by Joey Gibson, the founder of Patriot Prayer, who wore a JUSTICE FOR J hat. When Gibson passed us, shouting about Biden being a communist, Toni said, "Look at them. Full of hate, and proud of it." A woman waved a sign at Toni scrawled with GOD'S ARMY. Toni shook her head. "If God were here, he would smite these mother-fuckers."

Some thirty minutes later, a familiar foam MAGA hat came bobbing above the crowd. Underneath it was Stacey, the West Virginian I'd met in Harrisburg. She'd caught a ride to D.C. on the same Trump bus that had brought her to Pennsylvania. This time, fearing Antifa, she'd left her mother at home. "I'm sorry, I would have to knock the shit out of people," she told me. "You mess with my mom and you're in trouble."

I asked if she'd heard from the voter hotline.

"Nope. I also called the Justice Department and sent an email to Donald Trump. Hopefully, sooner or later they'll call me back." It was her first trip to D.C., but she had no plans for tourism. "Honestly, the only place I'd like to see is the White House," she said.

I left Toni and accompanied Stacey to Freedom Plaza, four or five blocks away, where we were immediately separated in a crush of tens of thousands of people. We'd just missed Trump, who had driven through in a motorcade, waving to protesters from behind the window of his limousine. "He looked right at me!" I overheard someone gush in disbelief.

The crowd was almost too dense to penetrate. Many people were forcing their way toward the south side of the square, and the raucous applause emanating from that direction made me wonder whether the president might be making another pass. After working my way there, I found Alex Jones standing on a planter box, ranting through a bullhorn.

All chest and no neck, with a round face that might have been described as cherubic if it were not permanently contorted by rage, Jones pumped a meaty fist in the air and screamed, "If the globalists think they're gonna keep America under martial law, and they're gonna put that communist Chinese agent Biden in, they got another thing coming!"

People cheered, chanted his name, and jostled to catch a glimpse of him. I was surprised by the intensity of their adulation, and even Jones seemed a bit taken aback. Not long ago, he'd appeared to be at risk of sliding into obsolescence. Facebook, Twitter, Apple, Spotify, and YouTube had all expelled him from their platforms after he accused the bereaved parents of children murdered at Sandy Hook of being paid actors, prompting Infowars fans to harass and threaten them. The bans curtailed his reach, but the pandemic and its attendant deluge of propaganda had drawn millions of people to his proprietary websites. For some of these Americans, Jones's dire warnings suddenly looked prophetic—an impression that Trump's election claims had only bolstered. "Alex Jones was right!" someone in the crowd yelled.

Across the plaza, Kylie Jane Kremer stepped to a lectern and promised "an incredible lineup of speakers," after which, she said, we would proceed up Pennsylvania Avenue, to the Supreme Court. But the event that Kremer had organized was no more under her control than the movement her Facebook page had catapulted. Less than five minutes into Kremer's speech, Alex Jones shouted over her, "The march starts now!" His usual security detail was supplemented by about a dozen Proud Boys, who formed a ring around him and cleared a narrow path through the crowd. Enrique Tarrio trailed behind him, grinning like a groupie. As usual, he seemed at a loss for words. His ammo vest contained a can of tropical-flavor Red Bull.

"The answer to their 1984 tyranny is 1776!" Jones cried. While he caught his breath, a man in his entourage raised his own megaphone: "Let's not forget what this country's made of—we stretch out ropes and hang people by them when they're treasonous pigs! Start getting out your rope, it's time to make a noose!"

The first person hanged for treason in the US had been the abolitionist John Brown, and thousands of African Americans were lynched by white vigilantes in the decades after slavery ended. In 1978, William Pierce, a former propagandist for the American Nazi Party, published *The Turner Diaries*, a novel that depicts "free men" mounting an insurgency against the government after its Jewish overlords devise a mass confiscation of guns. In an event called the "Day of the Rope," which bears a strong resemblance to the storm envisaged by QAnon, these white revolutionaries publicly hang "the lawyers, the businessmen, the TV newscasters, the newspaper reporters and editors, the judges, the teachers, the school officials, the 'civic leaders,' the bureaucrats, the preachers, and all the others" who "betrayed" or "defiled" their race by consorting with Black and non-Christian citizens. *The Turner Diaries* sold half a million copies and inspired a slew of terrorist attacks. Timothy McVeigh sold the novel at gun shows and carried pages of it with him when he blew up the Alfred P. Murrah building. The bomb that McVeigh built—a truckload of ammonium nitrate mixed with fuel oil—was almost identical to one used by Pierce's narrator against the FBI headquarters in D.C.

"Down with the deep state!" Jones intoned as we passed the headquarters. More and more people had abandoned Kremer and her scheduled speakers to follow him. Eventually, the avenue sloped up toward the US Capitol. At the top of the hill, I turned and peered down at a solid procession of Trump supporters stretching back for more than a mile. Flags waved like the sails of a bottlenecked armada. From this vantage, the Million MAGA March appeared to have been led by the Proud Boys and Infowars.

Another sound system was staged on the steps of the Supreme Court, and Jones did not hesitate to use it. "This march is the start of the Second American Revolution!" he told his riveted audience, which overflowed into the Capitol grounds. "This is the beginning of the end of the New World Order!"

A series of US representatives came next. Louie Gohmert, a congressman from Texas, could have been quoting Jones verbatim when he climbed onto the steps. "This is an information war," Gohmert said. "This is a multidimensional war that the US intelligence people have used on other governments. You not only steal the vote, but you use the media to convince people that they're not really seeing what they're seeing."

"We see!" a woman standing near me cried.

AFTER A WHILE, I made my way back toward Freedom Plaza. As I was walking down Pennsylvania Avenue, I fell in with a group of preppy-looking young men wearing plaid shirts, khakis, blazers, and sunglasses. Some carried rosaries and crosses, others held up royal-blue flags inscribed with AF in white letters. This was the logo for the web program *America First*, which was hosted by Nicholas Fuentes, a twenty-two-year-old college dropout who aimed to "restore traditional white society" and preserve a "core American identity centered around ethnicity and race." Fuentes viewed politics as a vehicle for ensuring the long-term demographic supremacy of white Christians, and reviled most mainstream Republicans for lacking sufficient commitment to this priority. (Neoconservatives were especially odious, due to their subservience to Jews.) His loyalty to Trump was "unconditional." As the America Firsters continued along Pennsylvania Avenue, they bellowed in unison, "Christian nation!" and "Emperor Trump!" They also chanted, "Groyper!" The name, which America Firsters often called themselves, derived from a variation of the Pepe the Frog meme fashionable among white supremacists.

Fuentes owed much of his ideological identity to Pat Buchanan, the right-wing author and politician who had championed America First nativism long before the rise of Trump. Both Fuentes and Buchanan were traditionalist Catholics who believed that Western values were under assault from nonwhite immigrants on the one hand, and from international Jewry on the other. Buchanan's book *The Death of the West: How Dying Populations and Immigrant Invasions Imperil Our Country and Civilization* highlights falling birth rates among whites and the "de-Christianizing of America" as acute perils to the republic. The phrase "America First" was initially popularized in 1940 by Nazi sympathizers lobbying to keep the US out of the Second World War. "The achievements of that organization are monumental," Buchanan, whose father was an original America Firster, wrote in a column. Before joining the Reagan administration, he championed accused Nazi war criminals and praised Hitler as "an individual of great courage" with "extraordinary gifts." When they ran against each other for the Reform Party nomination in 1999, Trump denounced Buchanan as "a Hitler-lover." Seventeen years later, when Trump co-opted both his slogan and his platform, Buchanan was enjoying a renaissance thanks to the Patriot Movement. At Proud Boys gatherings, Gavin McInnes and Enrique Tarrio both liked to read aloud from *The Death of the West.* Their favorite passage honored "the only hero" in the history of human bondage: "Western man," who "alone abolished slavery."

More than McInnes and Tarrio, though, it was Nicholas Fuentes who had most avidly regurgitated Buchanan's antisemitism. Fuentes had once dedicated a segment of his show to calculating how much time and how many ovens it would take to bake six million cookies—the number of Jews killed in the Holocaust—and had marveled at how COVID-19 outbreaks in Jewish communities were exposing their "secret gatherings" the way that some mouthwashes revealed bacterial plaque on teeth.

I did not see Fuentes on Pennsylvania Avenue, but when the Groypers reached Freedom Plaza one of them withdrew several sheets of paper from the pocket of his leather jacket and began to read an impassioned diatribe with a distinctly Fuentes-like sense of metaphor. His hair was slicked back with gel and his cheeks spotted with acne; his voice cracked and his hands shook as he raved about the "globalist scum engorging themselves as they ravish our beautiful nation," and the need to "strike down this foreign invasion" before it "extinguishes and smothers our way of life." When he finished, I noticed that two young men standing near me were giddily laughing. The response felt incongruous, until I recognized it as the juvenile thrill of transgression.

"He just gave a fascist speech!" one of them chirped.

OVER THE NEXT SEVEN HOURS, clashes between Trump supporters and counterprotesters throughout D.C. would see more than twenty people arrested, a few seriously injured, and one man hospitalized after being stabbed. While activists defending Black Lives Matter Plaza harassed and heckled Trump supporters, elsewhere in the city Proud Boys led by Enrique Tarrio brutalized antifascists. A livestreamer filmed one Proud Boy chasing after a young woman, tackling her, and repeatedly slamming her head into the pavement. When an officer pulled the man away and the woman again attempted to flee, two other Proud Boys grabbed and punched her in the face. Blood streamed from her brow. "Yeah, you stupid bitch!" one of the Proud Boys snarled. "Talk to your mommy, little fuckface!"

A second video captured another Proud Boy, a few feet away, swinging a motorcycle helmet into a Black woman's temple, knocking her unconscious.

"She went out like a light!" someone exclaimed.

Later, Trump tweeted, "ANTIFA SCUM ran for the hills today

when they tried attacking the people at the Trump Rally, because those people aggressively fought back."

At the time, I was following a pack of his supporters through the streets around the White House as they searched for more victims to beat up. A Proud Boy with a long wavy beard passed around Budweisers from a garbage sack; a man with a shaved head wore a T-shirt with the logo for Skrewdriver, a neo-Nazi punk band. When we reached Black Lives Matter Plaza, it was deserted. The antifascists had gone home, and police officers in riot gear guarded the fence. Large sheets of plywood attached to a labor union's office proclaimed BLACK LIVES MATTER, and soon the Trump supporters began tearing them down, dragging them into the plaza, and jumping on them until they splintered. "Our streets!" they yelled. One man wore a crisp white collared shirt and a dress tie under an ammo vest with a patch that read: GRAB THEM BY THE PUSSY.

I got back to my hotel around one in the morning. A few Trump supporters stood near the entrance, smoking cigarettes. As I passed them, one commented, "A grown man wearing a mask outside—*disgusting*." I turned to face her. She looked like she was in her early sixties and appeared pleasant enough. If you'd seen her in a library, you might have guessed she worked there. Holding my gaze, she said, "Pinko commie motherfucker."

WHAT IS COMING

From D.C., the Stop the Steal caravan proceeded to Georgia, another swing state that Biden had flipped. A few days after the Million MAGA March, Nicholas Fuentes appeared on an Infowars panel in an Atlanta hotel. On his own show, he had once insisted that he was "a kid at heart," admired his "boyish nature," and observed that it was "godly" to be "childlike." It was true that his face was usually creased in a mischievous smile, eyes gleaming with youthful amusement. But the fact that the smile broadened and the eyes brightened in proportion to the hatefulness and mendacity of whatever he was saying made them, to me at least, more wolfish than boyish. During the discussion in Atlanta, Fuentes lit up as he broached the subject of the "Great Replacement." This was the belief that white Christians in the US and Europe were being supplanted by populations incompatible with Western culture and identity. The same Jews behind the New World Order—the Rothschilds, George Soros—were orchestrating the demographic reversal in order to enfeeble gentiles and commit "white genocide." At the Unite the Right rally, in Charlottesville, neo-Nazis had chanted, "Jews will not replace us!" and the perpetrators of the New Zealand mosque massacre and the El Paso Walmart massacre, in 2019, both cited the Great Replacement in their manifestos. "If this transition is allowed to take place, that's it," Fuentes said in Atlanta. "There is nothing worse than what's coming."

"Submitting now will destroy you forever," Alex Jones agreed. It didn't matter that he was talking about the New World Order, Fuentes about the Great Replacement. By defining liberals as an existential menace, both Jones and Fuentes elevated their respective struggles above the realm of politics. The same could be said of evangelicals who exalted Trump as a messianic figure empowered to deliver the country from satanic machinations. Or the "church militant" movement, fostered by Steve Bannon, Trump's former chief strategist, which put Trump at the forefront of a worldwide contest between Western civilization and Islamic "barbarity." Or any of the politicians and pundits who situated partisan disagreements in the context of an eternal, cosmic struggle between good and evil. Religious maximalists, conspiracy theorists, and white nationalists all aspired to transcend democracy, with the same effect: they rendered constitutional principles of representation, pluralism, and the separation of powers less inviolable, given the magnitude of what was at stake.

In a speech announcing his candidacy for the Republican presidential nomination in 1992, Pat Buchanan had warned, "We must not trade in our sovereignty for a cushioned seat at the head table of anybody's New World Order." Back then, the New World Order was often referred to as the "ZOG," or Zionist Occupied Government. Louis Beam and Timothy McVeigh both understood themselves to be defending white Christians against the ZOG. So did the shooter at the Tree of Life synagogue, in Pittsburgh, who killed eleven Jews during a Shabbat service in 2018. "I can't sit by and watch my people get slaughtered," he'd explained. This has always been the way. Nazi propaganda blaming Jews for Germany's defeat in the First World War laid the groundwork for the Holocaust; *The Protocols of the Elders of Zion*, a fake blueprint for international Jewish hegemony, justified Russian pogroms in the early twentieth century; during the second bubonic plague, or Black Death, thousands of European Jews were burned alive for poisoning town wells (no evidence supports the calumny); and mobs throughout the Middle Ages regularly killed Jews after accusing them of abducting and consuming the blood of Christian children in secret rituals known as blood libels. At the state capitol in Pennsylvania, I watched a speaker implore the Trump supporters, "Do not become a cog in the ZOG!" and during the pandemic, Nicholas Fuentes had reminded his viewers about "rabbis and other Jewish people poisoning the wells with plague." Both Alex Jones and the QAnon community maintained that the Satanist pedophiles of the deep state practiced a modern form of blood libel, which involved kidnapping infants for their adrenochrome, a chemical compound that induced euphoria, prolonged youth, and allowed communion with fallen angels. Because the adrenal glands secreted the chemical only during states of extreme distress, torture preceded its extraction.

The moral of the adrenochrome story was the same as the moral of the Kenyan President story, or of the engineered pandemic story, or of the Antifa revolution story, or of the fraudulent election story. It was yet another episode in the never-ending saga of dispossession. Not satisfied with your land, guns, freedom, job, voice, heritage, religion, vote, and country, with adrenochrome they would take from you something even more precious. "I think the endgame for them is really about immortality," Fuentes said in Atlanta. "We are all going to die essentially. They will steal our life force so that they can perpetuate themselves."

Was this another metaphor? The Great Replacement or the New World Order? Jews or globalists? Aliens or immigrants? Black Lives Matter or Black lives?

"Whatever's behind it is not human," Jones offered.

The British antisemite and frequent Infowars guest David Icke contended that the planet was infiltrated by shape-shifting reptiles from outer space. But Jones's comment also recalled the Proud Boy position that "commies aren't people" and the popular Patriot tattoo "We the People." On January 6, shortly before dispatching his supporters to the Capitol, Trump would assure them, "You're the real people." The division of Americans into the real and the fake, coupled with the fear that the latter are becoming more numerous than the former, is the essence of the Great Replacement theory. Whether the distinction is understood literally or figuratively, violence is a predictable outcome. In 2019, a Proud Boy in Seattle became convinced that his brother was one of David Icke's lizard aliens and murdered him with a samurai sword. That same year, the El Paso shooter took twenty-three lives in hopes of stemming an "Hispanic invasion of Texas." Defending the gunman on *America First* two days later, Nicholas Fuentes asked, "At a certain point, what is the expectation?"

FOURTEEN

HIGHER LAW

As in Michigan, Wisconsin, and Pennsylvania, white and rural parts of Georgia had voted in person and for Trump, while the diverse city of Atlanta went overwhelmingly for Biden. Absentee ballots were processed in State Farm Arena, the home venue for the Atlanta Hawks. The stadium had been empty since March, when the NBA season was postponed due to the pandemic. On Election Day, a urinal that had gone unused for months overflowed. Water seeped through the floor, into the room below, where ballots were being tabulated. Although the toilet was quickly repaired and the counting soon resumed, false stories spread online of a "water-main break" and "dump of Biden votes" during the ensuing evacuation.

The presence of surveillance cameras only made things worse. On November 5, Donald Trump Jr. retweeted footage that showed Lawrence Sloan, a thirty-five-year-old election worker, crumpling up a piece of paper in frustration. The paper was an instruction sheet that someone had mistakenly returned inside an absentee envelope; nevertheless, the president's son wrote, "WTF?" When Sloan's number, address, and license plate were publicized, he dyed his hair and went into hiding. Conservative media outlets identified other election workers in the surveillance video, including a grandmother named Ruby Freeman and her adult daughter, Shaye Moss. *The Gateway Pundit* called Freeman and Moss "crooks" and accused them of smuggling in a suitcase containing thousands of fraudulent ballots. QAnon followers fixated on them. Freeman, Moss, and Sloan, like most of the election workers at State Farm Arena, were Black; according to Freeman, she was bombarded with death threats from people saying "the most vile and violent and racist things about me and my family—on the phone, on my social media accounts, on email, and in person. Things you wouldn't believe." One man reached Moss's fourteen-year-old son by phone. "You should hang alongside your nigger momma," the caller told him. After a QAnon influencer shared an innocuous video of another worker removing a thumb drive from a computer, the worker discovered a noose outside his house.

On December 1, Gabriel Sterling, a top election official in Georgia and a Republican who had voted for Trump twice, held a press conference to rebuke the president for having "lost the moral high ground." Warning that "it has all gone too far," Sterling beseeched Trump to "stop inspiring people to commit potential acts of violence. Someone's going to get hurt. Someone's going to get shot. Someone's going to get killed." A hand audit of all five million ballots cast in Georgia had confirmed Biden's victory, and that same day Attorney General Barr announced that investigations by the Justice Department and the Department of Homeland Security had found no evidence of widespread fraud. None of this made any difference. A few hours after Sterling's appeal, Trump tweeted, "Rigged Election . . . Expose the massive voter fraud in Georgia." Less than a week later, his personal attorney,

Rudy Giuliani, appeared via Zoom before Georgia state legislators for a publicly livestreamed hearing during which he played surveillance footage of Ruby Freeman and Shaye Moss withdrawing a bin from beneath a table, removing ballots, and scanning them—in other words, doing their job. Investigators had already looked into and dismissed preposterous online allegations regarding the clip. "There were no mystery ballots that were brought in from an unknown location and hidden under tables as has been reported by some," state authorities had concluded. Rudy Giuliani disagreed. "Look at them scurrying around with the ballots," he said of Freeman, Moss, and the other Black election workers in the video. "They look like they're passing out dope. It is quite clear they're stealing votes."

To write this, I rewatched the livestreamed hearing on YouTube. It has over a million views. On the chat replay, a running scroll of the original comments is preserved. Everyone seems to view Giuliani as a courageous defender of the downtrodden, speaking truth to power. Everyone seems as unable as Giuliani to fathom how any American can fail to see what he sees.

"BLM CROOKS lock them up."

"TREASON has a death penalty."

"Gabriel Sterling for the Hangmans NOOSE."

"Free Bananas!"

"EVIL."

BEFORE VOTING EVEN BEGAN, Trump had told reporters, "As soon as the election is over, we're going in with our lawyers." Giuliani and other attorneys duly filed more than eighty lawsuits in state and federal courts across the country. None held water. A Pennsylvania judge, whom Trump had nominated to the federal bench, wrote in one decision, "Calling an election unfair does not make it so. Charges require specific allegations and then proof. We have neither here." A Wisconsin Supreme Court justice, appointed by a Republican governor, declined to hear Trump's petition to nullify the vote in his state. "Such entreaties built on so flimsy a foundation would do indelible damage to every future election," the justice argued. After another Trump-nominated judge did grant the president an opportunity to make his case in Wisconsin, he ruled, "He has lost on the merits," and added that the "claims fail as a matter of law and fact." A Nevada judge, who'd recently sided with state Republicans against Democratic lawmakers in an unrelated matter, ridiculed affidavits submitted by the Trump campaign as "self-serving statements of little or no evidentiary value." As for the lawsuit filed by Karl Manke's lawyer on behalf of Republican challengers at Detroit's TCF Center, a circuit judge found that "the allegations simply are not credible."

Some allegations were less credible than others. In the days after the election, a QAnon theory had emerged that voting machines and software made by Dominion Voting Systems and Smartmatic had electronically reversed the results of the election. On November 12, Trump tweeted that Dominion had "DELETED" and "SWITCHED" millions of votes. In response, the US Cybersecurity and Infrastructure Security Agency asserted that the election had been "the most secure in American history," and that there was "no evidence that any voting system deleted or lost votes, changed votes, or was in any way compromised." At a press conference a week later, Giuliani linked Smartmatic to George Soros, Antifa, and Black Lives Matter. He also introduced one of the lawyers on his team, a former federal prosecutor named Sidney Powell. Wearing a black turtleneck and leopard-print cardigan, Powell declared with a patrician southern accent and a straight face, "What we are really dealing with here and uncovering more by the day is the massive influence of communist money through Venezuela, Cuba, and likely China." According to Powell, Smartmatic (which was founded in Florida) and Dominion (founded in Canada) "were created at the direction of Hugo Chavez," the Venezuelan leader who died in 2013. "An algorithm that probably ran all over the country" had "flipped" votes from Trump to Biden. "Globalists, dictators, corporations, you name it" were complicit in the scheme. "Everybody's against us," Powell concluded, "except President Trump."

Months later, when Dominion sued Powell for defamation, she would argue that "no reasonable person" could have mistaken any of her "outlandish" claims as "statements of fact." The validity of the claims, in any case, was less important than the overall climate of suspicion and distrust that they cumulatively generated. As the president doubled down on his increasingly ludicrous allegations, politicians and pundits unwilling to contradict him began to fall back on a kind of circular logic, citing the growing number of conservatives who believed that the election was stolen as proof that it had been, while pointing to the climate of suspicion and distrust in order to legitimize the falsehoods that had created it. One federal judge, dismissing a complaint filed by Powell as "an amalgamation of theories, conjecture, and speculation," admonished that "a belief is not evidence." But while this might have been true in the courtroom, politics was something else. During a Senate hearing at the Michigan state capitol, a Republican challenger from the TCF Center, offering no evidence of fraud himself, demanded to see evidence that none had occurred. "We believe," he testified. "Prove us wrong."

The witness was Randy Bishop, a Christian radio host, former county GOP chairman, and convicted felon. Of course, the absence of fraud could no more be proven than the absence of God—but this was likely Bishop's point. For him, and for millions of Americans like him, the existence of both was a matter of faith. I had watched Bishop deliver a rousing speech at the American Patriot Council rally on June 18. Outside the capitol that day, Bishop had talked a lot about the Constitution.

Now, inside the capitol, he implored Michigan's senators to defy the Constitution. Perhaps if they withheld delegates from the electoral college, they would be seen to have broken the law. However, Bishop assured them, "I'd say you responded to a *higher* law. You responded and appealed to God."

A REAL SOLUTION

While Trump's attorneys inundated battleground states with spurious litigation, one of them, during an interview on Fox Business, revealed the end goal of their strategy: "We're waiting for the United States Supreme Court, of which the president has nominated three justices, to step in and do something." This expectation—that nepotistic fealty would secure Trump's grip on power—was why the Million MAGA March had targeted the Supreme Court. And it was why, after the Supreme Court declined to second-guess any of the dozens of judges who'd ruled against Trump, the attorney general of Texas had petitioned it to invalidate every vote from Wisconsin, Georgia, Pennsylvania, and Michigan. Seventeen Republican-led states and 106 Republican members of Congress—well over half—signed on to the extraordinary attempt to summarily disenfranchise more than twenty million Americans. On December 11, the Supreme Court rejected their motion, though Samuel Alito and Clarence Thomas both dissented. Text messages obtained by *The Washington Post* would reveal that Thomas's wife, Ginni, had been pressuring the White House not to concede. In November, Ginni had written Chief of Staff Mark Meadows, "Biden and the Left is attempting the greatest Heist of our History"; urged him to collaborate with Sidney Powell; and relayed Louie Gohmert's contention that "this war is psychological. PSYOP." Meadows had assured Ginni, "Evil always looks like the victor until the King of Kings triumphs."

In spite of Alito and Thomas, the majority decision on December 11 dispelled once and for all the tenacious fantasy that the Supreme Court might annul the election. I was in D.C. when it was announced. Another MAGA rally had been planned for the next day, and in the morning thousands of Trump supporters again crowded into Freedom Plaza. On my way there, I stopped by Hotel Harrington, where the Proud Boys were staying. The street outside was filled with men in black-and-yellow polos, drinking Budweiser and White Claw. "We're going to own this town!" a bearded man in a flak jacket howled. It was something to behold. The first Proud Boys I'd met had been afraid to linger in a public park, in broad daylight, in their own hometown; a few months later, here they were, droves of them, determined to "own" Washington, D.C. They had the support of the president, who had the support of most Republican politicians, officials, and citizens. The Proud Boys Parler account had ballooned from about seventy thousand followers before the election to a quarter million. "I wanna see Trump drive by and give us one of these," said one Proud Boy, flashing an OK sign. A couple feet away, I recognized Brien James, the former neo-Nazi leader, wearing a Fred Perry scarf and singing a sea chantey. Other Proud Boys had on balaclavas, kilts, hockey masks, or batting helmets. Guns were illegal at protests in D.C., and the police had taped flyers to lampposts around downtown that warned: ALL FIREARMS PROHIBITED WITHIN 1000 FEET OF THIS SIGN. But many of the men were armed with solid wood sticks disguised as canes or flagpoles. Some carried bear mace, zip ties, and gas masks.

I continued to Freedom Plaza, where the America Firsters had assembled on one side of the square, holding crosses and AF flags. The Groyper who had ranted about the "globalist scum" at the Million MAGA March was there; so was the man with the GRAB THEM BY THE PUSSY patch. The crowd soon parted for Nicholas Fuentes, chanting his name. Diminutive and clean-shaven, in a blue suit and overcoat, he resembled a recent graduate dressed for a job interview. (He'd left Boston University after his freshman year, when other students became hostile toward him for attending the Charlottesville rally, in 2017, and for writing on Facebook that "a tidal wave of white identity is coming.") Fuentes climbed atop a granite retaining wall, and someone handed him a megaphone. Referencing the Supreme Court decision, he told the Groypers that the struggle in which they were engaged was no longer "a political battle." Rather, it was "a spiritual war for the soul of this country . . . a spiritual war between Satan—and evil—and us, the children of Jesus Christ." As his speech approached a crescendo of indignation, more and more Trump supporters gravitated to the Groypers. "It is *us* and *our* ancestors that created everything good that you see in this country," Fuentes said. "All these people that have taken over our country, we do not need them."

"Take it back!" the crowd roared.

"It's time for us to start saying another word again," Fuentes went on. "A very important word that describes the situation we're in. That word is 'parasite.' What is happening in this country is parasitism!" Arguing that Trump alone represented "*our* interests"—an end to all legal and illegal immigration, gay rights, abortion, free trade, and secularism—Fuentes distilled America Firstism into concise terms: "It is the American people, and our leader, Donald Trump, against everybody else in this country and this world." The Republican governors, judges, and legislators who had declined to leverage their authority to ensure Trump four more years in office—"traitors within our own ranks"—were on "a list" of enemies to be taken down.

After hearing so many conservatives shroud their assault on democracy in patriotic rhetoric, Fuentes's candor was almost refreshing. At least he was frank about his intentions: undoing not just the 2020 presidential outcome but also any form of representative government that allowed his opponents to obtain and exercise power. "Make no mistake about it," he emphasized, "the system is our enemy." Far from pretending to worship the Constitution, Fuentes readily acknowledged that the Constitution was a hindrance to long-term white Christian dominance; the Constitution enabled the very egalitarian multiculturalism that he wanted to eradicate; the Constitution had thwarted the autocratic ambitions of Donald Trump.

While conservatives might have balked at such iconoclasm, many of them also understood that true democracy was not in their interest, and had begun to turn against it. Republican voters had outnumbered Democrats *once* in the past three decades, and while more had shown up for Trump than for any previous candidate, they still were not enough. No wonder, then, Republican politicians had taken to quipping that the US was a republic, not a democracy. (In the sixties, the John Birch Society had advanced the same argument while warning that the civil rights movement would lead to "mobocracy.") With his war on the electoral process, Trump had brought the awkward relationship between conservatives and democracy into the open, and antiestablishment extremists like Fuentes were thrilled. Trump's refusal to concede was "the best thing that can happen," Fuentes had said in Atlanta, "because it's destroying the legitimacy of the system."

At Freedom Plaza, he told his audience that it was time "to galvanize the Patriots of this country behind a real solution to these problems that we're facing." He went on, "If we can't get a country that we deserve to live in through the legitimate process, then maybe we need to begin to explore some other options." In case anyone was still confused about what those other options might be, Fuentes spelled it out for them: "Our Founding Fathers would get in the streets, and they would take this country back by force if necessary. And that is what we must be prepared to do."

At some point while Fuentes was addressing them, the Groypers all turned their attention to the sky, beaming with delight at what they

saw there. It was Marine One, the presidential helicopter, circling Freedom Plaza with Trump inside.

GROUPS OF PROUD BOYS HAD begun migrating from the Harrington to the Washington Monument. When I got there, hundreds of them
covered the grassy expanse below the obelisk. Now that there was no
point in marching to the Supreme Court, they seemed unsure what
to do with themselves. After a while, someone suggested, "Let's take
Black Lives Matter Plaza!"

"Whose plaza?" the Proud Boys chanted as they headed down the
hill. "*Our* plaza!" A man with a derby hat and a gray goatee shouted,
"Fuck these gender-confused terrorists! They'll put the girls out
first—they think that's gonna stop us?" He was a Philadelphia Proud
Boy named Richard Schwetz, though he introduced himself as "Dick
Sweats." We soon reached Constitution Avenue, which separated the
National Mall from the Ellipse, a public park adjacent to the White
House. A Black pedestrian approached us on the sidewalk, minding
his own business. Several Proud Boys began shoving and jeering at him.
As the man ran away, they chased after him, swinging punches at his
back. Police officers intervened. It had happened so fast that I had
trouble processing what I'd just seen: a pack of white men, some wearing RIGHT WING DEATH SQUAD patches, attacking an African American, in the middle of the afternoon, in plain view of law enforcement,
steps from the Oval Office.

All but one of the Proud Boys were allowed to carry on. A few
blocks away, they arrived at Farragut Square, where half a dozen
antifascists—two men and four women—stood outside the Army and
Navy Club. Dressed in black bloc marked with medic crosses made
from red tape, they were much smaller and younger than most of the
Proud Boys, and visibly unnerved. As Schwetz and others closed in on

them, they retreated until they were pressed against a waist-high hedge. "Fucking pussies!" barked Schwetz, hitting two of the women. Other Proud Boys took his cue, assailing the antifascists, who disappeared into the hedge under a barrage of boots and fists. Policemen stopped the beating with pepper spray—which, inexplicably, they also used on the bloodied antifascists still lying in the bushes—but they did not arrest any of the Proud Boys, who staggered off in search of new victims.

They soon found one: another Black man, passing through on his bicycle. He wore Lycra exercise gear and looked perplexed by the scene he had stumbled into. Though he said nothing to anybody, "Black Lives Matter" was written in small letters on his helmet. The Proud Boys surrounded him. Pointing at officers watching from a few feet away, a man with a wood staff and a flak jacket said, "They're here now, but eventually they won't be. And we're gonna take this country back—believe that shit. Fuck Black Lives Matter. What y'all need to do is take your sorry asses to the ghetto."

A man carrying a Confederate flag joined in. "Get your dumb ass out of here," he told the cyclist.

This was basically the tenor of the next eight hours, as hundreds of Patriots marauded on the streets around the White House. The Metropolitan Police, Park Police, and Capitol Police did their best to separate them from the antifascists. Their interference enraged the Trump supporters, who called the officers "traitors," "piggies," "cunts," and "pieces of shit." Many of the insults were indistinguishable from those I'd heard in Portland.

"Fuck your paychecks!"

"Fuck the blue!"

"Vigilante justice will be king!"

"Defund the police!"

Since the death of George Floyd, backing the blue had become analogous with opposing the left. As anti-lockdowners had shown in Michigan, however, this alliance was conditional and tended to break down whenever laws intruded on conservative priorities. Patriots rationalized such inconsistency by assigning the epithet "oath breaker" to any American in uniform who executed his duties in a manner they disliked. Just as their reverence for the Constitution collapsed the moment it became an obstacle to their hold on power, their respect for law enforcement was contingent on absolute immunity from it.

When I returned to the Harrington, Proud Boys were yelling at an officer in the street. A minute earlier, they had ganged up on another Black man, who had withdrawn a knife in self-defense, wounding four of them. The officer had broken up the skirmish, and the Proud Boys were incensed that their punishing assault had been interrupted. "He's going to look different tomorrow," I overheard one of the assailants joke about the Black man's facial injuries, as if in consolation.

Enrique Tarrio was there. Someone handed him a Black Lives Matter banner, stolen from Asbury United Methodist Church. Bringing the banner to an intersection, Tarrio lit it on fire.

"Fuck Antifa!" the mob chanted.

Tarrio mutely watched the flames, his expression characteristically inscrutable. Though night had fallen hours ago, he still wore his sunglasses.

Joe Biggs, Tarrio's deputy, ordered the Proud Boys to line up in formation. He then led them to a Marriott hotel a few blocks away. Alex Jones stood beneath the portico, speaking to a crowd. Upon seeing the Proud Boys, Jones celebrated the violence that they had perpetrated throughout the day, and invested it with meaning: "Just like you've taken the streets back from those dirty murdering Antifa communist cowards, we pledge before God and our ancestors, and for our progeny, that we will restore the republic and defeat the globalists!"

"Seventeen seventy-six!" the mob responded.

I followed dozens of Trump supporters as they left the Marriott to stalk aimlessly through the city. Passing a rainbow poster outside a hair salon, a Groyper screamed, "This is sodomy!" and tore it to pieces. "Fuck the fags!" others cried.

By eleven p.m., I was with another group, which happened upon the Metropolitan African Methodist Episcopal Church. Built in the late nineteenth century, the steepled brick building had hosted Frederick Douglass's funeral and a memorial for Rosa Parks. In a small garden, a Black Lives Matter sign, illuminated by flood lamps, hung below a crucifix. Climbing over a low fence, several Proud Boys and Groypers in red MAGA hats ripped down the sign and pried off boards from its scaffolding to use as weapons.

Everybody cheered. More people piled into the garden, stomping on the sign and slashing it with knives. "Knife that shit up!" a woman screamed. "Fuck them!"

Amid the frenzy, a man removed another placard from a different display. It had a verse from the Bible: "I shall not sacrifice to the Lord my God that which costs me nothing."

"Hey, that's Christian," someone admonished.

The man nodded and gingerly set the placard down.

WHAT HAPPENED IN WASHINGTON, D.C., on November 14 and December 12 was almost entirely overlooked by journalists, editors, pundits, politicians, regular citizens, the Department of Homeland Security, and the FBI. Many news outlets would lament the predictability of January 6 after the fact. But none predicted it. The only Americans who truly rang the alarm about the insurrectionists were also the only ones who had physically confronted them in the weeks, months, and years before the insurrection: antifascists.

At one point on December 12, after hours of darting down alleys,

across parks, and around buildings, frantically attempting to circum-
vent police cordons, one group of Proud Boys finally succeeded. I was
walking with them on L Street, a few blocks from Black Lives Matter
Plaza, when a man up ahead flapped his arms and hollered, "They're
here! They're here!" Everyone broke into a sprint. "Let's go!" they
shouted. "It's on, boys!" I followed behind a Proud Boy in a helmet carrying a truncheon. The back of his shirt read: I AM A WESTERN CHAU-
VINIST AND I REFUSE TO APOLOGIZE FOR CREATING THE MODERN
WORLD. Running full tilt up the sidewalk, he turned to call over his
shoulder, "Women, stay back!" I could hear the adrenaline singing in
his voice. This was the moment about which many Proud Boys had
been fantasizing since their arrival in D.C. Or since the Million MAGA
March. Or since Portland or Charlottesville. It was why they had joined
the Proud Boys to begin with. But as we rounded the corner, the man
with the helmet and the truncheon pulled to an abrupt halt.

A large contingent of antifascists spanned the street. The first rank
held homemade shields spray-painted with messages: DEFEND BLACK
LIVES, SMASH FASCISM, JEWS WILL REPLACE YOU.

Out in front of the shields stood a solitary Black man. He wore a
knapsack, a zip-up sweater, and no armor or protection whatsoever,
apart from a blue medical mask. He looked almost comically out of
place—as if he'd taken a wrong turn walking home from a judicial
clerkship—except for one important detail: in his right hand he held a
long cable lock folded in half, ready to use as a whip.

"Let's crush 'em!" a Proud Boy yelled.

"Faggots!" screamed another.

Yet none of them moved. None attempted to attack the antifascists
or cross the Black man with the cable lock. As more and more Proud
Boys came careening around the corner, they too all froze in their
tracks. Even when a young woman in black bloc rhythmically pounded

her shield against the concrete, taunting them the way you might a pack of animals, the Proud Boys did not take the bait.

I often think back to this scene. I find comfort in knowing that there were those willing to stand up to the likes of the Groypers and the Proud Boys—to go where they went and place their bodies in front of them, impeding their way. During the lead-up to the Second World War, a popular precept among European antifascists was, "They shall not pass." It was used by French leftists in 1934 when far-right activists rioted in Paris and attempted to overthrow the government. It was used by defenders of the Spanish Republic, who resisted General Francisco Franco's putsch and military dictatorship. And it was used by the communists, socialists, and anarchists who, in 1936, refused to let the British Union of Fascists march through the East End of London, a traditionally Jewish neighborhood. On the day that Oswald Mosley and his Blackshirts assembled in the East End—escorted by London police officers—some twenty thousand counterprotesters successfully beat them back in bloody hand-to-hand combat that came to be known as the Battle of Cable Street. Eighty-four years later, only a few dozen Americans dared or bothered to square off against the Patriots as they ran roughshod over Washington, D.C. On L Street, though, that was enough. They did not pass.

FIFTEEN

LIKE A FLYNN

While the Proud Boys were still assembling outside Hotel Harrington, hundreds of other Trump supporters had gathered on the National Mall, where a concert stage and jumbotrons stood before the Capitol. The event had been organized by Robert Weaver, a thirty-nine-year-old Pentecostal who claimed to have received a divine vision two days after the election. In 2018, Weaver had been chosen by Trump to lead the Indian Health Service agency but withdrew his candidacy when it was revealed that he'd lied on his résumé. As Biden pulled ahead of Trump, Weaver later recounted on a Christian radio program, "I knew that something was wrong—so I went to God, and I cried out to him." The next morning Weaver heard "a spoken voice that said, 'It's not over.'"

The result was the Jericho March, which brought together Christians to "pray, march, fast, and rally for election integrity." In the Old Testament, Jericho was a Palestinian city that God promised to the

Israelites. When the Israelites marched on the city, God instructed them to blow trumpets made from hollow ram horns known as shofars. The stone walls surrounding Jericho crumbled, leaving it defenseless. The Israelites "destroyed with the sword every living thing in it: men and women, young and old, cattle, sheep, and donkeys." Then they burned it to the ground. The first time I'd heard a shofar had been at an anti-lockdown protest in Lansing. An evangelical retiree wearing cowboy boots, a white handlebar mustache, a cross necklace, a red MAGA hat, and a Jewish prayer shawl had held aloft the mythical-looking thing with both hands, filled his lungs, and emitted a pitch-perfect accompaniment to the moment's timeless lunacy.

The headliner at the Jericho March was the former three-star general Michael Flynn. Flynn had served as an army intelligence commander in Iraq and Afghanistan under George W. Bush, and as the director of the Defense Intelligence Agency under Obama. As a civilian, during the 2016 election, he became a devotee of both Trump and the conspiracy theories that propelled his candidacy. In the White House, Trump appointed Flynn to be his national security adviser, though Flynn was forced to resign after less than a month, for lying to the vice president about his interactions with the ambassador of Russia. Federal prosecutors charged Flynn with making false statements, and he admitted that he was guilty. He withdrew his plea, however, after replacing his attorneys with Sidney Powell. During Flynn's legal travails, "Fight like a Flynn" became a QAnon motto, and some followers appended three star emojis to their social media handles. The day after Trump's Mount Rushmore speech, Flynn posted a video of himself standing at a bonfire, reciting the QAnon pledge, "Where we go one, we go all." Trump issued Flynn a full pardon in November, and a week later Flynn tweeted a statement urging the president to "temporarily suspend the Constitution and civilian control of these federal elections," so that the military could "oversee a national re-vote."

On the National Mall, with the Capitol as a backdrop, Flynn declared, "We have penetrated the walls of Jericho." He called the election "a crucible moment in the history of the United States" and insisted,
"We are in a battle." A number of people had brought shofars, which
they raised and trumpeted.

In the audience was George, the Pennsylvania Three Percenter
who'd invited me to Freedom Biker Church. He wore knee-length
shorts that revealed a leg tattoo of a medieval crusader with a sword.
The cheerful optimism that had so impressed me the day after Biden's
victory was gone. "Bottom line is, we're ready to stack bodies," George
said. "If it has to be done, let it be done now, so our grandkids don't
have to do it."

Before becoming a police officer, George had served in the army.
When he said "we," he meant military veterans. "You have dudes out
there who have been training for twenty-five years and can put teams
together," he said. Veterans had always carried outsize weight in the
Patriot Movement. In *Bring the War Home*, Kathleen Belew describes
a similar phenomenon during the seventies and eighties. "One catastrophic ricochet of the Vietnam War," Belew writes, was a surge in
KKK, neo-Nazi, and far-right militia violence, as embittered veterans
sought "a literal extension of military-style combat into civilian space."
From the American soldier's perspective, Iraq and Afghanistan had
some qualities in common with Vietnam—most notably, the fact that
they were doomed from the start and continued long after everybody
knew it—but a crucial difference was the absence of a draft. Four days
after the invasion of Afghanistan, President Bush insisted, "The American people have got to go about their business," and the ensuing
insulation of US citizens from US wars required the creation of a professional warrior class. Whereas Vietnam consumed the conscience of
a generation, the most striking impact of the wars in Iraq and Afghanistan on American culture was the gap that they opened between this

tiny sliver of the population—less than one percent—and everybody else. While many veterans and active-duty service members experienced the distinction as a kind of painful alienation, some also enjoyed the prestige that it conferred. In conservative parts of the country, as the wars dragged on, the social rewards of belonging to the warrior class became a real incentive for joining it.

A similar elite status was arrogated by Three Percenters and other Patriots. "The way I look at it," a Boogaloo Boi in Michigan had told me, "joining the service was patriotic, and this is just an extension of that." He'd enlisted in the Marine Corps after high school and had deployed to Afghanistan as an infantryman. The M16 that he brought to protests had the same pistol grip, magazine, charging handle, and bolt carrier with which he'd customized his rifle overseas. He lived in Illinois but drove four hours to Michigan, alone in his SUV, for every anti-lockdown rally. Though I never doubted the sincerity of his convictions, I had the feeling that what made the trip worthwhile was the opportunity to display that weapon among people who had never heard of Musa Qala, the restive district in Helmand where he was stationed in 2012.

I'd been in Musa Qala a few months before he got there. The Marines with whom I was embedded had dealt with near-daily protracted firefights and endless IEDs. Despite their grit and courage, the district had fallen to the Taliban in 2015. The Boogaloo Boi had been unaware of this; when I informed him, he seemed neither disappointed nor surprised. The reaction was typical. An army veteran at Karl Manke's barbershop was equally unmoved when I mentioned that ISIS had occupied his former base in Mosul. Many veterans in the Patriot Movement seemed more attached to the idea of service, and to their identities as service members, than to the success or rectitude of the conflicts in which they had participated. At times, that success or rectitude felt almost immaterial. How else did one explain the complete indifference of Patriot veterans to Trump's denigration of the missions for which they had risked their lives, and to his policy of ending them at all costs, no matter how ignobly? The missions were not the point: being someone who had volunteered was. Belew writes that popular mobilization against the Vietnam War reinforced a "narrative of abandonment" among veterans returning stateside, which white supremacists exploited. But since Americans were allowed to go about their business after 9/11, no serious movement ever materialized against the Global War on Terrorism. I never had the sense that veterans of Iraq and Afghanistan were drawn to the Patriot Movement because they felt abandoned or betrayed. I had the sense that the Patriot Movement renewed their warrior-class status, if only in their own eyes.

Vietnam veterans in the white-power movement traveled to Latin America to support right-wing dictators and death squads because they conceived of their struggle against leftism on an international scale. In the aughts, Islamophobia similarly linked the wars overseas with the persecution of Muslims at home. For Patriots, though, the latter soon eclipsed the former. In 2015, when the Oath Keepers held armed rallies across the country to save the republic from an "invasion of Muslim colonization," ISIS occupied vast swaths of the Middle East. In Syria, Kurdish forces had invited Western volunteers to help them beat back the jihadists, and some Americans did answer the call. When I visited the front lines in 2017, I met a number of these fighters. A few were Christian veterans, but the majority were leftists, drawn to the socialist politics of the Kurds.

By reminding them of their duty to "defend the Constitution of the United States against all enemies, foreign *and domestic*," the Oath Keepers offered an appealing alternative to veterans whose identities had been forged in distant causes that no longer interested them. As Trump embellished the menace of Antifa and the Democrats to cartoonish proportions, many Patriot veterans seemed gratified for the chance to demonstrate, once again, their readiness to give their lives for something—whatever it might be. "If they think that we're not willing to die for this, they are sadly mistaken," George told me. Another veteran in Harrisburg had asked, "If I'm willing to go serve in a shithole, do you not think I'm willing to die here?" And Shane Moon, the Vancouver Proud Boy who stated at the rally in Portland that he would "die for this fraternity," had also served in the military.

I sometimes wondered how often and to what degree the desire of Patriot veterans to sacrifice themselves was a sublimation of the impulse to destroy themselves. When Moon made his declaration, Joe Biggs was standing next to him. On a podcast for veterans in 2018, Biggs had recounted his struggle with post-traumatic stress disorder, or PTSD. "This demon possessed me," he said. "I began having these night terrors. I remember screaming and crying and not knowing what the hell was going on." After becoming a "volatile, violent person" and "a ticking time bomb," he attempted suicide multiple times.

Biggs ascribed none of his torment to his experiences overseas, which he insisted he did not "dwell on." Rather, what had triggered his depressive spiral was being separated from his unit—losing that "family like no other, stronger than blood." With the Proud Boys, Biggs had found a new family.

So had George, who'd also suffered from debilitating PTSD. After the service at Freedom Biker Church, Pastor Jim had baptized one of the congregants, submerging him in a metal stock tank. George had then told me about his own baptism. As a young police officer in Maryland, he had killed a man after mistaking a BB gun for a real gun. He began to have severe panic attacks, left his wife and kids, and barricaded himself in a windowless room when not at work. "I made it seven years, then I had to retire," he said. Eventually, he was saved by Jesus and the Pennsylvania Three Percent.

About seven thousand Americans died in Iraq and Afghanistan.

Since 9/11, more than thirty thousand veterans and active-duty service members have killed themselves. There are many aspects of military service, beyond PTSD, that might have contributed to this epidemic. One that seldom gets talked about is selection bias: the likelihood that some portion of veterans suffered from self-destructive tendencies *before* they joined the military—and might have joined the military because of those tendencies. In my midtwenties, I served for three years in the New York National Guard. While attending the army's combat-medic school in San Antonio, Texas, I befriended a recruit from Utah who had volunteered because he was suicidally depressed and did not know what else to do. The man was a religious Mormon and believed that if he killed himself, he would go to hell. He had got it in his head that he could die a hero overseas. As soon as he'd arrived at boot camp, he'd regretted his decision. Though he petitioned to be discharged, his requests were all denied.

This was in 2008, when the military was strained by the troop surge in Iraq. To lure new recruits, the army had raised signing bonuses and lowered entry standards. Before coming to San Antonio, I'd gone through basic training at Fort Jackson, in South Carolina. The financial crisis had begun to squeeze the country, and nearly everyone in my platoon had enlisted for economic reasons. They needed salaries, or health care, or childcare, or help with student loans. Even housing was an enticement. One visibly emaciated private had been homeless when he was recruited. My assigned "battle buddy" was a recovering methamphetamine addict from Alabama whose teeth were corroded to rotten nubs. He could not afford dental insurance and had joined the army in the hopes of getting dentures. In San Antonio, my bunkmate was Kenyan. Military service might fast-track his naturalization, hastening the day that he could send for his wife.

Marginalized citizens have always been relied on, as much as patriotic citizens, to fight our wars. I never deployed, but most of the grunts

I met while reporting overseas were there because it was their job to be there, not because they believed they were degrading Al Qaeda, spreading democracy, or protecting the homeland. Joe Biggs served in eastern Afghanistan with the 82nd Airborne Division in 2009, as one of thirty-three thousand additional troops that Obama pumped into the country. In 2012, as the surge was winding down, I spent several weeks with a company from the 82nd, in the eastern province of Ghazni. What I found was near-unanimous disillusionment. The unit had already lost three men; any patrol that set foot outside the wire came under attack; and everyone, from senior officers to lowly privates, was clear-eyed about the likelihood that whatever modest gains they won would vanish as soon as they departed. That same month, President Obama visited Afghanistan and declared the surge a success. Across the country, direct-fire attacks were up, IED attacks were up, and insider attacks were up. Nevertheless, the president told Americans, "The tide has turned. We broke the Taliban's momentum." He'd just chosen General Michael Flynn to head the Defense Intelligence Agency.

In 2019, a classified audit obtained by *The Washington Post* revealed interviews with hundreds of officials admitting that the government had grossly and consistently misrepresented conditions in Afghanistan. One of the officials was Flynn. "There is a machinery behind what we do," he'd said, "and it keeps us participating in the conflict." He was alluding to special interests, the military-industrial complex, and probably, in retrospect, the deep state. But if that was how he felt about the war, why had he helped to oversee it for so long? Why hadn't he spoken out? Why had he sent men like Joe Biggs and Vincent Bell to kill and be killed year after year after year?

Maybe because it cost him nothing. Maybe because it enhanced his stature, influence, and power. Maybe because that is what it means to fight like a Flynn. Whether or not the people at the Jericho March were aware of the general's propensity for enlisting others in lost causes, they cheered and blew on their shofars when he told them, "There's going to be sacrifice. There already is sacrifice. We have men and women serving in our military all over the world tonight. Some of them are in harm's way. They don't even totally understand why they're out there. They're just out there because they love this country." Flynn held out his arms, opening them to the Trump supporters. "You represent that."

AT THE GATES

If some veterans were prepared to fight and die for Trump under the illusion that they were fighting and dying for their country, Flynn was not his only ally keen to put the broader citizenry on a similar war footing. After the Supreme Court declined to hear the petition from the attorney general of Texas, congressman Louie Gohmert filed a lawsuit asking a federal judge to affirm Vice President Pence's right to independently determine the result of the election. When the case was dismissed, Gohmert declared on television that the ruling had left Patriots with only one form of recourse: "You gotta go to the streets and be as violent as Antifa and BLM." The Arizona Republican Party, meanwhile, reposted a tweet from Ali Alexander, a chief organizer of the Stop the Steal campaign, which stated, "I am willing to give my life for this fight." The Twitter account of the Republican National Committee appended the following comment: "He is. Are you?"

Alexander was a convicted felon who had pled guilty to property theft in 2007 and to credit card abuse in 2008. In November, he had joined the Infowars panel in Atlanta with Alex Jones and Nicholas Fuentes, during which he warned that the New World Order would forcibly implant Americans with digital tracking microchips. "I'm just not going to go into that world," he asserted. Even then, well before the

Republican National Committee amplified his avowal of suicidal devotion to Trump, Alexander expressed jubilation and astonishment at how easily he, Jones, and Fuentes had converted mainstream Republicans to their quixotic enterprise. "We're the misfits, we are the crazy ones, rushing the gates," he marveled. "But we are winning!"

Alexander also spoke at the Jericho March, where he thanked Mo Brooks, a US representative from Alabama. Brooks had recently announced that he would contest the electoral college on January 6, when Congress met to approve each state's certified winner, the final step in formalizing Biden's victory and the last chance for Trump to subvert it. If one representative and one senator objected to a given state's results, both chambers would have to vote on whether to accept or reject them. Brooks, claiming that the election had been "stolen by the socialists," had pledged to use this mechanism to "fight and take it back." Two days after the Jericho March, he urged Patriots to follow his example, reminding them, "When it came time to fight in the Revolutionary War, beginning in seventeen seventy-six, people actually put their lives at stake."

Brooks's maneuver had no chance of working. The Democrats controlled the House of Representatives, and some Republican senators, including the majority leader Mitch McConnell, already considered Biden the president-elect. Hopeless though it was, the gambit became a test of loyalty. Since the election, any Republican who questioned Trump and his lies had been rancorously maligned. When the US Cybersecurity and Infrastructure Security Agency issued its statement discrediting the theories about Smartmatic and Dominion, Trump fired its director, Chris Krebs, and one of Trump's attorneys said that Krebs, a Trump appointee, "should be drawn and quartered—taken out at dawn and shot." Steve Bannon proposed a different method of punishing dissenters: "I'd put the heads on pikes. I'd put them at the two corners of the White House as a warning."

Rather than attract such ire, Republican legislators began lining up to back Mo Brooks: first sympatico fanatics like Louie Gohmert, Marjorie Taylor Greene, and Dan Meuser, but then many others—150 of them altogether, or more than two-thirds of the caucus. Trump continued inflaming the crazy ones at the gates, reiterating that "a crooked and vicious foe" was on the verge of installing an illegitimate and corrupt regime; that this was tantamount to "an act of war"; and that Republicans should be "up in arms" and "fight to the death." Finally, on December 19, in a tweet announcing that it was "statistically impossible" for him to have lost the election, he personally summoned the mob to D.C. for the explicit purpose of obstructing the congressional certification of the electoral college on January 6.

"Be there, will be wild!" the president wrote. The next day, he retweeted a post from a QAnon influencer with a quarter-million followers: "Justice is coming!"

ON DECEMBER 21, JOEY GIBSON, the leader of Patriot Prayer, offered a glimpse of what that justice might look like. As Oregon lawmakers convened to vote on extending certain pandemic measures, Gibson and more than a hundred other anti-lockdowners gathered at the statehouse in Salem. Some carried guns; one woman wielded a pitchfork. Cell phone footage showed them smashing open an entrance, assaulting journalists, and shattering windows with metal poles. I recognized a number of the rioters from Aaron Danielson's memorial. In one video, a Patriot Prayer member wearing a hat with Danielson's name attempted to kick through a door while clutching a rifle. Police were assailed with fists and pepper spray.

Surveillance tape from inside the capitol would later show Mike Nearman, a Republican state representative, opening a locked entrance and allowing the attackers to stream through it. In a video posted on

YouTube five days earlier, Nearman had shared his phone number and explained that if Patriots texted him and told him where they were, "somebody might exit that door while you're standing there." He went on to create an encrypted Telegram group called "Operation Hall Pass." Records from a state police investigation obtained by Oregon Public Broadcasting quote a number of exchanges between Nearman and the mob on the day of the attack.

"We are here," a woman messaged the lawmaker. "Which door shall we go to?"

The surveillance tape shows Nearman opening the entrance a few minutes later. State troopers appear, and a violent confrontation unfolds. One of the intruders sprays bear repellent. Others throw punches. The troopers look confused and caught off guard. No doubt they are wondering how the mob has breached the building. Nearman is gone, so they have no way of knowing that it was let in.

WINTER

SIXTEEN

THE WAR ON CHRISTMAS

My wife and I were in Nashville, Tennessee, visiting my brother for the holidays. On Christmas morning we awoke to a text from one of my wife's colleagues, Haroon, who lived in Afghanistan. "Checking in," Haroon had written. "Hope you didn't get blown up."

We assumed it was a joke. Six years ago, almost to the day, my wife's apartment in Kabul, where we had met a few months earlier, was badly damaged in a suicide bombing. We were not in the country at the time, and it was Haroon who had informed us. We both moved from Afghanistan not long after. Since then, whenever there was news of attacks in Kabul, Haroon was the first person my wife checked in with. The facetious note in Haroon's message—"Hope you didn't get blown up"—was exactly the sort of anxiety-belying humor that some people used in places where violence was a part of daily life to which you became habituated but never quite inured. The thing was, we weren't in such a place.

When we turned on the TV, we found footage from the aftermath of a "massive explosion" a mile from our hotel: burning wreckage, downed trees, collapsed buildings, smoking debris. By the time I got there, law enforcement had sealed off the blast site. Bomb squads and K-9 teams were sweeping the area for secondary devices. The streets were deserted. I joined some local news crews at an intersection a block away from the spinning lights of firetrucks and ambulances. Eventually, a spokesman from the Metropolitan Nashville Police Department arrived. "We do believe this to be an intentional act," he told us. I hung around a bit longer, then my brother picked me up and we went to his house to open presents.

The bomber was a sixty-three-year-old former computer technician named Anthony Warner. Before dawn, Warner had parked his RV on a street lined with tourist shops and honky-tonk bars. At around five thirty, a prerecorded message broadcasting from the vehicle warned people to evacuate; half an hour later, the message switched to a fifteen-minute countdown, interspersed with "Downtown," the 1964 pop song by Petula Clark. ("When you're alone and life is making you lonely / You can always go downtown.") When the fifteen minutes expired, the RV detonated in a soaring fireball that damaged or destroyed more than fifty buildings. The only fatality was Warner, who'd been inside the RV.

The question of his motive soon invited speculation. He had parked near an AT&T transmission hub, and for the next couple of days cell phone service throughout the region was disrupted. In Michigan, I had met anti-lockdowners who believed that 5G towers in Wuhan, China, were responsible for COVID-19, and that 5G networks globally spread the virus with their radiation. At my brother's house, when I mentioned that the bomber might have subscribed to such a theory, my wife replied, "Vous êtes malades"—"You're sick." *Vous* is the second-person plural in French. "You Americans," my wife was saying. *Malade*, or "sick," has the same double meaning as the English word.

Anthony Warner *was* sick. After a ten-week investigation, the FBI would conclude that the bombing had been "an effort to end his own life, driven in part by a totality of life stressors—including paranoia, long-held individualized beliefs adopted from several eccentric conspiracy theories, and the loss of stabilizing anchors and deteriorating interpersonal relationships." The FBI did not specify which theories, but a woman described as Warner's "best friend" told *The New York Times* that he was obsessed with David Icke's claim that alien lizards disguised as people roamed the planet. He'd even hunted them using an "infrared device." The woman said that Warner's delusions arose from a profound distrust of the government, centered around 9/11, which he deemed an inside job. Alex Jones, who often hosted Icke on Infowars, was also partial to this view.

According to the FBI, Warner's "actions were determined not to be related to terrorism." But clearly Warner himself was terrorized. It is possible that he would have committed the same act in a different political climate. But he did not. He committed the act at a moment of national hysteria, when much of the country, including the president, insisted that abominable monsters were lurking in the dark.

How many others like Warner were out there?

How many of us were, or had become, *malade?*

PLAGUE

On the same day that Trump called his supporters to D.C., Kylie Jane Kremer and her mother, Amy, who had put on the Million MAGA March, applied for a National Park Service permit to hold a rally at the Ellipse on January 6. For the stage, sound system, jumbotrons, and logistics, the Kremers engaged Event Strategies, a production company run by a former Trump campaign staffer named Tim Unes. A congressional committee would later subpoena Unes and the Kremers, alleging that they had "communicated with President Trump, White House officials including Chief of Staff Mark Meadows, and others about the rally and other events planned to coincide with the certification of the 2020 Electoral College results." One of those other events was organized by Ali Alexander, the convicted felon concerned about microchip implants, who acquired a separate permit from the US Capitol Police for a rally on Capitol Hill at a designated area, on the opposite side of the building from the National Mall, called Lot Eight. A substantial portion of the funding for the gathering on the Ellipse—about three hundred thousand dollars—was furnished by Julie Jenkins Fancelli, the wealthy heiress to Publix Super Markets and a major Trump donor. According to *The Wall Street Journal*, Alex Jones facilitated Fancelli's contribution, and also pledged fifty thousand dollars of his own money. Ali Alexander would later state that the plan agreed upon by the White House was for Trump to address his supporters at the Ellipse and then direct them to Lot Eight.

While the same Patriot groups that had descended on D.C. on November 14 and December 12 began mobilizing for a last hurrah, Josh Hawley, a freshman senator from Missouri, announced that he would join Mo Brooks and the other House Republicans who had pledged to contest the certification. With a senator on board, every member of Congress would be required to go on record affirming or rejecting the legitimacy of the election. A few days later, eleven more senators, led by Ted Cruz of Texas, declared that they would stand with Hawley to nullify the vote. Cruz and his colleagues cited no proof, evidence, or even specific complaints. Their decision, they explained, had been based on "unprecedented allegations."

That week, I called Michelle Gregoire, the former school bus driver and Michigan Home Guard member. It seemed to me you could draw a straight line from the current crisis back to April 29, eight months earlier, when Michelle entered the legislature in Lansing and had to be removed by David Dickson, enraging anti-lockdowners, who then stormed the statehouse.

Michelle had traveled to D.C. for the Million MAGA March but had missed the December 12 rally because she'd been in Georgia, canvassing for the state's two Republican Senate candidates. The race was of national importance: if the Democrats won both seats, the Senate would become evenly split between the two parties and effectively controlled by the Democrats (since the vice president serves as tie-breaker). No candidate had won a majority of votes in November, which meant that each race had advanced to a runoff, scheduled for January 5. Michelle planned to campaign until the very end. Even had she been free to do so, however, she would not have come to D.C. for the certification. "I highly recommend that if you go, be very careful," she said. "I've been avoiding it like the plague."

"Why?" I asked.

Michelle hesitated. I wondered what she was deciding not to tell me. "I don't know what's going to happen," she said. "But it seems like, whichever way it goes, it's not going to be good."

HISTORY

On the night of January 5, Ali Alexander stood on a stage at Freedom Plaza and led a crowd of Trump supporters in chants of "Victory or death!" I arrived in time to see Roger Stone. Shortly before Christmas, Trump had granted Stone a full pardon for his multiple felony convictions. A TV crew filmed Stone celebrating with Enrique Tarrio, the

Proud Boys chairman and a fellow Floridian. Ten days later, Stone re-
activated his original Stop the Steal website, from 2016, which began
collecting donations for "security" on January 6. He appeared at Freedom Plaza in a pin-striped suit and a feathered fedora. "This is nothing
less than an epic struggle for the future of this country between dark
and light, between the godly and the godless, between good and evil,"
he declaimed. "And we will win this fight—or America will step off
into a thousand years of darkness." While Stone held up two V signs in
homage to his mentor, Richard Nixon, someone in front of me waved a
flag with a cross and the words *Deus Vult*—"God Wills It"—a battle cry
from the First Crusade, in the eleventh century.

Throughout the day, Stone had been escorted by a team of Oath
Keepers led by Kelly Meggs, the head of the Florida chapter. After
Trump had tweeted his entreaty "Be there, will be wild!" Meggs had
written on Facebook, "He called us all to the Capitol and wants us to
make it wild!!!" A grand jury would later charge him and ten other Oath
Keepers with seditious conspiracy. The indictment cites encrypted
chats from late December in which the alleged conspirators assembled
a "quick-reaction force," or QRF, to stage "with an arsenal" outside the
capital. In a Signal group called "DC OP: Jan 6 21," Meggs posted a map
of the city and suggested potential routes for smuggling in weapons. On
January 5, the same day that he provided security for Roger Stone,
Meggs and another Oath Keeper booked three rooms at a Comfort Inn
across the Potomac River from D.C., in Ballston, Virginia. Hotel security cameras recorded several Oath Keepers hauling gun cases and what
appear to be rifles wrapped in bedsheets.

It remains unclear how seriously, how many, and which Patriots
intended in advance to assault the Capitol. On January 3, Meggs texted
his comrades about their "ammo situation." Using an acronym for "shit
hits the fan," he assured them, "If SHTF we got ample availability."
But he did not specify what would constitute shit hitting the fan. Nor

had Meggs—or Trump—spelled out what it might mean to "make it wild." There is no evidence in the charging documents that any Oath Keepers mentioned the Capitol or the certification of the electoral college. While this might be due to their having exercised a modicum of prudence—what they would have called "COMSEC," or "communications security"—it is also possible that the event for which they prepared was not the one that happened.

January 6 was the third D.C. rally in as many weeks, and many veterans of November 14 and December 12 were bracing for more street fighting with antifascists and Black Lives Matter activists. It's important to keep in mind the idiosyncratic Patriot worldview, according to which these leftists were not mere counterprotesters but frontline soldiers for the deep state and the New World Order. During a conference call with Oath Keepers ahead of the Million MAGA March, Stewart Rhodes, the group's founder, stated that he expected Trump to "declare an insurrection, and call us up as the militia." The more "kinetic" Antifa became, the better. "If they throw bombs at us and shoot us, great," Rhodes explained. "Because that brings the president his reason and rationale."

The Proud Boys, as well, appear to have been at least as preoccupied with antifascists around the Capitol as with the lawmakers inside it. On Parler, Enrique Tarrio wrote, "The Proud Boys will turn out in record numbers on Jan 6th but this time with a twist. We will not be wearing our traditional Black and Yellow. We will be incognito and we will spread across downtown DC in smaller teams." In a video addressed to D.C. antifascists, Joe Biggs added, "We are going to smell like you, move like you, and look like you." Upon arriving in D.C., Tarrio was arrested on a destruction-of-property charge related to his burning of the Black Lives Matter banner from Asbury United Methodist Church, and ordered to leave the city. (Before he did, prosecutors say, he met with Stewart Rhodes for approximately thirty minutes in an underground parking garage.) Proud Boys on Parler made plain that their days of backing the blue were over. "Every cop involved should be executed immediately," one commented. "Time to resist and revolt!" said another. A third wrote, "Fuck these D.C. Police. Fuck those cock suckers up. Beat them down. You dont get to return to your families."

There is no question that hundreds of Proud Boys, Oath Keepers, Groypers, Three Percenters, and other Patriots came to D.C. bent on committing violence—or that law enforcement would no longer be exempt. But I suspect that what took place on January 6 was a compressed version of what had been taking place throughout 2020. An amorphous rage, a communal delirium of fear and feverish self-righteousness, simply shifted from one target to another when it was offered a new outlet for expression. Joe Biggs and other Proud Boys would also face grand jury indictments, and one senior Proud Boy, Charles Donohoe, would plead guilty to conspiring to obstruct the certification. While they demonstrated their ability to attempt an insurrection, however, I have a hard time crediting them with the imagination necessary to conceive of one. According to Donohoe's plea, at 9:20 p.m. on January 5, Biggs messaged the Proud Boys leadership, "We have a plan." But he never stipulated what that plan entailed or offered Donohoe any practical guidance on how to execute it. What seems most plausible to me is that the Proud Boys were determined to do *something* but were waiting to be told exactly what. They were standing by.

MARTIN LUTHER KING WROTE MUCH of "I Have a Dream" while staying a block away from Freedom Plaza, in the Willard Hotel. The evening before he delivered the speech, he and his advisers refined the draft in the hotel lobby, cloistered behind potted plants that they paid a bellhop to arrange into a makeshift partition. On the night of January 5, more than half a century later, a quite different cohort, though one no less determined to change the course of American history, was staying at the Willard. Rudy Giuliani and other White House legal consultants had converted several suites into an operations center. While their options had narrowed considerably, they still saw a path to keeping Trump in power. In mid-December, Republican electors in seven swing states that Biden had won—including Michigan, Pennsylvania, and Georgia—had submitted to Congress documents naming Trump the victor. *The Washington Post* would later report that Giuliani had personally oversaw the scheme. Legally, these "alternate electors" were meaningless; however, John Eastman, another attorney at the Willard, had drafted a memo proposing that Vice President Pence, while presiding over the certification, could cite them as a reason to declare the seven contested states a wash. This would leave Biden with fewer electoral college votes in the remaining total. Anticipating "howls" from Democrats, Eastman explained that Pence could then refer the matter to the states, twenty-six of which were controlled by Republicans. "Trump is re-elected there as well," the memo advised.

Alex Jones had also reserved a room at the Willard, and while Giuliani and Eastman huddled in their suites, at times taking calls from Trump, Jones broadcast from the hotel an episode of Infowars featuring an interview with General Michael Flynn. Accusing China, Serbia, Spain, Italy, Iran, and Germany of "foreign interference," Flynn argued that "we are essentially in a national emergency," and repeated his line from the Jericho March that this was "a crucible moment" in American history. Steve Bannon, Trump's former chief strategist, was staying at the Willard as well. Earlier that day, he'd recorded an installment of his own web program, *War Room*. "All hell is going to break loose tomorrow," Bannon had assured his audience. "It's not going to happen like you think it's going to happen. It's going to be quite extraordinarily different. All I can say is, strap in."

SEVENTEEN

DAY OF THE ROPE

T rump was scheduled to speak at noon from the Ellipse. When I arrived a little before eight, the line to enter the permitted event organized by Amy and Kylie Jane Kremer already wrapped around the Washington Monument and extended as far as the National Museum of African American History and Culture. The first thing that caught my attention was the flags. Later, there would be much talk of people using flags as weapons. Actually, it was the other way around: they were using weapons—wood poles, metal pipes, baseball bats, two-by-fours, and axe handles—as flags. The axe handles were particularly striking. Chester Doles's KKK accomplice had used one against the Black man they dragged out of a car in Maryland; a white mob in 1960 had attacked peaceful Black demonstrators in Jacksonville, Florida, in an event remembered as "Axe Handle Saturday"; four years later, after passage of the Civil Rights Act, Lester Maddox, the owner of a fried-chicken restaurant in Atlanta, kept a barrel stocked with axe handles in his dining room so that he and his customers could fend off African Americans attempting to eat there. Maddox later became the governor of Georgia.

On the National Mall, men in flak jackets decorated with Three Percenter patches loitered in small groups. Their faces were wrapped in desert-camo shemaghs; some had walkie-talkies clipped to their ammo vests. "There'll be nothing left of this country," I overheard someone with an English accent say. "We'll be sitting in camps." At the base of the obelisk, a gravelly voice came through a megaphone: "Time to wake up, you guys. Donald Trump saw this coming." I turned to find a man whose face was painted red, white, and blue, carrying a spear. He wore a fur headdress with horns and a sweatshirt silkscreened with the image of a man wearing a fur headdress with horns. "We got 'em by the balls, baby," he went on, "and we're not lettin' go!"

It was Jacob Chansley, a thirty-three-year-old activist from Arizona, known as the "Q Shaman." Trump's call for a mass mobilization in D.C. had electrified the QAnon community, convincing it that the calm was over and the storm about to break. "This is not America's last stand—this is the communists' last stand in America!" Chansley shouted. "Where we go one . . ."

"We go all!" a chorus answered.

Thousands of Patriots had gathered in front of jumbotrons on Constitution Avenue. Young people had climbed the elm trees lining the street and straddled their leafless limbs; one man draped a Confederate flag from a high branch. Mo Brooks—who'd recently referred to the Civil War as the "war of Northern invasion" and said that a Biden presidency would be as catastrophic for the country as Lincoln's had been—appeared on the screens at nine o'clock. Peering out from beneath the brim of a camouflage hunting hat, Brooks warned that if the "heathenistic" Democrats were not stopped, they would make America "a godless, amoral, dictatorial, oppressed, and socialist nation." After

230 LUKE MOGELSON

theatrically reaching into his rain jacket and switching out his hunting hat for one that read FIRE PELOSI, he declared, "Today is the day American Patriots start taking down names and kicking ass!"

"Drag them out!" the people around me chanted.

Hoisted above the sea of heads was a life-size mannequin with duct tape over its eyes, "TRAITOR" scrawled on its chest, and a noose cinched around its neck. Heading that way, I found a man in his twenties holding up the dummy on a pole. He was with a woman about his age, who was talking to an older man wearing a Trump flag as a cape. They had driven all the way from Montana, the woman said.

"Do you follow Q?" the older man asked.

She nodded.

Other speakers continued to rile up the crowd. Amy Kremer: "We are here to save the Republic!" Donald Trump Jr.: "We're coming for you, and we're gonna have a good time doing it!" Rudy Giuliani: "Let's have trial by combat!" When Trump was impeached for "incitement of insurrection," his defense would hinge more on the meaning of the first word than the last. Had his supporters attacked the Capitol because of what he'd said, or would they have done so regardless? But by the time he addressed them, his supporters were so agitated that anything short of an unequivocal repudiation of the past three hours of propaganda and demagoguery—not to mention the past two months— would have failed to mollify them.

And yet: there was an element of suspense when the president stepped to the podium. If anyone could halt the momentum now careening toward some violent release, it was the person who had started it. The crowd waited in nervous expectation. Would he get cold feet? Cave to the deep state?

No. "We will never concede," Trump said. "It doesn't happen. You don't concede when there's theft involved. Our country has had enough.

We will not take it anymore, and that's what this is all about." The mood around me during this preamble was one of gratitude and relief. People were smiling and nodding. He was really going through with it. When they chanted "Fight-for-Trump!" I was reminded of the airfield in Grand Rapids, the night before the election, when the crowd had roared, "We-love-you!" The twin declarations—one of war, the other of affection—seemed to mean something similar for Trump as well as for them. He responded with the same two words as he had in Michigan:

"Thank you."

Promising his supporters "We will not let them silence your voices," Trump then rehashed some familiar grievances—Detroit, Philadelphia, Atlanta—but you could sense his impatience with the details. Details were no longer the point. They had never been the point. The matter was settled. It had been settled since the day after the election. From that moment on, allegations had substituted for evidence, theories had displaced reality. Now, doing away with allegations and theories, Trump summarized the wrongs committed against him, simply, as "explosions of bullshit."

"Bullshit!" the crowd bellowed. "Bullshit! Bullshit!"

It was the same elixir of emotion that had pervaded the other D.C. rallies and the Stop the Steal movement writ large: half mutinous rage, half gleeful excitement at being licensed to articulate and act on it. The profanity signaled a final jettisoning of whatever residual deference to political norms and respect for decorum had survived the past four years—and something else, a deeper inhibition, was also being shed. The man wearing the Trump flag as a cape told the couple from Montana, "There's gonna be a war." His tone was resigned, a bit weary, as if he were at last accepting an unsavory truth he'd long denied. "I'm ready to fight," he said as much to himself as to the couple.

The young man had lowered the lynched mannequin and was hugging it against his chest. He nodded but said nothing. He was mesmerized by the jumbotron, listening attentively.

"We want to be so *nice*," Trump said. "We want to be so respectful of everybody, including bad people. We're going to have to fight much harder. And Mike Pence is going to have to come through for us." The day before, Trump had tweeted, "The Vice President has the power to reject fraudulently chosen electors," endorsing the scenario laid out by John Eastman. Pence, however, had released a statement rejecting the plan as "entirely antithetical" to the Constitution. Undeterred, Trump insisted, "All Vice President Pence has to do is send it back to the states to recertify, and we become president."

When he told his supporters that he wanted them to proceed to the Capitol at the conclusion of his speech, Trump did not mention Lot Eight, the permitted demonstration zone. "I'll be there with you," he said. "We're going to walk down to the Capitol, and we're going to cheer on our brave senators and congressmen and -women. We're probably not going to be cheering so much for some of them, because you'll never take back our country with weakness."

"No weakness!" a woman cried.

Trump then explained that "what we're doing" was "much more important today than it was twenty-four hours ago." This was because the Democrats had won both runoff races in Georgia, thanks to high turnout from Black voters. The candidate Raphael Warnock—a pastor from Atlanta's Ebenezer Baptist Church, where Martin Luther King had preached until his assassination—would be the first African American to represent Georgia in the Senate. The losses in Georgia, said Trump, meant that the White House had become "the only line of demarcation—the only line that we have."

The time for innuendo had passed. The moment was at hand. "If you don't fight like hell," Trump told the Patriots, "you're not going to have a country anymore."

THOUSANDS OF PEOPLE WERE ALREADY moving up the National Mall, advancing over the long lawn slowly but steadily, as if pulled by a current. A few Trump supporters shouted out encouragements, but mostly there was an eerie sense of inexorability mixed with apprehensive hesitation. The mood was quiet and subdued. It reminded me of certain combat situations: the slightly stunned, almost bashful moment when bravado, expectation, and fantasy crash against reality. I'd left the Washington Monument a little before one o'clock. At roughly the same time, two pipe bombs were discovered outside the Democratic and Republican National Committee headquarters, a few blocks from the Capitol. While searching the area, officers found a pickup truck containing eleven Molotov cocktails, a semiautomatic rifle with a scope, a shotgun, three handguns, several high-capacity magazines, a crossbow, machetes, a Taser, smoke devices, hundreds of rounds of ammunition, and a piece of paper with a handwritten quote attributed to Abraham Lincoln: "We the people are the rightful masters of both the Congress and the courts, not to overthrow the Constitution but to overthrow the men who pervert the Constitution."

Later, police would arrest the truck's owner, Lonnie Coffman, a seventy-one-year-old army veteran from Alabama who'd done two tours in Vietnam. (A different person, captured on surveillance video planting the pipe bombs, remains at large.) The FBI had previously identified Coffman as a member of a Texas militia formed during the Obama administration to stop immigrants from crossing the border. In December, Coffman had contacted the office of Senator Ted Cruz, whom he viewed as an ally. Staffers who took notes on the call observed that

Coffman "did not seem threatening" but rather was "coming from the 'friend' angle in wanting to help with the election fraud."

As officers pulled weapons from Coffman's truck, and explosive ordnance technicians disabled the pipe bombs, and Ted Cruz and his colleagues settled into the House of Representatives for a historic joint session of Congress, Joe Biggs and a couple hundred Proud Boys fell in with a crowd of Trump supporters on the west side of the Capitol. Steel barricades cordoned off the grass. A few police stood nearby. Cell phone footage documents the ensuing confrontation. "Back the fuck off!" one man tells the officers; another removes his denim jacket, turns his red MAGA hat backward, and begins pushing and pulling the barricades as officers on the other side struggle to keep them upright. A female officer falls, hits her head, and suffers a concussion; the Trump supporters plow over her peers.

How is it possible that the perimeter of the US Capitol, on this day, could be so poorly defended and breached with such shocking speed and ease? Where was the militarized and vastly disproportionate force that had been marshaled to "dominate" racial-justice protesters in Minneapolis and Portland? Around twelve hundred officers were on duty. After the pipe bombs were discovered, many of them were moved from their posts to help evacuate nearby congressional buildings. During Senate testimony, Steven Sund, who resigned as Capitol Police chief after January 6, would speculate that the purpose of the explosives had been "to draw resources away," and that it was no accident that the Proud Boys assaulted the perimeter while his officers "were not at full strength." Sund would add, "I think there was significant coordination with this attack."

It's an interesting theory. But like many interesting theories, it distracts from an essential truth: after months of cracking down on antifascists and Black Lives Matter protesters, no federal or local authority viewed the Patriots as dangerous.

. . .

ON THE WEST SIDE of the Capitol, where presidential inauguration ceremonies had been held since 1981, two broad flights of marble steps descended from an outdoor terrace, on the third floor, to the National Mall. In anticipation of Joe Biden's swearing-in, huge bleachers had been erected over the steps and a ten-thousand-square-foot platform constructed between them. After the officers at the outer perimeter were overrun, they retreated to these bleachers, where they formed a back line with colleagues in riot gear and members of the Metropolitan Police Department.

"We need some reinforcements up here now," one officer told dispatch, in an audio recording made public during Trump's impeachment hearing. "They're starting to pull the gates down. They're throwing metal poles at us." Another officer reported "multiple law enforcement injuries." As I approached the melee, I could hear the dull thud of stun grenades and see their bright flashes. "It's us versus the cops!" a man in camouflage yelled. Someone let out what sounded like a rebel yell. A makeshift gallows stood near a statue of Ulysses S. Grant. People paused to climb the structure's wooden steps and take pictures of the Capitol framed within an oval noose.

"We the people make the law!" a man shouted.

"Trump won!"

Beside the gallows, a woman held a sign that read: THE STORM IS HERE.

Paramedics rushed by, pushing a stretcher loaded with equipment. A limping man was helped toward an ambulance. Scattered groups wavered, debating whether to join the confrontation. "We lost the Senate— we need to make a stand *now*," a bookish-looking woman in a down coat and glasses appealed to her friend. "This is it."

The bleachers had been wrapped in ripstop tarpaulin, creating a solid monolith that functioned as a kind of rampart. Trump supporters were using barricades as ladders to scale the balustrades and cutting through the fabric with knives. Officers blocked an opening at the bottom of the bleachers, but they were outnumbered and obviously intimidated as the mob pressed against them, screaming threats and insults, pelting them with cans and bottles. Some people shoved and punched individual officers; others linked arms and rammed their backs into the row of riot shields, eyes squeezed shut against blasts of pepper spray. A few Trump supporters countered with their own chemical agents. A man in a cowboy hat lifted his jacket to reveal a revolver tucked into his waistband. The stone slabs underfoot were smeared with blood. "To protect the Constitution of the United States against all enemies foreign *and domestic!*" someone yelled.

At 1:49 p.m., about ten minutes after I arrived at the base of the Capitol steps, Chief Steven Sund called General William Walker, the commander of the D.C. National Guard, and asked him for assistance. While each state's National Guard is controlled by its governor, units in D.C. answer to the White House. Typically, their activation is approved or denied by the secretary of the army and the secretary of defense, who do so on behalf of the president. Thousands of National Guard troops were mobilized in D.C. after George Floyd was killed. In December, Mayor Muriel Bowser had submitted a written request to General Walker for support with crowd control on January 6, in downtown areas beyond the Capitol Police's jurisdiction. Walker had sought approval from the secretary of the army, Ryan McCarthy, who agreed to make the troops available but imposed two caveats: there would be no quick-reaction force, or QRF—in this case, an element of soldiers equipped with riot gear, trained and organized to quell violent unrest—and if at any point Walker wished to move personnel from one location to another, McCarthy must first sign off on it. In a

Senate hearing in March, Walker would call both of these require-
ments "unusual." He would also describe the "frantic call" that he received on January 6 at 1:49: "Chief Sund, his voice cracking with
emotion, indicated that there was a dire emergency on Capitol Hill,
and he requested the immediate assistance of as many Guardsmen as
I could muster." After getting off the phone, General Walker immediately contacted the Pentagon and asked for permission to send troops
to the riot. He would receive the green light more than three hours
later.

While Sund was appealing to Walker, a man using a bullhorn plas-
tered with Infowars stickers made his way along the police line. "You're
a bunch of oath breakers!" he barked. "You're traitors to the country!"
Following behind him were Joe Biggs and half a dozen other Proud
Boys. Biggs wore a beanie and a plaid flannel with a radio clipped onto
the breast pocket. Seconds after he passed me, the mob overwhelmed
the officers at the opening in the tarpaulin, and everyone, including
Biggs, flooded into the understructure of the bleachers.

"Storm!" people yelled as they scrambled through the scaffolding's
metal braces and up the granite steps. Toward the top, a temporary security wall contained three doors, one of which was instantly breached.
Dozens of police stood behind the wall, using shields, nightsticks, and
chemical munitions to prevent the mob from crossing the threshold.
Other officers took up positions on the planks above us, firing a steady
barrage of pepper balls into the horde. As rounds tinked off metal and a
caustic miasma filled the space like the inside of a fumigation tent, more
and more Trump supporters crammed into the bleachers, crushing those
toward the front against the wall. A few people balked: "We need to retreat and assault another point!" But most remained resolute.

"Keep pushing!" they screamed.

"Shoot the politicians!"

"Push forward! We're winning!"

Martial bagpipes blared through portable speakers. I was tightly pinned, unable to move. Each time the mob heaved, it lifted me off my feet. One of the people I was pressed against wore a helmet, a gas mask, and an army combat uniform with a patch that read ARMOR OF GOD. At the beginning of the pandemic, Q had written in a post on 4Chan: "Be strong in the Lord and in the strength of His might. Put on the full armor of God so that you will be able to stand firm against the schemes of the devil."

I looked behind me. Tens of thousands of Trump supporters filled Pennsylvania Avenue, stretching as far back as I could see. Although the people at the rear had no way of knowing what was happening here, from my vantage they all bled together, comprising a single entity animated by one purpose. In the video I recorded at this moment, individual features become progressively more distinct as they approach the foreground. A man with meticulously coiffed silver hair, in a military dress coat adorned with medals; a man wearing swimming goggles and a motorcycle helmet printed with a skull and crossbones; a man in wire-frame bifocals, clothed from head to foot in animal pelts; and then, a couple of feet away, leaning all his weight into the bodies directly beside me, a corpulent and goateed man whose black baseball hat is embroidered with the letters TAT.

The meaning of the acronym—"Take Action Today"—had changed somewhat dramatically since Jason Howland first started wearing the hat as a marketing gimmick for the Jason Howland Corporation. In one promotional video, three years before he cofounded the American Patriot Council, Howland had averred, "I want to be an example of Christ for people in business, show people that you can become a master in your market space through honesty and integrity and doing the right thing every time." I now watched that would-be example of Christ drop his head, plant his feet, and add his considerable mass to the human thing churning over the Capitol Police. Balanced on a crossbeam above Howland was his partner, Ryan Kelley, who, in June, had thanked law enforcement "for standing up for our communities" and insisted, "We are here demanding peace." A cell phone video would capture Kelley yelling at rioters, "This is war, baby!"

While I was under the bleachers, Lauren Boebert, the newly elected congresswoman from Colorado, rose to deliver the first speech of her career in the House of Representatives. The lawmakers had broken off from the joint session after Ted Cruz objected to the votes from Arizona, the third state in the certification process, which proceeds alphabetically. Both chambers were now debating independently, after which they would reunite and continue to Arkansas. "The members who stand here today and accept the results of this concentrated, coordinated, partisan effort by Democrats, where every fraudulent vote cancels out the vote of an honest American, has sided with the extremist left," Boebert warned her fellow Republicans. But she also had a message for Nancy Pelosi: "Madam Speaker, I have constituents outside this building right now."

SOME PEOPLE HAD MANAGED to go over the top of the security wall, and through the open door I could see men in flak jackets brawling wildly with about a dozen officers—tumbling down the stairs, grappling and punching. Focused on recording the scene with my phone, I failed to realize that I had moved to the front of the fray, and suddenly one of the officers protecting the door hit me with a copious payload of chemical irritant. I was blinded and had to feel my way back out of the bleachers. Somebody sat me on the ground and emptied a bottle of water on my head. It was about fifteen minutes before I could open my eyes. The crowd around me was cheering. "They're up there!" someone yelled ecstatically.

Trump supporters had reached the top of the bleachers. One waved a thin-blue-line flag—a symbol of solidarity with law enforcement—while another, wearing a Captain America costume, raised his round shield in triumph.

In front of me, an elderly lady with thin white hair and large square glasses told her male companion, "They better get the fucking message." Moving forward, I passed people retreating with red eyes and minor injuries. Some were bleeding. A woman wrapped bandages around a man's arm that appeared to be broken. "What are you here for?" someone with a bullhorn chastised those hanging back. "Is tear gas worse than being a slave?"

"This is a day of reckoning!" added a woman in designer jeans, a purse on her shoulder. Beside her, another woman screamed, "Grab them by the fucking hair and pull them out here!" Both were blond and bundled in knitted scarves; they looked like they'd been teleported from a PTA meeting.

Back under the bleachers, people were now streaming through all three doors. A man wearing a Kevlar helmet with a Confederate flag painted on its side filmed himself with his phone. "We're storming!" he said. "We're taking the Capitol!"

Raucous throngs swarmed the open terrace at the top of the steps, taking selfies and celebrating. A man paraded around with a large flag for the white-nationalist website VDARE (named for Virginia Dare, the first English child born in North America). Several Groypers waved AF flags. Some Trump supporters were scaling the stone walls; at the back of the terrace, others clambered into the building through a shattered window. Forty-four-year-old Dominic Pezzola, a Proud Boy and former Marine from Rochester, New York, had smashed it with a riot shield. Pezzola had stolen the shield from an officer on the steps, where I'd seen him using it to provide cover for rioters from rubber bullets.

A wheelchair ramp led up to a door. As people waited in line to enter, they pounded their staffs on the metal incline at a plodding tempo: *boom, boom, boom, boom.*

It was 2:23 p.m. One minute earlier, General Walker had convened a conference call with Capitol Police Chief Sund, Metropolitan Police Chief Robert Contee, and senior army leaders at the Pentagon. "Chief Contee and Chief Sund passionately pleaded for District of Columbia National Guard to get to the Capitol with all deliberate speed," Walker would testify. The Secret Service had already escorted Mike Pence from the Senate floor to a secure loading dock. (Accompanying the vice president was an air force officer with the briefcase containing the nuclear launch equipment and codes.) Lawmakers were donning gas masks, hiding behind chairs, and removing their congressional pins—"out of fear that they would be seen or taken by the mob," one later recounted. Nevertheless, General Walker recalled, "The army senior leaders did not think that it would look good—that it would be a good optic" to deploy the National Guard. Chief Robert Contee testified that he was "stunned at the tepid response" from the Pentagon. According to Walker, one of the military officials who advised against sending troops to the Capitol was the deputy chief of staff for army operations, General Charles Flynn, a younger brother of Trump's former national security adviser, Michael Flynn.

Charles Flynn has denied Walker's account—and the acting defense secretary at the time, Christopher Miller, claims that the three-hour delay was a result of preparations and planning. Whatever the case, someone who seems clearly to have been uneager to send the National Guard was the person with whom the authority to do so ultimately rested. After his speech, Trump had returned to the White House, where he followed TV coverage of the siege from a dining room next to the Oval Office. Mitch McConnell, the Republican

Senate minority leader, would later condemn him for having "watched television happily—*happily*—as the chaos unfolded." According to Jaime Herrera Beutler, a Republican representative from Washington, the House minority leader Kevin McCarthy reached the president by phone and begged him to "call off the riot." Trump refused, telling McCarthy, "Well, Kevin, I guess these people are more upset about the election than you are." In the Senate chamber, after Pence was whisked away, Republican Mike Lee of Utah held a prayer with colleagues; when they finished, Lee's phone rang. It was Trump, looking for the Alabama senator Tommy Tuberville. Lee gave his phone to Tuberville, who informed Trump that the vice president had been evacuated and that the senators were about to abandon the chamber as well. Some minutes later, Trump tweeted, "Mike Pence didn't have the courage to do what should have been done to protect our Country and our Constitution. . . . USA demands the truth!"

On the outdoor terrace, a line of people were waiting their turn to climb through the broken window. I recognized a man with gelled hair and a severely geometric beard. He'd spoken at the Patriot Prayer memorial for Aaron Danielson in Vancouver. "We must continue to separate ourselves from this evil, and be the better side, with God as our guidance," he'd told the assembled mourners. I followed him through the window, into the Capitol.

We emerged into a long hallway ringing with pandemonium. The first person I encountered wore a flak jacket and waved an axe handle in the air. "Whose house?" he roared.

The man would later be identified as a member of the Kansas City Proud Boys. Antifascists would publish screenshots from his Facebook page, which was rife with QAnon theories, anti-lockdown diatribes, and derogatory comments about George Floyd.

"*Our* house!" answered the Trump supporters, their cries echoing through narrow corridors.

"Where's the traitors?"

"Bring them out!"

"Get these fucking cocksucking commies out!"

"Hang Mike Pence!"

A dozen officers guarded a staircase to the left of the window. I didn't know it at the time, but these stairs led directly to the Senate. The first rioters into the building had ascended them, while a lone officer, Eugene Goodman, attempted to stall their progress. In a video filmed by a *HuffPost* reporter, a coterie of white men advances on Goodman, who is Black, as he lures them away. "This is *our* America," someone shouts at him. The senators were still being evacuated; brandishing a telescopic night stick, Goodman diverted the group from a passage that connected to their unprotected chamber. One Republican senator would later credit Goodman, a combat veteran of the Iraq War, with having "single-handedly prevented untold bloodshed."

Rather than go through the officers, the rioters with whom I entered the building all turned right, down the hallway, which delivered them into a circular, vaulted room lined with marble statues and brightly lit by chandeliers.

"God is with us!" exclaimed a young man with long blond hair and a Burberry coat. He was Christian Kulas, whose family owned Kulas Maids, a high-end residential cleaning company in the suburbs of Chicago. On Instagram, Kulas had described himself as a "Yogi" and "Spiritual Catalyst."

"If God is with us, who can stand against us?"

"Amen, brother, amen!"

Various nondescript corridors branched off in different directions. "Stand down," a tall, husky man in a MAGA hat told officers blocking one of them. "You're outnumbered." The man looked familiar, and later I'd realize that he had taken part in the attack on the Oregon state capitol on December 21. A video from that day had captured him assaulting a reporter from the *Statesman Journal*. Now the man warned the officers in his path, "There's a fucking million of us out here, and we are listening to Trump—your boss."

"We can take you out," someone else said.

"I will not let this country be taken over by globalist communist scum!" yelled another man. He sported a thick beard and a Pittsburgh Pirates hat. "They want us all to be slaves! They're gonna haul us to camps when the time comes! Everybody's seen the documentation—it's out in the open!" He was hoarse and trembling. He could not comprehend why the officers were interfering in such a virtuous undertaking. "You *know* what's right," he told them. Then he gestured vaguely at the rest of the rampaging mob. "Just like these people know what's right."

"Sellouts!"

"When did you stop being Americans?"

Eventually, the officers capitulated, backpedaling the length of the corridor. When we arrived at a marble staircase, they moved aside. "We love you guys, take it easy!" a rioter told them as he bounded up the steps. "Stay safe: *stand down*."

The steps led to the central rotunda, whose soaring light and space opened skyward. Beneath the high dome, surrounded by statues of former presidents and life-size oil paintings depicting such historical scenes as the embarkation of the Pilgrims and the presentation of the Declaration of Independence, Trump supporters chanted, "USA!" (Earlier, Mo Brooks had ended his speech with the same chant, after asking the crowd, "What are the words that cause socialists and weak-kneed Republicans on Capitol Hill to shake in their boots and cower in their foxholes?") Nearly everyone I watched enter the rotunda was momentarily dumbstruck by its beauty. A number of mouths literally hung open. More selfies were taken. During the *gilets jaunes* demonstrations, in 2018, many of the French citizens who rioted in Paris had never been to the capital before; throughout the protests, I'd overheard several out-of-towners, some carrying illustrated street maps normally sold to tourists, grudgingly acknowledge how magnificent it was. Although French and American populists despised Paris and D.C. as swamps of elitism, they also took pride in their splendor as symbols of the nation. Amid violent clashes with the gendarmerie on the Champs-Élysées, one man enshrouded with tear gas had taken a moment to concede, "It's not bad, after all, the Arc de Triomphe."

In the exact center of the rotunda—easy to locate within the concentric rings of waxed sandstone tiles—a Trump supporter stood stock-still, his palms pressed together and head hinged back, gazing straight up at a detailed fresco of George Washington ascending to heaven while clutching a sword.

"White people will not let this country fail!" a woman in a fur-lined ski parka shouted.

Tall double doors linked the rotunda to a wide anteroom across which stood the eastern entrance to the Capitol, on the opposite face of the building from the inauguration platform and the National Mall. Lot Eight was located nearby. Earlier, a reporter had photographed Senator Josh Hawley raising his fist to Trump supporters gathered at the perimeter there. The crowd had subsequently overwhelmed the police and rushed up the steps. The eastern entrance consisted of a pair of solid bronze doors inset with glass window panels. The windows had been shattered, and beyond them I could see police being crushed by the mob. Videos from outside would capture people chanting "Take their shields!" and dousing them with pepper spray. Some Trump supporters had already forced their way into the anteroom, including Christopher Warnagiris, an active-duty major in the Marine Corps stationed in Quantico, Virginia. Surveillance footage captured Warnagiris shoving and boxing out officers so that others could follow him. By the time I reached the anteroom, three officers had barricaded the doors with wrought-iron benches and stood between them and the Trump supporters coming from the rotunda.

"Let them in!" people yelled.

They surged toward the officers, crushing them against the doors on the other side of which a mirror image of the same scene was taking place. The result was that the police were back-to-back, facing countervailing onslaughts. In the anteroom, a Trump supporter turned his flagpole horizontally and rammed it into an officer's chest. Seconds later, the entrance gave. The officers caught in the breach fought desperately to fend off the mob while more Trump supporters attacked them from behind. One man repeatedly whacked an officer on the head with a length of plastic conduit wrapped in an American flag. Besieged from the front and the rear, the police could do little other than attempt to stay on their feet while using their bodies as obstacles to slow the stampede.

From a high mezzanine overlooking the anteroom, a man droned down at us through a powerful bullhorn, "We will not be denied! We will not be denied!"

One of the officers in the doorway stumbled backward, pursued by rioters while he flailed as if at a swarm of bees. He wore a helmet with a transparent face shield, behind which his expression was a clinched rictus of animal panic. After that, the line broke and the mob poured into the building unimpeded.

"It's fucking on! This is *our* country!"

"Naaaancy, I'm hoooome!"

Kelly Meggs and other Oath Keepers moved through the rioters in a military formation known as a "stack": single file, each with a hand on the back of the person in front of him. The grand jury indictment would quote recordings of their communications on Zello, an app that converts phones into walkie-talkies. "We have about thirty to forty of us," one Oath Keeper said. "We are sticking together and sticking to the plan." Stewart Rhodes, the Oath Keepers founder, was on the Capitol grounds but remained outside. Though he would also be indicted for seditious conspiracy, Rhodes appears to have been flummoxed by the absence of Antifa columns and Trump's failure to impose martial law. "Patriots are taking it into their own hands," he posted on Signal. From the Comfort Inn across the Potomac River, where the group had stashed their guns and ammunition, an Oath Keeper texted, "QRF standing by at hotel. Just say the word . . ." On his way to D.C., Rhodes had spent six thousand dollars on firearms equipment. Yet he never said the word.

After Meggs and his team were inside, an unknown Oath Keeper urged them on Zello, "You are executing a citizen's arrest. Arrest this assembly. We have probable cause for acts of treason, election fraud." It's unclear, though, if this was the aforementioned plan or improvisation; the indictment accuses the Oath Keepers of searching for Pelosi, but it does not contemplate to what end.

Joe Biggs and his cadre were also in the anteroom. While the Oath Keepers headed for the rotunda, I followed behind Biggs as he led a stack up a flight of stairs, then down a carpeted hallway, back toward the Senate wing. People banged on doors, kicking some of them open. All the offices appeared deserted.

"Where the fuck are they?"

"Where the fuck is Nancy?"

A witness would later tell the FBI that, after the insurrection, Dominic Pezzola and other Proud Boys maintained "that anyone they got their hands on they would have killed, including Nancy Pelosi." (They also "would have killed Mike Pence if given the chance.") Pelosi's office was located at the opposite end of the Capitol, and other Trump supporters had already broken into it. Pictures would show a sixty-year-old man from Arkansas, wearing a nine-hundred-thousand-volt stun gun on his hip, sitting in Pelosi's chair, a foot up on her desk.

A twenty-two-year-old native of Harrisburg named Riley June Williams would be arrested for stealing Pelosi's laptop. According to the FBI, Williams hoped to sell the computer to Russian intelligence. She had been with Nicholas Fuentes at Freedom Plaza on December 12, and on January 6 she wore a T-shirt that read I'M WITH GROYPER. The investigative website Bellingcat would uncover a video of her giving the Nazi salute and pledging allegiance to Hitler in front of a book about the Waffen-SS.

Some Trump supporters converged on another pair of wood-and-glass doors, which accessed the Speaker's Lobby, adjacent to the legislature. Desks and chairs had been heaped against them. In video recorded by one of the rioters, fleeing lawmakers can be seen hurrying across the Lobby, away from the mob.

"Break it down!" someone yells.

"Let's fucking go!"

A middle-aged man with a long graying beard wears a sweatshirt printed with a skull below the words CAMP AUSCHWITZ. The back reads: STAFF.

"Drag them out!"

As the rioters smash the window panels in the door, a lone officer stands on the other side, behind the piled-up furniture, warding them off with a pistol.

"There's a gun!"

"He's got a gun!"

A woman wearing a Trump flag as a cape attempts to lunge into the lobby. The officer fires a single round. The woman falls backward, bleeding from her upper torso.

A thirty-five-year-old air force veteran from San Diego, California, Ashli Babbitt had spent most of her adult life in the military, deploying to both Iraq and Afghanistan. Discharged in 2016, she embraced Trump and took to maligning immigrants on social media. During the pandemic, she became a committed anti-lockdowner. Her online activism led her to QAnon and, after the election, to conspiracy theories advanced by Rudy Giuliani, Sidney Powell, and Michael Flynn. The day before her death, Babbitt had tweeted, "Nothing will stop us . . . they can try and try and try but the storm is here and it is descending upon DC in less than 24 hours . . . dark to light!"

BABBITT WAS KILLED at 2:46 p.m. At 2:48, a Groyper in the group of Trump supporters I was with pushed through a series of unlocked doors. "Praise God!" someone shrieked.

A narrow, short passageway opened onto the US Senate. Emerging into the chamber was like entering a music hall. It had its own atmosphere, acoustics, light. The powerful feeling of distortion that had prevailed throughout the day—in scene after scene of iconic, venerable settings transformed into circus rings of demented abandon—was even more arresting here. Not because of what was happening but because of what wasn't. There were signs of a hasty evacuation: bags and purses under chairs, personal belongings on some of the desks. A black duffel sitting on the floor was marked N.A.A.K. PACK. The Nerve Agent Antidote Kit contained enough auto-injectors to treat all fifty senators for sarin gas exposure.

From the gallery, a Trump supporter called down, "Take everything! Take all that shit!"

"No!" an older man, wearing body armor and holding several plastic flex-cuffs, responded. "We do not take anything." He was Larry Rendall Brock Jr., a retired air force lieutenant colonel. His flak jacket was decorated with a unit patch for the 706th Fighter Squadron, in which he'd been a pilot.

A Groyper in a red MAGA hat went to the elevated dais and sat in the leather chair recently occupied by Vice President Pence. His friend filmed him extemporizing a speech: "Donald Trump is the emperor of the United States..."

"Hey, get out of that chair," said a man about his age, with a Southern drawl. He wore cowhide work gloves and a hunting jacket that was several sizes too large for him. Gauze hung around his neck. Large amounts of dark blood, leaking from an open wound on his cheek, encrusted his beard. Later, when another rioter asked for his name, he replied, "Mr. Black."

The Groyper turned and regarded him uncertainly.

"We're a democracy," Mr. Black said.

"Bro, we just broke into the Capitol," the Groyper pointed out. "What are you talking about?"

"We can't be disrespectful," Lieutenant Colonel Brock said. Using the acronym for "information operations," he explained, "You have to understand—it's an IO war. We can't lose the IO war."

The Groyper was Christian Secor, a student at UCLA who lived with his mother in Costa Mesa. The founder of the America First Bruins club, Secor had once recounted on a far-right podcast his political activation at the age of nineteen, after being yelled at by antifascists for bringing a Rhodesian flag to a protest against racism in the wake of Charlottesville. White supremacists revere Rhodesia, the apartheid state that preceded the founding of Zimbabwe, and Dylann Roof wore a Rhodesian patch when he murdered nine members of a Black church in South Carolina. On January 6, Secor had a different flag. As he reluctantly left the vice president's chair, he picked it up, displaying its white-and-blue AF emblem.

One hundred mahogany desks with engraved brass nameplates were arrayed in four tiered semicircles; swinging open the hinged tops, the Trump supporters rifled through documents, taking pictures of private notes, appointment schedules, and manuals on Senate procedure. One senator had a copy of *Dreyer's English*, another a partly completed crossword puzzle. Someone found a signed letter, on official stationery, addressed from "Mitt" to "Mike"—presumably, Romney and Pence. It was an excerpt of the speech that Romney, the senator from Utah and former Republican presidential nominee, had delivered when he voted to impeach Trump for pressuring the president of Ukraine to produce dirt on Biden. "Corrupting an election to keep oneself in office is perhaps the most abusive and disruptive violation of one's oath of office that I can imagine," Romney had written.

On January 3, Romney had released a statement disavowing the "egregious ploy" of his colleagues Josh Hawley and Ted Cruz, and warning that their decision to reject electors "dangerously threatens our Democratic Republic." He also denounced "the President's call for his supporters to come to the Capitol," which he said could "lead to disruption, and worse." Some of those supporters had been on Romney's flight when he traveled from Salt Lake City to D.C. two days later, on January 5. They filmed themselves harassing him in the airport and chanting "Traitor!" on the plane. During his speech from the Ellipse, Trump had ridiculed Romney, to the delight of the crowd, sneering, "I wonder if he enjoyed his flight in last night."

A number of senators had printed out prepared remarks for the certification debate. A man with a cardboard sign asked me to take a picture of a statement from Idaho senator James Risch.

"Looks like somebody on our side," he said.

The sign read:

WE HAVE A REPUBLIC, IF WE CAN KEEP IT.
LET'S MAKE SURE WE KEEP IT!
—BENJAMIN FRANKLIN

While a version of the first line is famously attributed to Franklin, he never said the second part—at least, not in this world. The Freedom from Religion Foundation would later trace the quote to a Christian nationalist preacher who, a week before January 6, claimed to have had a dream in which a statue of Benjamin Franklin, located outside the Trump International Hotel in D.C., came alive, "shaking with fury as he clinched his fists" in anger over mail-in ballot fraud. Then, the preacher had recounted, Franklin "looked me in the eye as if to say, 'Let's make sure we keep it.'"

As the Trump supporters scoured the desks, Jacob Chansley, the Q Shaman, appeared above us in the gallery. He'd discarded the sweatshirt he'd been wearing on the Mall; his bare chest was covered with Viking and pagan tattoos. Pumping his spear up and down, he let loose a throaty, barbarian wail—the consummate berserker—interspersed with cries of "Freedom!"

"Quit actin' a fool!" Mr. Black shouted up at him.

But Chansley wasn't acting a fool. He was carrying out a highly specific and consequential mission, from which he would not be deterred. Two days later, on Infowars, he'd tell Alex Jones that Washington, D.C., was built on "ley lines"—tracts of electromagnetic energy that link together the world's ancient religious and cultural sites. The "shamanic song" that he sang from the gallery engaged these mystical veins, "literally affecting the quantum realm, because sound supersedes electromagnetic activity." In this way, explained Chansley, he "actually took back the Capitol for God."

While the Q Shaman might have known exactly what he was doing and why, the other Trump supporters seemed less sure. When a man in a green construction hard hat lifted out a stack of documents from Republican senator Marsha Blackburn's desk and began putting them in his backpack, a woman wearing a bicycle helmet and sunglasses asked him, "Can you get in trouble for that?"

The man hesitated. Another woman warned, "They can get you for stealing."

After some reflection, the man in the hard hat removed the documents from his backpack and returned them to Blackburn's desk. A few minutes later, he had moved onto Ted Cruz's desk. Withdrawing a piece of paper, he announced, "He was gonna sell us out all along!" People gathered around. The man in the hard hat traced the words with his finger while he read aloud: "'Objection to counting the electoral votes of the state of Arizona.'" He paused, furrowing his brow. "Oh, wait, that's actually OK."

"He's with us," a Groyper confirmed.

A third man, wearing an undershirt and baggy sweatpants, seemed unconvinced. Flipping through a three-ring binder from Cruz's desk, he muttered, "There's gotta be something in here we can fucking use against these scumbags."

"Cruz would want us to do this, so I think we're good," someone assured him.

"Yeah, absolutely."

A woman with a QAnon sign—THE CHILDREN CRY OUT FOR JUSTICE—called people on a walkie-talkie. "We did this in vain if you guys don't come!" Another began to sing: "Jesus, Jesus, you make the darkness tremble. Jesus, Jesus, you cast out fear . . ."

Mr. Black wandered around in a state of childlike wonder. "This don't look big enough," I heard him say to himself. "This can't be the right place." Two weeks later, Joshua Black would be arrested in Leeds, Alabama, where he ran a lawn-care service with his brother. Authorities tracked him down after he posted a confession on YouTube. "I just felt like the spirit of God wanted me to go in the Senate room," he'd explained.

A young man whose hooded sweatshirt was printed with a crucifix and HERSHEY CHRISTIAN ACADEMY noticed Black's wound and handed him a plastic bottle. "Here, drink some water," he said. He was Leo Bozell IV, the son of the frequent Fox News guest Leo Bozell III. Leo

Bozell III's own father, Leo Bozell Jr., had ghostwritten *The Conscience of a Conservative*, Barry Goldwater's bestselling manifesto for the reactionary Republican politics of the 1960s, which had emerged in opposition to the civil rights movement. Bozell III had remained faithful to his father's legacy, telling Sean Hannity in 2011 that Barack Obama looked like "a skinny ghetto crackhead." In December, along with more than seventy other prominent conservatives, he'd signed an open letter exhorting Republicans in Michigan, Pennsylvania, Georgia, Arizona, Wisconsin, and Nevada to "appoint clean slates of electors," in accordance with John Eastman's strategy. His son, Leo Bozell IV, was the first Leo Bozell to reach the Senate.

AFTER A WHILE, most of the Trump supporters grew bored and left the chamber. For a surreal interlude, just a few of us remained. Black's cheek was grotesquely swollen, and as I looked closer, I glimpsed the smooth, yellow surface of a plastic projectile embedded deeply within it. Blood seeped around the edges.

"Is it drippin'?" he asked.

"Yeah," I said. "You're bleeding."

"I'm gonna call my dad," Black responded.

He sat down on the plush blue carpet and leaned his back against the dais. His hunting jacket hung open; underneath it he wore a T-shirt printed with BLACKS FOR TRUMP.

A moment later, the door at the rear of the center aisle opened and the Q Shaman strode through. "Fuckin' A, man," he said, looking around with an impish grin.

A young police officer followed close behind. Pudgy, with glasses and a medical mask over red facial hair, he approached Black, who was still talking on the phone. "You good, sir?" the officer asked with concern. "You need medical attention?"

"I'm good, thank you," Black answered. Then, returning to his call, he explained to his dad, "I got shot in the face with some kind of plastic bullet."

"Any chance I could get you guys to leave the Senate wing?" the officer inquired. His tone was supplicating—that of a negotiator luring someone down from a ledge.

"We will," Black assured him. "I been making sure they ain't disrespectin' the place."

"OK," said the officer. "I just want to let you guys know: this is, like, *the* sacredest place."

Chansley had climbed onto the dais. "I'm gonna take a seat in this chair," he announced. "Because Mike Pence is a fucking traitor." Handing his phone to another Trump supporter, he said, "I'm not one to usually take pictures of myself, but in this case, I think I'll make an exception."

The officer looked on with a pained expression as Chansley flexed his biceps.

A skinny man in dark clothes remarked, "This is so weird—like, you should be stopping us."

The officer appeared offended. Pointing at each person in the chamber, he counted, "One, two, three, four, five." Then he pointed at himself: "One."

Throughout the day, I'd been recording the Trump supporters with my phone while keeping interactions with them to a minimum. I never lied or misrepresented myself, but neither had I advertised that I was press. Clearly, they'd all assumed that I was one of them. Now so did the police. Not only had the officer explicitly identified me as a potential threat—he'd stated that I accounted for 20 percent of the potential threat that was preventing him from taking action.

"Come on, let's go," I told the other 80 percent.

That didn't work. After Chansley had his pictures, the officer asked him, "Now that you've done that, can I get you guys to walk out of this room, please?"

"Yes, sir," Chansley replied. He stood and took a step, but then a thought seemed to occur to him. Setting down his spear, he found a pen and wrote something on a sheet of paper.

"I feel like you're pushing the line," the officer said.

Chansley ignored him. I went behind the vice president's desk to see what message he had left. Over a roll-call list of senators' names, the Q Shaman had scrawled:

> ITS ONLY
>
> A MATTER
>
> OF TIME
>
> JUSTICE
>
> IS
>
> COMING!

I was still standing with Chansley on the dais when a Proud Boy in biker gloves and a black-and-yellow flannel walked in. "This is our Capitol, let's be respectful to it," he told Chansley. Turning to the officer, he said, "We love you guys. We love the cops."

"I appreciate your help."

"Yeah, I know. I'm running the show."

"You're running the show?"

"No," the Proud Boy said.

Everybody laughed. "I was about to say," chuckled the officer, "'Holy shit, I found the golden goose.'"

"There is no centralized command," Chansley said.

"That's a shame."

When dozens more Trump supporters entered the chamber, pounding staffs on the floor and howling rowdily, "Kill the traitors!" the officer withdrew to a discreet remove, whispering into his radio. Several young men joined Chansley on the dais. "Jesus Christ, come into this building!" one of them screamed repeatedly. "Jesus Christ, we invoke your name! Amen!"

"Amen!"

Not to be outdone, Chansley proposed, "Let's all say a prayer in this sacred space." He raised his megaphone: "Thank you, Heavenly Father, for blessing us with this opportunity . . . Hold on, let me . . ." Lowering the megaphone, Chansley removed his fur headdress and set it on the desk. "Thank you, Heavenly Father, for this opportunity to stand up for our God-given, inalienable rights," he continued. The Trump supporters bowed their heads; a couple kneeled. Joshua Black held up his hands, surrendering to the moment, the spirit. In his YouTube confession, he'd recall, "I praised the name of Jesus on the Senate floor. That was my goal. I think that was God's goal." He and Chansley were more alike than he might have thought. As for me, it was during the communal prayer that my sense of dislocation became the most acute that day. Though we were all witnessing and participating in the same events, the people around me inhabited a magical reality that under normal circumstances I would have probably dismissed as "alternate." Yet here we were, at the US Capitol, in the US Senate, living it.

"This is how Donald Trump becomes the next president!" someone yelled after Chansley thanked God for helping them "to send a message to all the tyrants, the communists, and the globalists—for this is our nation, not theirs."

"Yes, Lord!"

A Bible lay on Pence's desk. Some of the men took turns posing for pictures with it—consciously or not, reenacting Trump's visit, in June, to St. John's Church.

· · ·

AT LAST, MORE OFFICERS ARRIVED. A sergeant with a shaved head entered the chamber and consulted with his red-bearded colleague. The sergeant's uniform was half-untucked and missing buttons, his necktie ripped and crooked. A man wearing a TRUMP beanie with a furry pompom approached him. "Got a little situation?" the man asked jokingly. He had removed one of the gold-tasseled American flags from its stand on the dais and was holding it over his shoulder. Sticking out the back pocket of his jeans were rolled-up documents that I had seen him take from a senator's desk.

"I've had better days," the sergeant laughed.

"You all right, man?"

"Yeah, I'm good."

"You sure?"

The sergeant pointed at another officer. "I feel better than he looks." The officer was covered with a white powdery substance, as if a sack of flour had been dumped on him.

"Some dude got me with a fire extinguisher," he said.

"I think I ate a whole container of pepper spray," the sergeant added, with similar good cheer. It was as if they were recounting some long-ago, amusing experience that had nothing to do with the people in the Senate chamber.

Officers have characterized such bizarre scenes as part of a "de-escalation" strategy. The problem with this explanation is that there was no strategy, to de-escalate or otherwise. According to a Senate review, the Capitol Police "received little-to-no communication from senior officers during the attack." As ranking members of the force became consumed with repelling the violent offensives outside, no one stepped in to coordinate the overall defense after the building was breached. One officer told senators, "We were on our own. Totally on our own." Another wrote, "I was horrified that NO deputy chief or above was on the radio or helping us. . . . Officers were begging and pleading for help." A lieutenant asked repeatedly throughout the day, "Does anybody have a plan?"

Although the FBI and the Department of Homeland Security had been tracking "online posts calling for violence at the Capitol," and an FBI informant had even traveled to D.C. with the Proud Boys, the Senate review found that no federal agency had deemed the threats "credible," which meant that "no formal intelligence bulletins about the potential for violence" were issued ahead of January 6. The Capitol Police, with an annual budget of roughly half a billion dollars, had its own intelligence division, and in late December it had provided the department's command staff with a report that included screenshots of a discussion on a pro-Trump blog. "Anyone going armed needs to be mentally prepared to draw down on LEOs," someone, referring to "law enforcement officers," had commented. A map of the Capitol campus had been posted. Concerned citizens had also emailed the Capitol Police about what they were seeing on chat forums; one individual had alerted its Public Information Office to "tweets from people organizing to 'storm the Capitol' on January 6." Despite all this, the Capitol Police, like the FBI, did not "assess the threat as likely to occur" and "failed to prepare a department-wide operational plan" or "comprehensive staffing plan" to protect the premises.

In the absence of guidance, officers had to decide for themselves how to engage with the mob. Several would be placed under investigation and reprimanded for their conduct. One officer posed for pictures with rioters inside the building. Others removed a barricade from the perimeter on the east side of the grounds to allow a restive crowd through. A lieutenant was filmed donning a MAGA hat and coordinating his beleaguered platoon's retreat with a group of Oath Keepers. In the video, the crowd cheers as the officers leave the Capitol, and a woman gives each of them a hug.

My impression was that a simple contract—sometimes tacit, sometimes explicit—governed most interactions between Trump supporters and law enforcement on January 6: the former would only attack those among the latter who stood in their way, while bestowing the usual respect and deference upon those who stood down. This was why the dynamic between the two sides ranged from homicidal belligerence to something like camaraderie, depending on where you were and whether the officers in that place chose to accept or reject the ultimatum—a schizophrenic vacillation that compounded the dark unreality of the day.

Little mercy was shown to those who fought back. A hundred eighty officers were wounded. Some sustained brain injuries. According to the Capitol Police Labor Committee, one suffered "two cracked ribs and two smashed spinal disks." Another lost an eye. "Another was stabbed with a metal fence stake." An officer quoted in the Senate review said that the weapons used against him included "frozen cans and bottles, rebar from the construction, bricks . . . sticks of various widths, pipes, bats." Body cam footage captured a Trump supporter assaulting officers with a metal whip. Bear spray, mace, insecticide, and other caustic agents left some officers with lasting vision and respiratory complications. The chemical burns that scarred one captain's face took months to heal. Officer Brian Sicknick, who had two strokes after fighting with Trump supporters on the steps and being attacked with pepper spray, died the next day. Four officers who defended the Capitol committed suicide in the following months. The family of one of them attributed his sudden depression to the concussion he suffered after a Trump supporter struck him with a crowbar.

Black officers faced unique enmity. Before a House select committee, Officer Harry Dunn recalled being subjected to "a torrent of racial epithets" from "a crowd of perhaps twenty people." Officer James Blassingame, a seventeen-year veteran of the Capitol Police, sued Trump for the lingering trauma of what he experienced while fighting with a racist mob on the ground floor of the building. As "insurrectionists struck Officer Blassingame in his face, head, chest, arms, and what felt like every part of his body," they also berated and belittled him, Blassingame's attorneys claim. "For the first time in his life, people were yelling into his face, calling him a 'nigger' repeatedly and throughout the attack. . . . He lost count of the many times the racial slur was hurled at him."

Some of the most intense violence occurred on the inauguration platform. After breaking through the police line between the bleachers, hundreds of Trump supporters swarmed onto the plywood stage and an elevated promenade above it. A tunnel with an arched opening led inside the Capitol—it was from here that Joe Biden and Kamala Harris would emerge to be sworn in during the public ceremony. Cramming into the tunnel, the mob encountered a platoon from the Metropolitan Police. Cell phone video captured a man clawing at Officer Daniel Hodges and ripping off his gas mask while the mob rocked back and forth to cries of "Heave! Ho!" Hodges became pinned in a doorway, howling in agony, blood dripping from his mouth. He later testified that someone grabbed his baton and beat him over the head with it while he was immobilized. Worried that he would be "dragged out into the crowd and lynched," Hodges recalled, "I did the only thing that I could do and screamed for help."

It took the officers almost an hour to repulse the mob. But that was only the beginning of their ordeal. Determined to retake the tunnel, Trump supporters launched projectiles at them and assailed them with blunt instruments. One man savagely hacked at the forward-most police with a hockey stick wrapped in a TRUMP 2020 flag. (Another would attack an officer with a lacrosse stick taped to a Confederate flag.) Someone else swung an aluminum crutch. Others used sharp metal poles as lances and javelins. A wooden table was hurled. Breaking off one of its legs, a Trump supporter employed it as a club. A man was filmed kicking an officer's shield with the flat of his boot while he yelled, "You're going to die tonight!"

When rioters got ahold of Michael Fanone, a D.C. narcotics officer with almost twenty years of service, they dragged him headfirst down the steps, yanking off his helmet and magazines, striking him with fists, feet, sticks, and flagpoles.

"USA!" the crowd chanted.

Fanone testified that one Trump supporter "repeatedly lunged for me and attempted to remove my firearm." He heard shouts of "Kill him with his own gun!"

"I've got kids!" Fanone pleaded.

He was shot with a Taser multiple times in the neck—"electrocuted again and again and again," he testified. Then he was beaten unconscious. Before a few men intervened, Fanone suffered a brain injury and a heart attack.

About an hour later, amid ongoing frenzied hand-to-hand combat at the tunnel mouth, a thirty-four-year-old woman from Georgia named Rosanne Boyland was trampled to death. Body cam footage shows Boyland's friend crouched over her inert body, desperately appealing to their fellow Trump supporters. "She's dead!" he cries out. "I need somebody!"

Ignoring him, a man sprays mace at the police while another yells, "Knock their masks off!" Then someone charges over Boyland to wrestle away an officer's baton.

"No! No!" Boyland's friend begs.

They pay no heed. "I'll fucking kill you!" a Trump supporter tells an officer. Like Fanone, the officer is dragged down the steps, past the dead woman, and set upon by the mob.

THE EXPERIENCES OF OFFICERS like Michael Fanone and James Blassingame make the passivity of some of their colleagues all the more confounding. I'd been in the Senate chamber for about twenty minutes when a large phalanx of Metropolitan Police entered and the Trump supporters were suddenly outnumbered. Corralled with no avenue of escape, I assumed that we would all be detained and that our phones would be confiscated. I withdrew my wallet and prepared to show my press card. But no arrests were made. No one was searched. Nobody questioned. The red-bearded officer approached Jacob Chansley and spoke to him privately, after which Chansley announced, "We gotta go, guys, otherwise we're going in handcuffs." As we filed out through the main door, the sergeant with the shaved head told us, "Be safe. We appreciate your being peaceful."

The man in front of me wore a cap with a WE THE PEOPLE patch. I had watched him gather papers belonging to various senators and put them in a blue folder. He walked right past the sergeant, with the folder in his hand. The corridor outside was also full of police. "This way," invited one of them, extending his arm. Another officer led us to a staircase. His hair was disheveled, he looked exhausted, and he was limping. "We support you guys, OK?" the Proud Boy in the black-and-yellow flannel kept telling him. "We support you guys. We support you guys."

"Thank you," the battered officer replied.

I followed the man with the blue folder through an emergency exit and out of the building. Police in riot gear stood beneath a portico; as I filmed them while walking backward, a female officer jabbed her finger in the air, pointing emphatically at something behind me. I turned to look. Had she spotted the blue folder? Was she signaling a colleague?

No. There was a low step, and she was worried I might trip.

Strategic forbearance is one thing. But can we really attribute such outright solicitude, in the midst of what one officer later called "a medieval battle," to some tactically shrewd charade intended to beguile a volatile adversary? I don't think so. I think that the complex, often contradictory actions of officers on January 6 flowed from their complex, often contradictory relationship with that adversary. The day after the attack, one member of the Capitol Police contacted an insurrectionist who had bragged on Facebook about entering the building. Introducing himself as someone "who agrees with your political stance," the officer advised deleting the confession. "Just looking out!" he explained.

No evidence suggests that either the Capitol Police or the Metropolitan Police was an exception to the overwhelming support for Trump among law enforcement agencies nationwide. Eleven thousand D.C. officers belonged to the Fraternal Order of Police, which enthusiastically endorsed Trump twice. In 2019, the organization's D.C. branch held its annual winter holiday party at the Trump International Hotel. Nor is there any reason to assume that the Capitol Police or the Metropolitan Police was immune to the kind of infiltration by white supremacists and more insidious bigotry that plagued other departments, such as in Portland and Minneapolis. In a 2001 class-action lawsuit, over 250 Black officers claimed that "racial discrimination is rampant in the ranks of the U.S. Capitol Police," and a similar complaint filed in 2012 alleged "continuous, pervasive, and egregiously discriminatory actions." Two months after January 6, a Jewish congressional staffer photographed a Capitol Police officer reading a copy of *The Protocols of the Elders of Zion*, the century-old antisemitic text that had inspired fascists from Adolf Hitler to Nicholas Fuentes, and that William Potter Gale distributed to members of the Posse Comitatus.

A number of law enforcement officers and their relatives participated in the insurrection. Half a dozen members of the Seattle Police
Department traveled to D.C., among them a lieutenant with the Major
Crimes Unit and a detective from the vice squad. Two officers from
Virginia took selfies inside the Capitol. One of them posted on Facebook, "The right IN ONE DAY took the f** U.S. Capitol. Keep poking
us." A Pennsylvania officer was photographed marching up Pennsylvania Avenue in a hat emblazoned with TRUMP / MAGA / 2020 /
FUCK YOUR FEELINGS. A sheriff's lieutenant from Texas published a
picture of herself amid the violence below the bleachers, and wrote,
"Aside from my kids, this was, indeed, the best day of my life." Before
taking selfies inside a senator's office, a Chicago police officer messaged his friends about having "knocked out a commie." A former police officer from Oakland who had gone to D.C. appeared on a local
news program that same night to defend the riot. "What do you think
is worse," he asked, "storming the Capitol with a flag or committing
treason against your country?" A retired and highly decorated New
York City police officer was filmed beating a member of the Metropolitan Police with a metal pipe, calling him a "fucking piece of shit"
and "fucking commie motherfucker," and digging his thumbs into his
eyes. An assistant district attorney general from Tennessee watched
idly from the inauguration platform as the tunnel was attacked. A special agent on leave from the Drug Enforcement Agency posed for pictures on the Capitol grounds with a LIBERTY OR DEATH flag while
pulling back his coat to display his federal badge and government-
issued sidearm. A former member of the Salt Lake City Police Department who'd been named Officer of the Year was arrested after
appearing in a photo beside a bust of Abraham Lincoln inside the Capitol. An ex-military policeman from the Marine Corps was accused of
assaulting officers on the steps while yelling at them, "I'm a military
fucking police! I'm a military police!" A grand jury indicted Alan

Hostetter, an ex–chief of police for La Habra, California, on multiple charges related to the siege. "People at the highest levels need to be made an example of with an execution or two or three," Hostetter had declared on social media. The wife of a Pennsylvania detective assigned to an FBI task force was caught on tape in the rotunda, and Scott Fairlamb, the son of a New Jersey state trooper, was filmed punching an officer in the head and stealing his baton. Fairlamb's brother was a senior agent in the Secret Service, who had led Michelle Obama's security detail. A lawyer representing Fairlamb would later tell *HuffPost* that his client donated to law enforcement charities and shared "the same ideological viewpoint" as the police.

One way to think about January 6 is as the consummation, in real time, of a tumultuous passage between two distinct eras of conservatism. Before 2020, most conservatives celebrated law enforcement as the protectors of a system that was, on balance, reliably favorable to their interests; by the end of 2020, many conservatives had come to see that system as corrupt and tyrannical—perhaps even satanic. At the same time, so long as Trump was still in power and weaponizing law enforcement against leftists, neither conservatives nor the police were forced to confront what this meant for their alliance. That reckoning could no longer be avoided on January 6, and it is unsurprising that a number of people on both sides of the line persisted in respecting the terms of a compact now obsolete. The platoon that was cheered and hugged by Trump supporters seconds after being assaulted by them must have experienced the same disorientation as some victims of abusive relationships, and one wonders how many officers at the Capitol believed that the people trying to kill them also loved them. During his Senate testimony, Officer Harry Dunn described a rioter who "displayed what looked like a law enforcement badge, and told me, 'We're doing this for you.'" As if to memorialize the dissonance, Trump, a couple of minutes after I exited the Capitol, tweeted, "Remember, WE are the Party of Law & Order."

The afternoon was cold and blustery. I followed several people around a corner, to the north end of the building. Incredibly, a renewed offensive was being mounted here, and some of the intruders who had just been politely escorted from the Senate chamber promptly joined the attack. Using metal barricades for battering rams, the mob charged a group of officers in riot gear guarding an entrance, was repulsed, and charged again.

"Choose a side!" people cried.

"We stood behind you, now stand behind us!"

A man with a high-and-tight military haircut, whose face was covered with camouflage paint, yelled for people to push. He wore a bulletproof vest with a patch that read: BLESSED BE THE LORD, MY ROCK, WHO TRAINS MY HANDS FOR WAR, AND MY FINGERS FOR BATTLE. His name was Samuel Lazar, and he was a diehard supporter of Doug Mastriano, the Pennsylvania state senator who'd spoken at the Stop the Steal rally in Harrisburg. Later, online sleuths would unearth several pictures of Lazar and Mastriano together, sometimes with their arms around each other. Lazar had also been in Harrisburg when Representative Jim Jordan visited. Wearing a Trump flag as a cape, he'd stood on the steps behind the congressman and saluted as Jordan asserted, "We are not timid folk. We are people who take action." The same House committee that would subpoena the Kremers and others would later obtain a text message sent by Jordan to White House chief of staff Mark Meadows on January 5, advising that Vice President Pence "should call out all electoral votes that he believes are unconstitutional as no electoral votes at all."

"Hang the traitors!" Lazar now bellowed.

Suddenly, a gaunt and somewhat tremulous officer, from the Metro

Transit Police, asked to borrow a rioter's megaphone. He had something that he wished to say.

"Ladies and gentlemen, can I have your attention, please?" The obsequious request was met with jeers and insults. The transit officer persisted: "Like President Bush said after 9/11, '*We hear you.*'"

This was a remarkable reference. Three days after the attack on the World Trade Center, Bush had visited Ground Zero. Standing amid the ruins, he had borrowed a megaphone to address the firefighters, paramedics, and other rescue workers clearing debris. "I can hear you," Bush told them. "The rest of the world hears you. And the people who knocked these buildings down will hear all of us soon." It was an expression of solidarity with victims of a grave injustice, and it was a vow to the bereaved that their dispossession would be avenged. We now know that Bush was also uniting the country against an imaginary enemy, honoring American patriots while invoking their injury to legitimize a bogus war. His audience had chanted, "USA."

What an oddity the transit officer was. The first person I'd met in Minneapolis, outside the burning Third Precinct station, told me, "Hopefully, they hear us." But this was the only member of law enforcement I had seen offer an assurance that they *had* heard anyone.

Black protesters in Minneapolis had taken heed of the indiscriminate violence with which the police and military responded to their appeals; they had believed the president when he threatened their lives ("When the looting starts, the shooting starts"); and they had reasonably surmised that demonstrating came with a risk of being killed. Conversely, on January 6, Trump's followers also listened to him ("We have truth and justice on our side"); took heed of the military's absence and law enforcement's restraint; and reasonably surmised that they could proceed with impunity. None of the Trump supporters I observed appeared to experience fear—certainly, nothing resembling the physical terror that police and soldiers had awoken in Minneapolis in May. When Simone Hunter, Tony Clark, Deondre Moore, and other peaceful marchers were surrounded by troops in armored Humvees and brutalized with less-lethal munitions at the Mobil gas station downtown, many of them thought—because they were meant to think—that the bullets were real. The Trump supporters who attacked the Capitol, on the other hand, assumed that there was a limit to what could be done to them, and ingratiating state agents like the transit officer and the sergeant with the shaved head confirmed this assumption again and again.

While testifying before the House Administration committee, an inspector general would reveal another likely reason for why so many insurrectionists were so undaunted: the Capitol Police had not availed itself of sting-ball grenades and forty-millimeter launchers capable of shooting beanbags, sponge bullets, and other large-bore projectiles, all of which had been regularly deployed against Black Lives Matter protesters over the summer, including in D.C. (The projectile that struck Cornell Griffin in the neck and damaged his vocal cords while he was evacuating peaceful demonstrators in Minneapolis was probably forty millimeters; a sergeant's body cam that night recorded him telling officers, "You got to hit them with the forties.") Such weapons "would have helped us that day to enhance our ability to protect the Capitol," the inspector general explained. Nonetheless, they had been forbidden because of their potential to "cause life-altering injury and/or death." While I was under the bleachers, the rounds that rained down on us, whatever caliber they were, did nothing to repel or even discourage the attackers from breaching that critical choke point. "Is that all you got?" one Trump supporter had taunted. The answer was no—but it was all that they were willing to use.

Even if the docility of law enforcement on January 6 could be chalked up to a good-faith attempt at de-escalation, it was a profound misjudgment that only emboldened those it was intended to pacify. After telling the Trump supporters that he heard them, the transit officer said, "We are not here to kick you out or use force. That is not why we are here."

"We have guns, too, motherfuckers!" a man yelled over him. "With a lot bigger rounds!"

Another added, "If we have to tool up, it's gonna be over! We're coming heavy!"

A few minutes later, I overheard a woman say into her phone, "We need to come back with guns. One time with guns, and then we'll never have to do this again."

I WAS SHOVED against two men in the middle of an argument. One had a white goatee and wore a Texas Longhorns hat; the other was in his twenties, cheeks flushed with cold. The younger man, I realized, was the older man's son. He wanted to move forward, toward Samuel Lazar and the point of contact with the police.

"Wait," his father said. "Wait. Just wait here."

"Let go of me."

"Wait."

"We have to *push*."

Many parents had brought their children to D.C. Two of the men at the front of the mob that I saw crushing officers in the anteroom by the rotunda were fifty-one-year-old Daryl Johnson and his twenty-nine-year-old son, Daniel. "Lol Dad and I were one of the first ones inside," Daniel wrote on Facebook the next day. Court documents in another case would include a picture of twenty-eight-year-old Antony Vo posing with his mother in the rotunda. "My mom and I helped stop the vote count for a bit," Vo had bragged on social media. Jason Owens flew from Texas with his twenty-one-year-old son, Grady. Both men would be charged with assaulting officers, Jason with his fists and

Grady with a skateboard. Five members of another Texas family would be arrested. Thomas and Dawn Munn drove sixteen hundred miles to D.C., with their son and two daughters. According to the FBI, the Munns followed the mob up the steps beneath the bleachers and into the building through the broken window. The mom later wrote on Facebook, "We went in and stormed capital!"

Yet the scene before me on the north end of the premises was something different. In a way, it could not have been more prosaic. The yearning child, the anxious parent. Even the father's appeal expressed a universal apprehension: "*Wait . . . wait.*" As if he wanted to pause the world whose transformation seemed to be accelerating. Stop time. Take stock. He was grabbing his son's arm, physically holding him back. But from what, exactly?

Someone stepped between them. "Hold on," he said. It was the man in the TRUMP beanie with the furry pom-pom, who had paraded around the Senate with the gold-tasseled flag. "Look at this," he told the father and son. From his back pocket he withdrew the purloined documents. "I took this off the fucking halls of the Senate just now," he said. "I've already been in there."

The son gaped at the thing before him:

SENATE OF THE UNITED STATES

ONE HUNDRED SEVENTEENTH CONGRESS

CALENDAR OF BUSINESS

WEDNESDAY JANUARY 6, 2021

"Yeah?" he asked.

The man patted his back. "Yeah," he said.

The son nodded. Then, breaking loose from his father, he joined the insurrection.

. . .

MOST OF THE PEOPLE who stormed the Capitol hoped to forestall the peaceful transition of power. Some intended to harm lawmakers. Though neither of these goals was achieved, the man in the beanie was exultant. He had penetrated "the sacredest place," an affirmation of dominance so emotionally gratifying that it was an end in itself. While the Trump supporter with the stun gun was in Pelosi's office, he left her a note: "Nancy, Bigo was here, you bitch." The next day, another rioter sent a video to his friend in which he pounded his chest and boasted about having urinated in Pelosi's toilet. Perhaps no tribunals had been held. Perhaps no traitors had been hanged. But they had proven whose house it still was, who was still in charge, and to whom the country still belonged.

Proof—what else had the man in the beanie been offering the father and his son when he showed them that piece of paper from the Senate chamber? Ultimately, the affirmation of dominance was not only for the dominated—it was also, and maybe first and foremost, for each other and for themselves. While being escorted out of the Capitol, I had overtaken an elderly woman carrying a TRUMP tote bag. "We scared them," she said, "that's what we did. We scared the bastards." She sounded like she was reassuring someone doubtful of the value of their work. But she was talking to herself.

During the riot, the Proud Boys chairman Enrique Tarrio, who was no longer in D.C., had posted on social media, "Make no mistake . . . We did this." The many Trump supporters who published incriminating pictures in the days following the attack also felt compelled to say, "Look at this." One resident of New York was arrested after publishing an image from the inauguration platform with a photoshopped arrow and the words "THIS IS ME." While Officer Fanone was being assaulted, another New Yorker tore off his badge; back home in

Buffalo, he sealed the memento in a ziplock bag and buried it in his backyard.

Lynchings of African Americans often ended with the murderers posing for photographs around the bodies of their victims. Some kept souvenirs—a length of rope, limbs of the tree from which it had hung. American guards at Abu Ghraib routinely photographed themselves with the Iraqi detainees they tortured and humiliated. In Afghanistan, members of a platoon that executed civilians for sport posed for pictures with one of their quarry, holding up his head by fistfuls of hair. I watched dozens of Kurdish soldiers, in 2015, pull a mortally wounded ISIS fighter out of a house in Sinjar. His arms splayed behind him as he was dragged into the street. The Kurdish soldiers swarmed around him, bringing out their phones and taking pictures while he died. Some smiled for the camera while stepping on his head. "Get one of me," a man told his comrades before squatting beside the fighter and spitting in his face. "Did you get it?"

Mob violence is theater. Officer Fanone was beaten unconscious and Rosanne Boyland was trampled to death on a literal stage. Many images of the mayhem on the inauguration platform were taken from the "center stand"—a tall scaffolding tower erected for camera crews to document Biden and Harris's swearing-in. On January 6, some Trump supporters joined professional photographers who had climbed the tower to gain a cinematic, bird's-eye view of the action. These people were simultaneously perpetrators and spectators. They were performing for each other. I had the same feeling in the Senate chamber when Jacob Chansley delivered his prayer from the dais. It did not come as a surprise when I learned that Chansley had once been an aspiring actor.

As with any tragedy, participation brought catharsis, which both purges and elucidates emotions. When the transit officer, seeing that Bush's words had failed to produce the same effect as they had at

Ground Zero, relinquished the megaphone and withdrew behind his embattled men, the mob resumed its offensive. As waves of Trump supporters hurled epithets, objects, and their own bodies at the police, one stood among them, rooted to the earth, his face aglow with feeling. He was in his late twenties, short, and overweight, with vaguely porcine features that must have led to much unhappiness in school. Throwing back his head and squeezing shut his eyes, he screamed, "Fuck George Floyd! Fuck Breonna Taylor! Fuck them all!" The release looked emetic. He was overcome, at last giving expression to something he had lived with and suppressed too long.

ONE OF THE SPEAKERS outside the Supreme Court at the Million MAGA March had been Jack Posobiec, a young Republican operative who rose to prominence in 2016 while promoting the Pizzagate conspiracy theory. Pizzagate, which held that Hillary Clinton and other leading Democrats were running a juvenile sex-trafficking ring out of the basement of a D.C. pizzeria, had been a kind of antecedent to QAnon, which emerged from the same right-wing message boards and fascination with pedophilia. On November 14, Posobiec excoriated a different villain, though one no less perverse than child-molesting politicians. The mainstream media, he told his audience, "will call you every name in the book. They'll say you're racists. They'll say you're Nazis. But do you know what the worst thing the mainstream media does? They say that you do not exist." Posobiec went on, "I think we're all here today to tell them that we *do* exist."

On January 6, the first words of Trump's speech were these: "The media will not show the magnitude of this crowd." He continued, "We have hundreds of thousands of people here, and I just want them to be recognized." For Trump, Posobiec, and their followers, it was the media's negation of their existence, not its lies and libel, that made it "the

enemy of the people." A similar fear of erasure lay behind the Great
Replacement, ZOG, and New World Order theories. The performative
quality of the insurrectionists, meanwhile, arose from the same desire
"to be recognized" that fueled their hatred of the press.

We did this. Look at this. THIS IS ME.

After a wall of Metropolitan Police in riot gear, half a dozen ranks
deep, finally dispersed the Trump supporters from the north end of the
Capitol, some shifted their attention to a collection of TV journalists
in a small park on the east side of the grounds. A man had already accosted an Israeli reporter in the middle of a live broadcast there, calling him a "lying Israeli" and telling him, "You are cattle today." Now
the mob chased off crews from the Associated Press and other outlets,
smashing their equipment with bats and sticks, fulfilling the president's
directive to "get them straightened out."

There was a ritualistic atmosphere as they gathered in a circle
around the piled-up cameras, lights, and tripods.

"Burn that shit!"

"Torch it!"

Someone attempted to set the equipment on fire, but the plastic and
metal wouldn't catch. A man wielding a thick tree branch declared, "We
are the media now!"

Another man, in a black leather jacket and wraparound sunglasses,
shouted, "Start makin' a list! Put all those names down, and we start
huntin' them down, one by one!"

"Hang 'em!"

When a TV crew was spotted about a hundred feet away, everyone
left the heap of destroyed gear and hurried over. It was a Middle Eastern network. The Arab correspondent, in a suit and tie and a long winter coat, smiled nervously under bright lamps.

"God bless you," he said.

"No," a young man told him. "Say 'Trump 2020.'" He wore goggles and biking gloves. A pair of binoculars hung from his neck. In his hand was a wooden club.

"Say 'Trump 2020,'" he repeated.

A man with a shovel stepped forward. "Say it."

The correspondent pointed at the microphone in his ear. "I'm just waiting on the newsroom," he explained.

"Traitors get the rope!" somebody yelled at him.

Though the correspondent was bravely maintaining his smile, his mouth had begun to twitch. Whether or not he understood what "the rope" was, he knew that he didn't want to get it. He must have felt the same dangerous energy vibrating through the crowd that I did: its loose power, supercharged from the electric day, still unexpended, searching for an outlet.

"NBC's over there!" a voice called out.

The mob moved on. The reporter stopped smiling.

It was dark and lights were glowing in the windows of the rotunda when, at 5:40 p.m., three hours and nineteen minutes after the Capitol Police requested their assistance, 154 National Guard soldiers arrived. By then, with the help of officers from Maryland and Virginia, the building had been secured. I linked up with the photographers Balazs Gardi and Victor Blue. Balazs and I had walked together up the National Mall from the Washington Monument but were separated in the chaos under the bleachers. He had entered the Capitol on the same level as I but ended up in a space beneath the rotunda known as the Crypt. Victor had gone to the Capitol earlier that morning. He had witnessed Joe Biggs and the Proud Boys overpower the officers on the outer perimeter, and had been with the mob that tried to break into the Speaker's Lobby. While I was following the Groypers into the Senate chamber, Victor was taking pictures of Ashli Babbitt as she died.

Four years earlier, when Trump defeated Clinton, Victor and I had been in Mosul, where the immediacy of the civil war raging around us seemed to dwarf the significance of the American election. That felt like a long time ago now.

Mayor Bowser had imposed a curfew, and as the three of us headed back toward our hotel, downtown D.C. was quiet. Scattered bands of Trump supporters roamed the streets. We were walking up the middle of Pennsylvania Avenue, talking about where we had been and what we had seen, when a young man ahead of us stopped and turned around. I think we all expected some kind of confrontation. The man, however, only wanted to share something with us. "Check this out," he said excitedly, holding forth a black cube with a plastic lens. Balazs, Victor, and I leaned over to inspect the object. It appeared to be a body camera.

"I took it off a cop," the man said.

We stood there mutely staring at the thing. I was aware that I should be asking questions. I knew the questions that I was supposed to ask. Who was he? Where, when, and how had he done it? *Why?* But I did not want to hear his answers. I didn't care. After a while, our failure to congratulate the man seemed to make him regret showing us his prize. He shoved it back in his coat pocket. A cold wind was gusting down the avenue. The man shrugged and continued on his way. We watched him disappear into the empty city.

EIGHTEEN

THINGS AND EVENTS

When Congress reconvened at eight p.m., Mike Pence— sitting in the chair recently occupied by Jacob Chansley, having presumably read the note that Chansley left for him—addressed the Senate. "Even in the wake of unprecedented violence and vandalism at this Capitol, the elected representatives of the people of the United States have assembled again on the very same day to support and defend the Constitution," Pence declared. But as the certification of the electoral college resumed, it became clear that he had misconstrued the situation. In the end, 147 Republicans voted to overturn the election. One hundred forty-seven—still a substantial majority of the caucus—sided with the Proud Boys, the Groypers, the Three Percenters, the Oath Keepers, QAnon, the man in the CAMP AUSCHWITZ sweatshirt, the sieg-heiling woman who stole Nancy Pelosi's laptop to sell to the Russians, and the mob that brutalized and tried to kill the police officers protecting them. "To those who wreaked havoc in our Capitol today, you did not win," Pence said. "Violence never wins." The second claim is demonstrably false; the first looks increasingly doubtful.

In *The Turner Diaries*, after white insurgents lob mortars at the US Capitol from across the Potomac, the narrator observes that "the real value of all our attacks today lies in the psychological impact"—in the knowledge imparted to politicians "that not one of them is beyond our reach." A couple of hours before Pence's speech, Trump tweeted, "These are the things and events that happen when a sacred landslide election victory is so unceremoniously & viciously stripped away from great patriots who have been badly & unfairly treated for so long." The statement was not only a defense of the insurrection and a tribute to its perpetrators. It was also a threat. This is what happens, this is what *will* happen. No justice, no peace.

Pete Meijer, a Republican congressman from Michigan, later told the libertarian magazine *Reason* that many of his colleagues "knew in their heart of hearts that they should've voted to certify, but some had legitimate concerns about the safety of their families. They felt that that vote would put their families in danger." A week later, House Democrats held another vote, to impeach Trump for incitement of in-surrection. Representative Jason Crow said on *Meet the Press* that dur-ing his conversations with Republican lawmakers, "a couple of them broke down in tears, saying that they are afraid for their lives if they vote for this impeachment." Only ten Republicans did so. One of them was Pete Meijer, who told NBC News, "Our expectation is that some-one may try to kill us." Another was Liz Cheney, the third-ranking Republican in Congress. Death threats obliged her to hire a private security detail.

Political survival was another concern. On January 20, Joe Biden traversed the tunnel where Daniel Hodges had been crushed and beaten, stepped out from the archway where Rosanne Boyland had been trampled to death, descended the steps where Michael Fanone had been electrocuted ("again and again and again"), and took the oath of office on the stage where hundreds had obeyed Trump's injunction to fight like hell. Yet Trump's failure to remain in the White House had by no means diminished that obedience. When Cheney cautioned her colleagues not to "let the former president drag us backward and make us complicit in his efforts to unravel our democracy," they revoked her leadership position and gave it to a Trump loyalist. "She's made a determination that the Republican Party can't grow with President Trump—I've determined we can't grow *without* him," said Senator Lindsey Graham, who in 2016 had denounced Trump as "a race-baiting xenophobic religious bigot."

At least fifty-seven Republican officials had traveled from two dozen states to be in D.C. on January 6. Some had marched on the Capitol, including Senator Doug Mastriano, who crossed the perimeter of barricades after a mob, skirmishing with officers, tossed them aside. A member of the West Virginia House of Delegates livestreamed himself barging past police, yelling Trump's name. A secretary for the California Republican Assembly was interviewed on camera after being expelled from the Capitol. "We broke windows," he boasted. "We pushed our way to Nancy Pelosi's office. It was pretty badass." A county commissioner from New Mexico filmed himself on the inauguration platform; a few days later, he posted another video on social media, warning that Trump supporters might return to the Capitol armed. "If we do, it's gonna be a sad day," he said. "Because there's gonna be blood running out of that building."

Republicans nationwide closed ranks behind Trump and against those who would hold him accountable. The Wyoming GOP formally censured Liz Cheney, and the Arizona GOP did the same for the state's Republican governor, Doug Ducey; former senator Jeff Flake; and the widow of John McCain. Mitt Romney, who voted to impeach Trump a

THE STORM IS HERE

second time, was booed and heckled at the Utah Republican Convention. Some politicians who'd initially condemned Trump began to walk back or reverse their positions, following the same well-trodden trajectory as Mike Shirkey, the Senate leader from Michigan who had called militia members in his state "at best a bunch of jackasses," only to tell them a month later, "We need you now more than ever." Meijer, Cheney, and Romney were exceptions. The vast majority of Republicans, fearful of the mob, opted to join it. A week after January 6, House minority leader Kevin McCarthy told the country, "The President bears responsibility for Wednesday's attack on Congress by mob rioters." By the end of the month, McCarthy would change his position to: "I don't think he provoked it." By the end of the year, he'd be blaming Nancy Pelosi. Former UN ambassador Nikki Haley disavowed Trump the day after January 6, in a speech before the Republican National Committee, saying that he would "be judged harshly by history." She went on to tell *Politico*, "We shouldn't have followed him, and we shouldn't have listened to him." A few months later, Haley would criticize Mike Pence for reiterating that Trump had been wrong to ask him to overturn the election. "I'm not a fan of Republicans going against Republicans," Haley would say on Fox News.

As more and more politicians cravenly acceded to Trump and the lies and the hate that had spurred the attack against them, I was reminded of something that I'd witnessed at the D.C. rally on December 12. Toward the end of his speech at Freedom Plaza, Nicholas Fuentes had noticed a drag queen in a blond wig and an evening gown standing in the crowd. An embroidered sash identified her as "Lady MAGA." I had met her at the previous rally, in November, when Trump supporters had lined up to have their pictures taken with her, showering her with compliments. Now Fuentes yelled, "That is disgusting! I don't want to see that!" and dozens of young men wheeled on her, chanting in unison, "Shame!"

It was the sort of thing I'd come to expect from the Groypers. But there were a lot of other people there, as well. Many of them resembled the customers in Karl Manke's barbershop: hardworking Americans who believed in God and loved their country. Most observed the public shaming with a mix of discomfort and amusement. A few laughed. None of them—not a single Patriot—objected or defended Lady MAGA.

IN FEBRUARY, TRUMP APPEARED at the Conservative Political Action Conference in Orlando, Florida, which featured a golden statue of him holding a scepter and a copy of the Constitution. He received a long ovation and put to rest speculation that he might start a new political party. "The Republican Party is united," he said—and it was. Polls showed that most Republicans still supported him. They also still believed that he had won the election. Instead of withering after January 6, the lie became an ever more salient issue for conservatives everywhere. In March, Republican senators in Arizona hired Cyber Ninjas, a private company owned by a QAnon supporter, to conduct a private audit of two million ballots cast in Maricopa County, which Biden had won. The audit took place in a Phoenix stadium, where ballots were inspected with high-magnification cameras. "What they're doing is to find out if there's bamboo in the paper," an official told a local news channel, explaining that forty thousand ballots from "the southeast part of the world" were thought to have been "flown in" and "stuffed into the box." Ballots were also scanned with ultraviolet lights in a search for "watermarks," which QAnon followers contended Trump had used as a secret identifier of authenticity.

Republican officials in other states began pushing for similar reviews, which the former president maintained would bring about his "re-instatement." It seems doubtful that many of the career politicians and operatives allied with Trump shared this delusion. The erosion of public trust in the electoral process, however, afforded them a pretext for modifying that process to their advantage. Within six months of the insurrection, Republican-controlled legislatures in thirty-six states introduced over two hundred election-reform bills. In Georgia, a sweeping law made requesting absentee ballots more onerous, dramatically limited access to drop boxes, criminalized offering food or water to voters in long lines, and imposed additional constraints on in-person voting. The new provisions targeted populous urban districts, such as Atlanta, which were majority Democrat and Black. While the Republican governor, Brian Kemp, was signing the bill into law, Park Cannon, a Black legislator from Atlanta, knocked on his closed door. Cannon wished to know why the governor was not formalizing such a momentous law in public. Several Georgia state troopers, all white and male, promptly detained the congresswoman, escorted her through the capitol in handcuffs, and brought her to jail.

No arrests, incidentally, had been made on January 6, when armed militia members gathered at the Georgia statehouse and Secretary of State Brad Raffensperger had to be evacuated by the Georgia Capitol Police. Chester Doles, the former National Alliance leader and imperial wizard in the KKK, was seen stalking the halls of the building with a piece of paper that he wanted to deliver to Raffensperger. Doles later told me that the paper was a "writ of grievance," and that state troopers had let him in through the front door.

A few days earlier, Raffensperger had released a recording of a phone call in which the president told him, "I just want to find 11,780 votes," or one more vote than Biden's margin of victory. "It's just not possible to have lost Georgia," Trump said. "It's not possible." He went on to mention Ruby Freeman—the Black election worker in Atlanta whom QAnon followers had slandered and harassed—eighteen times. "You know the internet?" Trump asked Raffensperger, before explaining that Freeman was "trending" on it. He called her a "known scammer" and accused her of fabricating over fifty thousand votes for Biden. "She stuffed the ballot boxes," he said. "They were stuffed like nobody has ever seen them stuffed before." When Raffensperger maintained that this was false—that both the FBI and the Georgia Bureau of Investigation had examined the surveillance footage from State Farm Arena, conducted interrogations, and found nothing inappropriate on the part of Freeman or her colleagues—Trump countered by questioning Freeman's "reputation."

In addition to the obstacles that the new Georgia law placed between citizens and the ballot box, it also divested Raffensperger of the authority that had enabled him to resist Trump's demand to manufacture votes. Elected secretaries of state would no longer oversee Georgia's election board; instead, the general assembly—reliably Republican, due to severely gerrymandered legislative districts—would appoint a majority of members. A raft of bills in other states similarly aimed to suppress Democratic turnout and transfer oversight powers from independent administrators to Republican legislatures. Texas banned drive-through and twenty-four-hour voting outright. In 2020, such facilities had been used (without incident) by 140,000 residents of Harris County, which includes Houston, the most diverse city in America.

Outside the Supreme Court during the Million MAGA March, the Texas congressman Louie Gohmert had granted that Biden had prevailed in New York and California; however, Gohmert went on, if you didn't count "those two fringe states," Trump had "won the popular vote." Such arithmetic echoed Robin Vos, the top Republican in the Wisconsin state assembly, who, after his party lost control in the 2018 midterms, said, "If you took Madison and Milwaukee out of the state election formula, we would have a clear majority." Never mind that Madison and Milwaukee were the most populous cities in Wisconsin, or New York and California the most populous states in the country.

Because of redistricting and the electoral college system, the votes of people who lived in those places had always mattered less than the votes of rural conservatives; it was a difference of degree, not of category, to propose that they shouldn't matter at all. (Applying the same logic to the pandemic, Trump had said of COVID-19 rates, "If you take the blue states out . . . we're really at a very low level.") On January 6, after returning to the Senate and declaring that "violence never wins," Mike Pence had concluded, "This is still the people's house." But the incoming Senate's fifty Republicans represented forty million fewer Americans than its fifty Democrats (and in June, when the Democrats introduced legislation to protect voting rights, it would fail along partisan lines, fifty to fifty). Such obscene inequity in representation did not offend conservatives who valued kind over number. Noting that some Americans were "uninformed on the issues," John Kavanagh, a Republican lawmaker in Arizona, told CNN, "Quantity is important, but we have to look at the quality of votes, as well." He added, "We don't mind putting security measures in that won't let everybody vote. . . . Everybody *shouldn't* be voting."

The Voting Rights Act of 1965 outlawed practices, common in Southern states, designed to disenfranchise Black citizens—among them, literacy and comprehension tests. Passage of the legislation enraged many Southern whites, who considered every gain by African Americans a personal deprivation. (Lauren Boebert articulated the same zero-sum calculus on January 6, when she told Congress, "Every fraudulent vote cancels out the vote of an honest American.") Three years later, the presidential candidate Richard Nixon saw an opportunity to leverage white backlash against the Voting Rights Act for partisan advantage. "The more Negroes who register as Democrats in the South, the sooner the Negrophobe whites will quit the Democrats and become Republicans," Nixon's political strategist told *The New York Times.* Nixon won the presidency, and the Southern Strategy—ceding the Black vote to

Democrats while exploiting racial polarization to consolidate the white vote—became a blueprint for national elections. Nixon called his supporters "the silent majority," and it was true that they had turned out in higher numbers than the Democratic coalition. But cities have since grown and diversified even as rural populations decline, and conservatives can no longer claim to constitute a majority, silent or otherwise. Instead, by focusing on "quality" over quantity, some have embraced the ethos of a privileged minority, their right to power deriving not from popular mandate but from identity. Like Three Percenters, they deserve authority *because* they are elite—they are Patriots—and this minoritarian status makes them, as Trump called the Capitol rioters on January 6, "special."

ON HIS SHOW the day after the insurrection, Nicholas Fuentes hailed the attack as "the most awe-inspiring and inspirational and incredible thing I have seen in my entire life." Far from discrediting the Groypers, January 6 expanded their influence. In May, Fuentes partnered with Alex Jones, and *America First* was incorporated into the same online platform as Infowars, formalizing the symbiosis of New World Order paranoia and white-nationalist hate and violence. Jones was not alone in recognizing the Groypers as the vanguard of a rising force in right-wing politics and culture. At the same time that the Conservative Political Action Conference took place in Orlando, Fuentes held an America First Political Action Conference at a hotel up the road. The lineup included Paul Gosar, a US representative from Arizona. During the joint session of Congress on January 6, Gosar had been the first lawmaker to contest the electors from his state. It was this objection, cosigned by Ted Cruz, that sent the senators and representatives to debate the certification in their respective chambers. In Orlando, Gosar denounced the "shadowy elites," "the deep state," and the "angry, violent communists" on the left. To uproarious cheers and applause, he then intoned the Groyper slogan: "America First is inevitable."

Fuentes followed the congressman at the podium. "If it loses its white demographic core, and if it loses its faith in Jesus Christ, then this is not America anymore," he said. "White people founded this country, this country wouldn't exist without white people, and white people are done being bullied."

In contrast to Liz Cheney, Gosar, who had skipped a vote on a pandemic relief bill in order to join the Groypers, was neither punished nor rebuked by his caucus. Only eleven Republicans, meanwhile, voted to discipline Marjorie Taylor Greene after a watchdog group uncovered antisemitic Facebook posts that she had published in 2018 attributing the devastating wildfires in California that year to "laser beams" shot from outer space "solar generators" paid for by the Rothschilds. Greene went on to open for Trump in Wellington, Ohio, during his first public rally since leaving the White House. The venue was packed to capacity. Thousands of people from across the region waited in line for hours, and traffic was backed up for miles.

FRIGHTENING PARALLELS

When Balazs, Victor, and I got back to our hotel on January 6, the lobby was full of guests, and wall-mounted TVs were playing footage from the Capitol. Victor and Balazs went upstairs to file their pictures, and I took an escalator to a lower level, where to-go meals were being served at an impromptu buffet. (Because of the curfew, all the restaurants downtown were closed.) I waited in line between a middle-aged couple in matching MAGA hats and a young man wearing an ammo vest and a holstered Taser on his hip. After a while, the three of them, having seen the same CNN coverage in the lobby, began commiserating over how the media was already distorting what had transpired.

"They're making us out to look violent when that's not what happened," the woman said.

The man with the Taser agreed. "I'm here with my mom. Everything I saw was peaceful."

A picture of the man would later spread online, showing him vaulting over a row of chairs in the Senate gallery, carrying several pairs of plastic flex-cuffs. After becoming immortalized on the internet as "Zip-Tie Guy," he would be identified as a thirty-year-old bartender from Nashville named Eric Munchel. Citing video from Munchel's own cell phone, the FBI would claim that he and his mother, Lisa Eisenhart, appeared to stash weapons on the Capitol grounds. When someone in the mob bragged about punching two officers in the face, Eisenhart responded, "Good." Munchel added, "We ain't playing fucking nice no goddamn more." During a search of his home, agents found assault rifles, a sniper rifle, pistols, shotguns, and hundreds of rounds of ammunition.

Around the same time that I was waiting in the buffet line with Zip-Tie Guy, Florida congressman Matt Gaetz addressed the reconvened House of Representatives. Some of the rioters, alleged Gaetz, had been "masquerading as Trump supporters and in fact were members of the violent terrorist group Antifa." Republican lawmakers gave him a standing ovation. The next day, Fox News and other right-wing outlets repeated the theory. Mo Brooks, who'd implored the crowd on the Mall to start "kickin' ass," tweeted, "Evidence growing that fascist ANTIFA orchestrated Capitol attack with clever mob control tactics." Texas attorney general Ken Paxton, who'd also spoken from the Ellipse, wrote on Facebook, "Those who stormed the capitol yesterday were not Trump supporters. They have been confirmed to be Antifa."

A couple of hours later, I received a call from Stacey, the West Virginian I'd met at the rally in Harrisburg. Stacey had been unable to come to D.C., owing to a recent surgery. She asked me if I could tell her what I'd seen, and if the stories about Antifa were accurate. She was upset. She did not believe that "Trump people" could have done the things that the media was claiming. Before I replied, she put me on speaker. I could hear other people in the background. I tried to picture them—these Americans no longer capable of believing anything they saw on the news, huddled around a phone in a West Virginia living room, waiting expectantly to hear from someone who'd witnessed the event with his own eyes. They had no agenda; they only wanted to know the truth. I did my best to convey it to them as I understood it. Stacey responded with skepticism when I said that Trump supporters had in fact committed violence. How could I be sure that they were Trump supporters? We went back and forth for a while, until, losing patience, I said that I had to go. About thirty minutes after I hung up, Stacey texted me a screenshot of a CNN broadcast with a bulletin at the bottom: "ANTIFA has taken responsiblitly for storming capital hill." The image, which was circulating widely on social media, was crudely photoshopped and poorly spelled. "Thought you might want to see this," Stacey wrote.

WHILE THEIR BRETHREN WERE LEADING the charge in D.C., Proud Boys in Oregon had clashed with police and counterprotesters outside the statehouse in Salem. Gary, the Black Lives Matter activist I had met in Portland over the summer, was hospitalized after a Proud Boy shot him in the face with a paintball gun, fracturing his eye socket. Kyle Brewster, the neo-Nazi who beat to death Mulugeta Seraw in 1991, was photographed spraying hornet pesticide at antifascists. None of this prevented the Oregon GOP from passing a resolution declaring January 6 "a 'false flag' operation designed to discredit President Trump, his supporters, and all conservative Republicans." The purpose of the operation had been "to advance the Democrat goal of seizing total power, in a frightening parallel to the February 1933 burning of the German Reichstag."

Some politicians who had spent the past year denying the reality of COVID-19, racism, and Trump's electoral defeat had little trouble revising the events of January 6. During a committee hearing in May, Andrew Clyde, a US Representative from Georgia, said that Trump supporters had behaved "in an orderly fashion," as if on "a normal tourist visit." Images later surfaced of Clyde barricading the main door of the House of Representatives as the mob attempted to break it down. When Democrats sought to form a bipartisan commission to produce a definitive report on the siege, the family of Brian Sicknick, the Capitol Police officer who died from a stroke the day after fighting with Trump supporters, lobbied Congress to support it. Sicknick's mother, Gladys, wrote a letter to lawmakers reminding them that her son "died because of the insurrectionists," and that "he and his fellow officers fought for hours and hours against those animals" while "congressmen and senators were locking themselves inside their offices." Gladys went on, "Not having a January 6 Commission to look into exactly what occurred is a slap in the faces of all the officers who did their jobs that day." All but six Republican senators voted against the bill, and a Republican filibuster blocked its passage.

Beyond shifting blame and evading accountability, Republican obfuscation served to incorporate January 6 into the same right-wing narrative of oppression that had inspired it in the first place. Rather than a liability, the attack became yet another grievance to invoke for political points. Echoing his sympathetic words for the neo-Nazis who'd marched in Charlottesville in 2017, Trump hailed the rioters as "great people," guilty only of "hugging and kissing the police." If anyone was a villain, it was Nancy Pelosi, whose failure to coordinate an effective defense of the Capitol amounted to a dereliction of duty. "The American people deserve to know the truth that Nancy Pelosi bears responsibility as Speaker of the House for the tragedy that occurred on January 6," Representative Elise Stefanik declared not long after replacing Liz Cheney as the chair of the House Republican Conference. From this premise, it followed that the Trump supporters who were arrested for their roles in the attack—many of whom had wished to find and kill Pelosi—were the real victims. In July, a group of Republican lawmakers marched to the Justice Department and held a press conference in honor of these "political prisoners." Paul Gosar emotionally described Trump supporters charged with crimes related to the insurrection as "being persecuted and bearing the pain of unjust suffering." Later, a Texas realtor who'd traveled to D.C. on a private jet would compare her six-month jail term to the treatment of "the Jews in Germany."

Paul Gosar also condemned the officer who had defended the Speaker's Lobby as Gosar and his fellow lawmakers fled from the mob, claiming that the officer had "executed" Ashli Babbitt after "lying in wait" and giving "no warning before killing her." This was false, but Babbitt had become an idealized martyr for Patriots—their own Breonna Taylor, an equivalence that some on Parler, such as Gavin McInnes, promoted by co-opting the phrase "Say her name." The reverence for Babbitt and derision of the officer who shot her was the exact inverse of how the right viewed Kyle Rittenhouse and his victims. After Rittenhouse killed two protesters in Kenosha, Gosar had called the shootings "100% justified."

Predictably, Trump piled on. "Who is the person that shot an innocent, wonderful, incredible woman, a military woman, right in the head?" he demanded on Fox News, and suggested that it had been Pelosi's chief of security. Another lie. Some Americans, however, knew all they needed to about the officer. While his face was not visible in the livestreamed video of Babbitt's death, the two Black hands that aimed the gun were. After living in hiding for several months, Lieutenant Michael Byrd, a twenty-eight-year veteran of the force, appeared on NBC, where he said that he would have done the same for Trump and Trump's family as he had for the lawmakers whose lives he may have saved. Trump supporters on right-wing message boards responded with racial slurs and calls for Byrd to be lynched.

JUSTICE

At least eight hundred Americans were arrested in connection with January 6. They came from almost every state and an array of backgrounds. A beautician from Beverly Hills, a CEO from Florida, a Peace Corps alum from New Jersey, a Connecticut nurse, a New York transit worker, a TV actor and director, a former State Department aide, a Boy Scouts leader, a winery owner, a retired firefighter, four male models, a Gideons International Bible salesman on parole for burglary, and a two-time Olympic gold medalist were just some of the individuals charged with crimes ranging from trespassing to conspiracy. More than two hundred people were accused of assaulting law enforcement officers, and more than seventy-five of using weapons against them. Prosecutors estimated damages at around $1.5 million. Doors had been splintered, windows shattered, furniture smashed, antique light fixtures broken, walls defaced, offices vandalized, and objects stolen. Rioters had urinated on the floors, smeared blood on statues, and tracked feces through several hallways.

Some of the accused expressed contrition. "I'm a piece of shit!" the man who had electrocuted Officer Michael Fanone sobbed to FBI agents during his interrogation. "I'm an asshole!" Others were less remorseful. "I do not feel a sense of shame or guilt," the Texas realtor told a local news station. In her view, she added hopefully, "We all deserve a pardon." Before his last day in office, Trump pardoned a lengthy roster of Republican donors, lobbyists, celebrities, friends, business associates, hedge-fund managers, and executives convicted of such felonies as tax fraud, mail fraud, bank fraud, wire fraud, insurance fraud, securities fraud, health-care fraud, bribery, extortion, racketeering, and money laundering. So it was not altogether unreasonable for those who had fought on his behalf, and at his direction, to expect a similar deliverance. On January 20, when Trump left D.C. for his resort in Palm Beach, Florida, without having granted it to any of them, some felt understandably betrayed. Ethan Nordean, one of more than three dozen Proud Boys indicted for the insurrection, wrote on social media, *"I've got some of my good friends and myself facing jail time cuz we followed this guys lead and never questioned it. . . .* Fuck you trump you left us on the battle field bloody and alone."

Trump had been lying when, after dispatching his followers to the Capitol, he told them, "I'll be with you." Almost none of the Stop the Steal leaders exposed themselves to any real physical or legal risk on January 6. Ali Alexander, who had insisted that he was "willing to give my life for this fight" and inflamed Trump supporters with chants of "Victory or death," watched the insurrection from a rooftop. Stewart Rhodes, who for months had been gearing up his outfit for civil war, disavowed the Oath Keepers who entered the Capitol as "dumbasses." Nicholas Fuentes, who'd urged his followers to "take this country back by force," also remained outside. So did Alex Jones. On January 5, Roger Stone promised the crowd at Freedom Plaza, "I will be with you tomorrow, shoulder-to-shoulder." During the attack, he was at Dulles International Airport, waiting for a flight to Florida. Michael Flynn, who'd urged his sycophants to "fight with courage," was nowhere to be seen on the field of battle. Of course, generals seldom are.

An investigation by the Intercept would uncover an "online business empire" of lucrative websites, corporations, and LLCs linked to Flynn that had capitalized on his stature in the QAnon community. Similarly, the Oath Keepers crowdfunded $350,000 for expenses related to January 6, and *The Wall Street Journal* reported that Stewart Rhodes used money from the organization to pay for a home deposit, dental work, alcohol, and sex-shop purchases. As Nicholas Fuentes's profile rose throughout 2020, he earned at least $140,000 from the livestreaming site DLive, and in December a French programmer gave him $250,000 in Bitcoin before committing suicide. Alex Jones likely raked in tens of millions of dollars hawking male vitality pills and other supplements to his viewers, while Enrique Tarrio sold more than $350,000 worth of Proud Boys merchandise. In Michigan, a report authored by senate Republicans recommended criminal investigations into "those who have been utilizing misleading and false information" about the election "to raise money or publicity for their own ends." Other politicians had few qualms about trafficking in falsehoods themselves. "Many of them were fundraising off this," Representative Pete Meijer said, in *Reason*, about his Republican colleagues. "I'm just at a loss for words about how some of them have acted." Republicans in Arizona used the Cyber Ninjas audit as a pretext to solicit millions in contributions from constituents and wealthy donors alike. No one monetized the lies more avidly than Donald Trump. With a relentless avalanche of texts and emails urgently calling on "*REAL* Patriots" to donate to his "Election Defense Fund" or "risk giving up the Election, and ultimately the Nation," Trump raised $200 million in November alone. Aggressive fundraising continued into 2021. Most of the money went not to legal challenges, as suggested, but to a new political action committee, under Trump's purview, with few restrictions on how he could spend it.

Because so many right-wing personalities go to such lengths to convert their activism into cash, it can be tempting to dismiss the ideas that they espouse as mere grift. Often, though, grifting is fundamental to the ideas that they espouse. The first anti-lockdown protest in the country was funded by Richard and Betsy DeVos, whose family fortune comes from one of the most successful boondoggles in the history of capitalism. Pyramid schemes like Amway are, by definition, hierarchical: there are people at the top and people on the bottom, and one category of person cannot exist without the other. Amway is an abbreviation of "American way," and that is how those who give their money, allegiance, love, and even sometimes their lives to the likes of Trump and the DeVoses appear to see it. *REAL* Patriots do not support Trump in spite of his unending swindles, scams, and shakedowns; they admire him for them. Jason Howland went from pitching get-rich-quick schemes to storming the Capitol because making a killing and killing commies were both integral to the American way. Few citizens demonstrated this principle better than Betsy DeVos's younger brother, Erik Prince, whose private military company, Blackwater, made over a billion taxpayer dollars while taking lives in Iraq.

On my first visit to Karl Manke's barbershop, I had been impressed by the wicker basket on his counter and the growing pile of money to which visitors kept generously adding. Something about the largesse of the contributors—blue-collar types unemployed because of the pandemic—felt backward. After all, Manke was working and they were not. At the time, Manke presented himself as an apolitical everyman struggling to pay his bills. But somewhere along his journey, he took to the role of conservative cultural icon, appearing on *Fox & Friends*, *The Ingraham Angle*, and *Cavuto Live* (where he warned, "It happened in the nineteen forties, with the Jewish people in the Warsaw Ghetto, and it'll happen again unless we are diligent"). His bills, by then, were likely paid. A GoFundMe page had raised over seventy thousand dollars for his legal fees, while karlmanke.com sold T-shirts with his image framed by the words ᴀᴍᴇʀɪᴄᴀ's ʙᴀʀʙᴇʀ. After Glenn Beck plugged *Age of Shame*, Manke's Holocaust novel, the book sold out.

The last time I visited Owosso, a MAGA hat had been added to Manke's shelves of bric-a-brac, the basket was piled high, and a line snaked out the door. Manke was even more garrulous than usual. The Michigan Supreme Court had recently ruled that he could keep his business open. While he clipped a customer's bangs, I asked whether he might draw on his recent experiences for his next book. Actually, said Manke, an idea had been percolating in his mind that he was eager to develop. "I'm trying to parallel the lives of two young men in eighteen fourteen," he explained. "One is from Ghana, and he is kidnapped out of his village by a group of slavers. The other is a young man in Northern Germany whose father has indentured him to be a blacksmith—in other words, the same type of slavery." The story, Manke went on, would compare how the two men responded to their respective states of bondage, with the African submitting and the German, because of his distinct "mindset," resisting. Manke paused, lifting the scissors away from the customer, mulling. "I haven't completely worked all that out yet," he admitted. "But I want to make that connection there. Human beings are capable of a lot of different adjustments, adapting to certain conditions. I see that now with this."

NINETEEN

NEVER FORGET

Though it was a windfall for Alex Jones and Nicholas Fuentes, more than nine million Americans lost their jobs during the pandemic. One of them was Michael Lynn Jr., the firefighter from Lansing. Since escorting Representative Sarah Anthony from her office to the Michigan state capitol after the first American Patriot Council rally, Lynn had sued the city of Lansing for "repeated and continuous discriminatory treatment" by his white colleagues and superiors (such as the placement of a banana on the windshield of his fire truck). Over the summer, spurred by Lynn, eight other Black firefighters, including four chiefs, filed a separate lawsuit alleging that they "were constantly being targeted due to their race," and that three of them had been "terminated and/or forced out of their positions" and "replaced by Caucasian employees."

In January, Lynn became the colead for the Lansing chapter of Black Lives Matter. During his first meeting with the Democratic mayor, he brought up his childhood best friend, Aldric McKinstry, who had been killed by the police when he and Lynn were teenagers. Lynn mentioned the memorial for the German shepherd that the police department posted on its Facebook page every January 23, on the anniversary of the shooting. He explained that the tradition re-traumatized Mc-Kinstry's family and friends each year, and he asked for it to stop. Lynn then made the same request of the Lansing chief of police, who was Black and whom Lynn viewed as a good-faith ally. Three days after Biden's inauguration, the police department posted the same tribute to the dog as always, under a banner that read: "We Shall NEVER Forget."

Lynn texted the police chief to complain. When he received no reply, he posted the chief's number on Facebook and urged residents to share their feelings about the page. In a written statement, the chief alleged, rather improbably, that this had "jeopardized the safety of many in our community." A few weeks later, the fire department, accusing Lynn of breaking his oath to protect citizens, sent him a letter of termination.

In March, I visited Lynn and his wife, Erica, at the offices of their nonprofit organization for local youth, the Village Lansing. Erica was busy organizing a vaccination drive; Lynn, a group trip to the gun range. The Facebook page he'd started at the beginning of the pandemic, "Black and Brown 2a Advocates," had evolved into a larger-scale operation. One wall of the office was covered with certificates from the National Rifle Association, an "executive protection" academy, and a state firearms-training instructor workshop. Lynn estimated that he had helped around seventy people obtain concealed pistol licenses. More and more Americans had been arming themselves since the summer, particularly in Michigan, where background checks for new gun owners were up 155 percent. Overall gun sales had also reached record levels in 2020, with more than twenty-three million firearms purchased nationwide. January 6 had heightened Lynn's wariness of the militias, but he was no less concerned about more proximate dangers. "We had thirty homicides last year," he said, "and not one white person killed a Black person."

In 2020, gun violence killed almost twenty thousand Americans and injured almost forty thousand, more than any year since 1995. (Around twenty-five thousand Americans also committed suicide with guns.) Shootings soared in Portland, to about nine hundred, more than double that of the previous year. Midway through 2021, with the city on track to surpass its 1987 record of seventy homicides, Black community leaders would hold a March Against Murder, at Peninsula Park. Economic hardship was clearly a factor—but so was the deteriorating relationship between citizens and the state. Most of the Americans I'd met in 2020, no matter their politics, had one thing in common: a diminished faith in the government as a reliable authority, whether to administer justice or to ensure their safety.

This breakdown of confidence in sources of stability long taken for granted intimated the kind of social fracturing I'd covered overseas. One emotional feature of contemporary conflict is the ever-present, low-frequency dread of random catastrophe: the mortar whistling out of the sky, the missile tearing through the roof, the IED erupting from the earth, the bomber detonating in a crowd. When no place is immune from haphazard demolition, more abstract structures—the invisible schema that holds societies together—also become precarious. After trips to war zones, I often found that it took time to regain my trust in the soundness and solidity of things. And you never *fully* regained it. Even a city as architecturally splendid and rigorously circumscribed by cultural norms as Paris could feel imbued with the threat of collapse. I don't think of this as a psychological phenomenon; I think that war reminds us how things are not as sound and solid as we believe.

A few weeks after I returned to Paris from Raqqa in early 2020, the president of France, Emmanuel Macron, had appeared on TV to announce a severe countrywide lockdown. "We are at war," he insisted half a dozen times during a twenty-minute speech. In the hours before the new restrictions went into effect, residents of my neighborhood in the Eighteenth Arrondissement made the most of their last opportunity to freely walk the streets. The air smelled bracingly of spring. This would have been the day when restaurants, bars, and cafés moved their furniture outdoors—when their customers, plantlike, rotated their heads in superslow unison along the trajectory of the sun. The mood was festive. Something different was happening. Many Parisians had already fled the city, and a feeling of solidarity connected those of us who'd stayed. Near the Jules Joffrin metro station, a florist raised the metal shutter of his shop and stepped out to distribute flowers. They would wither, otherwise, during the quarantine. People gathered. Citing the one-meter "distance of security" prescribed by the authorities, the florist asked us, "Form a line, please."

But as the crowd grew, a troubling realization took hold: there were more of us than there were flowers. Jostling ensued. Each bouquet was wrapped in cellophane, which crinkled as people snatched them from the florist's arms. "Move back," he pleaded, his expression darkening. Concern that he might retreat into his shop, taking the flowers with him, caused the crowd to surge. People bumped and shoved each other, straining for the blue and white lilies, the orange and yellow tulips. Two women gripped a bouquet, tearing the cellophane in opposite directions. Suddenly, the florist seized a bucket and slung its contents across the sidewalk, splashing legs. An elderly woman staggered backward. She looked as if she were about to weep. "Some people got two, and I didn't get any," I heard her mutter.

SACRED SPACE

From Michigan, I headed to Minneapolis, retracing the nine-hour drive I'd made the year before. The Third Precinct house was still closed, its entrance sealed behind huge slabs of concrete, its windows covered with sheet metal, its flagpole tall and naked. Target was back in business. Migizi, the after-school program for Indigenous youth, had moved to a new location. A chain-link fence enclosed the empty lot where its former offices had burned. I continued down Lake Street, the long commercial boulevard leading to the Fifth Precinct. Many of the businesses damaged during the rioting had reopened, though not all. A few were charred shells. The Stop-N-Shop remained boarded up, and the police station, surrounded by twin perimeters of barricades topped with concertina wire, resembled a military outpost in hostile territory. You would never have guessed that the skeleton of I beams across the street, listing amid mounds of bulldozed earth and twisted scrap metal, had once been a bank—if not for the still-standing sign with the image of a stagecoach in full gallop, heading west.

The last time I was in Minneapolis, the city council had made its historic promise to "begin the process of ending" the police department. That had turned out to be easier said than done. Polls showed that most residents, and Black residents more significantly than others, opposed reducing the number of officers in the city, let alone eliminating them. As council members walked back their ambitious pledge and bureaucratic headwinds inevitably arose, the initiative atrophied. All the while, the police were disappearing on their own. Since the summer, about two hundred officers—a quarter of the force—had quit, retired, or gone on extended medical leave, in many cases for PTSD. A decline in police responsiveness corresponded with a surge in crime. In 2020, more than 550 people were hit by gunfire in the city, and 84 were murdered—the highest toll in at least a decade and a half. Shortly before I returned to Minneapolis, the same city council that had vowed to abolish the police department allocated $6.4 million to hire new recruits. In November, voters would resoundingly reject a ballot measure, championed by Black Visions and other activist groups, to replace the remaining police in Minneapolis with a "Department of Public Safety." A few months later, an officer who'd been temporarily dismissed for abusing his authority while heading the Metro Gang Strike Force would be promoted to "training commander."

Much of the violence in the city was said to be gang related. When I showed up at Thirty-Eighth Street and Chicago Avenue, the intersection was closed to outsiders due to a recent fatal shooting. A block away from the crossroads, barricades and fences stood in front of a plywood guard booth. A wheeled metal gate could be retracted for authorized vehicles. A sign affixed to the gate read: YOU ARE NOW ENTERING THE FREE STATE OF GEORGE FLOYD. A white woman with a radio came out of the booth to explain that visits were discouraged because "people are mourning up there." I said that I was meeting friends, and she allowed me through.

"Watch your six," she advised.

A tall iron statue of a raised fist occupied the center of the intersection where, in June, the Ojibwe women had performed their jingle-dress dance. Flower beds lined the road. Under the canopy of the Speedway, benches and chairs stood beside a large firepit stocked with chopped wood. A small greenhouse contained planter boxes and Christmas trees. Cards, stuffed animals, bouquets, and mementos still crowded the sidewalk, and ropes and stanchions cordoned off the painting on the asphalt of the winged body whose hands were permanently manacled behind its back.

A couple feet away, young people were arranging candles near a pile of red roses encircled by traffic cones. It took me a minute to realize that they were not adding to Floyd's memorial but creating a new one. Two days earlier, thirty-year-old Imez Wright had been shot so close to where Floyd died that their shrines were contiguous; it was impossible to say where one ended and the other began. Prosecutors, claiming that both Wright and his killer belonged to the Bloods, would attribute the shooting to "an internal dispute." Friends and relatives told reporters that Wright had recently left the Bloods and begun mentoring local youth.

Simone Hunter, whom I'd come to the intersection to see, had witnessed the homicide. After the protests had dissipated and the press had packed up and the country had moved on and the weather had turned harsh, Simone had continued to spend nearly every day at Thirty-Eighth and Chicago—watering the plants, swapping out dead flowers, and tending the firepit for homeless people who wandered over from Lake Street looking for reprieve from the snow and subzero cold. "If I'm not here, it's because I'm at home asleep," Simone told me while we sat on one of the benches between the pumps at the Speedway (now identified with red paint as the "People's Way"). She'd been the first to respond after Imez Wright was gunned down. "When I got to him, I took off his mask to see who he was," she recalled, "turned him over, saw how much he was bleeding." Wright had been hit multiple times in the chest and hand. Simone had applied pressure to his wounds and accompanied him in the backseat of a car to the nearest hospital, where he died.

Calls had been growing louder for the city to reopen Thirty-Eighth and Chicago to traffic and law enforcement. A couple of days after I saw Simone, a local resident writing on behalf of people from the neighborhood published a letter in the *Star Tribune* describing near-nightly gunfire; "ducking for cover behind our houses, children in tow"; men on rooftops surveilling the area with tripod-mounted assault rifles; and stray bullets "kicking up dust in the street." The letter lamented that "the spiritual health of our community, the feeling of being connected to something larger than ourselves, is collapsing." Still, when I asked Simone whether she felt that the uprising she'd helped instigate had been a net positive for her city, she did not hesitate to respond.

"Hell fucking yeah."

DEREK CHAUVIN'S TRIAL STARTED the next week. The prosecution was led by Minnesota's attorney general, Keith Ellison, who had previously represented Minneapolis as the first Muslim in Congress. His political activism dated back to the late eighties, when he'd headed the Minnesota chapter of the National Black Law Students Association. It was in this capacity that, in 1989, he marched with Mic Crenshaw and the Baldies, the young skinheads who became Anti-Racist Action, which became Rose City Antifa. Although Ellison inspired more trust than other prosecutors would have, none of the locals I knew believed that Chauvin would be convicted. Extensive security preparations seemed to anticipate the backlash to an inevitable exoneration. The governor had deployed the National Guard, and a million dollars had been spent on fortifying the courthouse and other buildings. Walking around downtown, it was hard not to compare the impenetrable defenses with the freestanding safety barriers that had stood between the mob and the Capitol on January 6.

Two weeks into the proceedings, a white officer in Brooklyn Center, which borders Minneapolis, shot and killed a twenty-year-old Black man, Daunte Wright, after stopping him for a tag violation. Over the next several nights, protesters gathered outside the Brooklyn Center police headquarters, where some threw rocks and fireworks at officers, who responded with tear gas, rubber bullets, and stun grenades. Stores were looted, a Dollar Tree was set on fire, and a drive-by shooting shattered the windshield of an armored National Guard Humvee, lightly injuring two soldiers inside. Then, on April 20, Derek Chauvin's jury rendered its verdict: guilty of second-degree manslaughter, guilty of third-degree murder, and guilty of second-degree unintentional murder. Thousands of people filled the intersection at Thirty-Eighth and Chicago, where, however fleetingly, a year of anger, tension, and sorrow gave way to elation and relief.

Daunte Wright was buried two days later. The officer who killed him, Kimberly Potter—who claimed to have confused her gun with her Taser—had been arrested for second-degree manslaughter. Many people in Minneapolis considered this insufficient. After the Chauvin verdict, protesters congregated in a suburb of Saint Paul, across the Mississippi River, where the district attorney prosecuting Potter lived. Most of the demonstrators were Black. As they peacefully marched through the prosecutor's neighborhood, one of them filmed a man and his wife emerging from their house to accost them in the street. The man, wearing American flag shorts and a Minnesota Department of Corrections T-shirt, would later be identified as a prison guard who had worked in a state penitentiary for the past twenty-six years. In the video, he waves his middle finger and drunkenly shouts, "Fuck you!" His wife slurs, "Get out of here, all you fucking niggers!"

If the video was shocking to me, it was hardly revelatory to Simone Hunter, for whom Thirty-Eighth and Chicago, far from an isolated zone of chaos, represented a refuge of security amid multiplying threats. At the Speedway, across the street from where she had stanched Imez Wright's fatal chest wounds two days earlier, Simone told me that racist whites and police frightened her far more than any crime on the Southside. "Black people don't kill Black people because they're Black," she said. What was indisputable was that Simone felt more safe, not less, within the barricades, and that the world beyond them seemed to her more dangerous, not less, since they'd been erected. Of January 6, she said, "It just confirmed what I already knew."

As evidence, Simone cited the Asatru Folk Assembly, a whites-only pagan organization that had recently purchased a Lutheran church in Murdock, about a hundred miles west of Minneapolis. On my last day in town, I drove out there. Tractor dealerships, grain elevators, and feed mills bordered the interstate. Dense snow gusted over rolling fields tilled for corn and soybeans. Trump flags still whipped in the fierce wind. So did a couple of upside-down American flags. Others announced: BIDEN IS NOT MY PRESIDENT, MY GOVERNOR IS AN IDIOT, LIBERTY OR DEATH, and 1776. By the time I reached the outskirts of Murdock, I was unsurprised to see, even this close to Canada, a Confederate flag hoisted high in a well-kept front yard.

The Asatru Folk Assembly's new place of worship stood opposite a row of silos on a deserted two-lane highway. Nothing about the place suggested the gods to whom it was now consecrated. A plaque affixed to its foundation gave a construction date of 1951; few improvements appeared to have been commissioned in the interim. The door was locked. Behind the property stood a small wood-frame house with a TRUMP 2020 banner hanging on its porch.

The only business in town seemed to be a gas station with a cramped convenience store. I went inside, bought a drink, and asked the clerk if she knew anything about the church.

"It's a church," she said.

"Is it open?"

"It's open to certain people."

Realizing that she might think I was an Asatru Folk Assembly congregant—in which case her hostility would be reason for encouragement—I said, "I'm a journalist."

The clerk stiffened. "No comment."

"I'm just trying to—"

"No comment. Would you like your receipt?"

When they voted to grant the Asatru Folk Assembly a zoning permit,

Murdock City Council members had made a point of condemning "racism in all its forms: conscious, unconscious, any place, any time, now and in the future," while explaining that the First Amendment left them no choice. I admit I was skeptical. After I left Minnesota, I kept thinking about that house with the TRUMP 2020 banner. I've never been the type of reporter to show up unannounced at people's homes, but in this case I regretted not having done so. Who lived there, and what did they think about the Asatru Folk Assembly? The more time that went by, the more convinced I became that I had a pretty good idea. They were white, they were Christian, and they condemned racism in all its forms. They also got along fine with their new neighbors, who were not at all what the media alleged.

In February 2022, I went back to Murdock. Most of the same flags still lined the roads. A couple new ones read: LET'S GO BRANDON (a euphemism for "Fuck Joe Biden"). The church was empty, and the banner on the little house was gone. It was getting late. Heavy snow slanted through the night. A dog started barking when I knocked, and a man with a shaved head opened the door, holding back a pit bull. He wore slippers, sweatpants, and a sweatshirt with the logo for the New England Patriots. It was four degrees outside, and he looked equal parts confused and cold.

His name was Felix. As we stood on the porch, shivering and watching rabbits hop across his driveway, he told me that he had moved to Murdock from Massachusetts, where he'd been raised by a foster mother after his parents, who were both Puerto Rican, abandoned him. He'd served in the National Guard for over a decade. He had planned to make a career of the military, but two deployments to Iraq had left him with extreme PTSD, and he'd been chaptered out in 2012. "That began a five-year fight to just try to find my grounding again," Felix said. An equine-assisted therapy program changed his life by introducing him to the healing power of horses. He had come to Minnesota

in 2017, with a dream of starting a grass-fed cattle farm staffed by veterans struggling with trauma. In the meantime, he worked as a ranch
hand at local dairies and feed lots.

"It's been incredible here," he said. "I love it."

When I asked about the church, Felix told me that it had been vacant
for a few months but that over the summer dozens of people from out of
state had gathered there on Saturdays. "I went over and confronted
them," he said. "I asked them, 'Are you guys white supremacists?' I don't
buy their bullshit. It looked like a lot of bad apples—people who had
done time, biker dudes and stuff." He'd asked the city council to plant a
row of lilac bushes between his property and theirs; if the flowers didn't
grow fast enough, he was going to build a fence.

As far as Felix was concerned, there was no connection whatsoever
between the Asatru Folk Assembly and the politics of Donald Trump.
He was forty-three years old, and 2020 was the first election in which
he'd ever voted. He believed that it had been stolen.

I mentioned the banner that I'd seen above his porch the last time I
was in Murdock. It had been damaged in the weather, Felix said. "I got
a new one I'm gonna throw up this year."

ONE EVENING DURING MY FIRST visit to Minneapolis, about a
week into the protests, I'd passed by Thirty-Eighth Street and Chicago Avenue a little after midnight. The uprising's initial heady energy had started to subside. Everybody was exhausted. Emotions were
raw. Reality imposed. "Am I fucking dreaming?" a demonstrator had
asked outside the burning Wells Fargo. Now the dream was ending.
For several days, these people had made the world stop—but they
could not make it disappear. Although a global movement had ema-
nated from their streets, from their actions, for many locals the stresses

and pressures that had defined their lives before Floyd's murder were no less consuming than before.

An argument led to a fight. Bystanders became involved. Soon, dozens of young people were swinging punches, weapons were drawn, and a dire outcome looked imminent.

Then, as abruptly as it had begun, it was over. A tall, burly figure with a commanding voice appeared to have single-handedly diffused the brawl. When he ordered everyone to gather around him in the intersection, nobody argued.

He was Corey Moore, a forty-four-year-old veteran combat medic who'd been wounded in Iraq. With the neighborhood youth sitting around the ring of candles and flowers, Moore paced in a circle, dressing them down. "I don't give a fuck who bumps into you, who talks about your mama—that's your brother!" Softening his tone, he went on, "Every OG out here knows: we failed y'all. But it won't happen another night. We got your back, come hell or high water."

Eventually, Moore sat down. He and about twenty others remained there until dawn. People stood one at a time to speak. There were also interludes of silence. Squad cars periodically approached the barricades but never crossed them. It felt like an oasis.

A year later, almost to the day, municipal workers with heavy equipment descended on Thirty-Eighth and Chicago and dismantled the gates and guard booths. The move was the initial stage of what Mayor Jacob Frey called "a phased reconnection." He did not specify to what. After meeting Felix in Murdock, I returned to Minneapolis to see what had become of the intersection. Not much had changed. A traffic circle diverted the occasional car around the iron fist. New ropes divided Floyd's memorial from Wright's. Frozen snowdrifts half covered the displays. At the Speedway, the message on the letter board had been updated. It read: AMIR LOCKE WAS LYNCHED! Three days earlier, a SWAT team with a no-knock warrant—the same controversial authorization that led to Breonna Taylor's death—had burst into an apartment in downtown Minneapolis and killed the twenty-two-year-old Black man while he was lying on a couch. He had committed no crime and was not who they were looking for.

TWENTY

WE TRIED

After Timothy McVeigh was linked to the Michigan Militia, most of its leaders and members, like those of other far-right armed groups, went to ground. "The feds started kicking down doors, and they disappeared," one Michigan Home Guardsman told me. "All those old guys are probably still in their bunkers somewhere." January 6 had a rather different effect. Some extremist outfits did strain under the pressure of prosecutions, public blowback, and internal recriminations. Brien James, the president of the Indiana Proud Boys and former skinhead gang leader, put out a video in which he called Enrique Tarrio, the Proud Boys chairman, "the lowest fucking form of piece of shit that there is." The rebuke had nothing to do with January 6, however. James was incensed by a Reuters investigation revealing that Tarrio, in order to reduce his sentence for selling stolen medical devices, had served as an FBI informant. After the exposé, Proud Boys in Nevada, Missouri, and Alabama also splintered off. Because each chapter was already functionally autonomous, though, the fragmentation was more symbolic than structural. And James had a message for those who'd held up Tarrio as evidence that the Proud Boys could not be racist: "In reality, Enrique was a spokesman as much as anything else." When Tarrio stepped down in July, the organization remained intact and open to greater influence by the likes of Brien James.

The very next month, armed Proud Boys again mobilized and battled with antifascists in Portland. Videos showed men in body armor racing around downtown in the backs of pickup trucks, smashing up vehicles with baseball bats, and shooting semiautomatic paintball guns on busy streets. A year earlier, Mic Crenshaw, the Anti-Racist Action founder, had told me that he viewed the right-wing use of paintball guns as "a symbol of what's to come"—practice for real guns. In his book *Warrior Dreams*, the scholar James William Gibson chronicles the rise of paintballing in the 1980s, with parks in California like War Zone and Sat Cong Village, where young men could pretend to kill pretend communists in pretend Cambodias, Nicaraguas, and Vietnams. Portland served as an arena for a similar kind of simulation, and with each iteration, the line between fantasy and reality became more porous. In August 2020, a Proud Boy in Portland had ditched his paintball gun and brandished a pistol at antifascists; in August 2021, a man *shot* a pistol at antifascists, some of whom withdrew their own sidearms and returned fire.

Though the shootout took place five blocks from the Portland Police Bureau headquarters, officers were slow to intervene. This was by design. Two days earlier, the department had released a statement telling Proud Boys and antifascists that it would not "keep people apart" should they choose to assault one another. The hands-off policy, which effectively assured the Proud Boys that they would receive a wide berth to commit violence when they came to town, underscored how little January 6 had changed law enforcement blindness to the threat that Patriots represented. This was also by design. The efforts of Trump and his allies to diminish the events of January 6 precluded any meaningful reckoning with right-wing extremism, and all but guaranteed that it would continue to metastasize irrespective of the specific groups, movements, and causes through which it found expression. In early 2022, with the number of Americans killed by COVID-19 approaching a million, I attended an anti-vax rally on the National Mall where thousands of citizens from around the country listened to speakers on the steps of the Lincoln Memorial compare themselves and their cause to Martin Luther King and the civil rights movement. Groypers waved AF flags; Proud Boys wore black and yellow. One man held a sign with an image of Anthony Fauci resembling Hitler above a swastika made of syringes. "Every capitulation is a signal to the oppressors to impose new forms of torment or torture," the keynote speaker, Robert F. Kennedy Jr., warned. "The hill that you're gonna die on is the hill that you're on right now."

"There's only one way," an older man standing beside me told his female companion, who nodded in agreement. "You think they're gonna be *voted* out? Give me a break."

"And they're coming for our children," Kennedy went on.

A few weeks earlier, uniformed members of Patriot Front—a white-nationalist organization opposed to "the dysfunctional American democratic system"—had paraded from the Lincoln Memorial to the Capitol with flags bearing the emblem of Mussolini's National Fascist Party. If it wasn't vaccines, it was masks or critical race theory or transgender bathrooms. At the same time that some Oath Keepers were turning on Stewart Rhodes, the Constitutional Sheriffs and Peace Officers Association began more aggressively reaching out to law enforcement. In March, for the "special price" of $149, CSPOA founder Richard Mack offered a six-week digital course on "how to create a Liberty movement in your county." Later, Mack partnered with Robert Steele, a major QAnon figure and former CIA officer, for the Arise USA tour. Steele rejected "the Holocaust myth" and promoted "the eradication of the Zionist parasite," and his beliefs were a natural complement to the Posse Comitatus principles of the CSPOA. During the tour, he often talked about "satanic pedophilia and child trafficking" before Mack took the stage to advocate for local independence from government authorities. One of the stops was in Oklahoma. A Republican senator there, warning of a "full totalitarian leftist takeover," later introduced legislation empowering county sheriffs to form posses and arrest federal employees.

Arise USA demonstrated the persistence of QAnon despite none of its promises having come to pass. With each day, the phenomenon resembled less a social movement and more a shared psychosis. In April, a woman in Los Angeles drowned her three infants after becoming consumed with paranoia about child sex trafficking. "I prefer them not being tortured and abused on a regular basis for the rest of their lives," she told a local TV station from jail. In May, another mother, in New Hampshire, was accused of trying to burn down her house with her young son and daughter inside; investigators found messages on her phone referencing QAnon and the election. In September, a California man was arrested for murdering his two-year-old son and ten-month-old daughter with a spearfishing gun. According to authorities, QAnon had convinced him that his children had "serpent DNA" and "were going to grow into monsters." A national poll conducted by the Public Religion Research Institute found that 23 percent of Republicans agreed that "the government, media, and financial worlds in the U.S. are controlled by a group of Satan-worshipping pedophiles who run a global sex trafficking operation." Twenty-eight percent thought that "true American patriots may have to resort to violence in order to save our country."

The rationale for such violence offered by Representative Louie Gohmert in the lead-up to January 6—that the legal and political mechanisms to redress their grievances were no longer viable—only gained resonance in its wake. "The ballot box, we tried as hard as we could try," a militia leader in Georgia told *The Atlanta Journal-Constitution.* "It's not working." The militia had previously provided security for Representative Marjorie Taylor Greene; now it was joining forces with Chester Doles, the former KKK imperial wizard. "We both have the same objective," the militia leader explained.

Some politicians more or less promised violence if Democrats continued to win office. The Arizona state representative Wendy Rogers tweeted in July, "The election fraud will either be exposed and stopped and many people will go to jail or they will keep doing it ushering in a new era of 1776." The following month, a man parked his truck near the Capitol, told police it contained explosives, and accused Democrats of "killing America." In a statement on the bomb threat, Congressman Mo Brooks wrote, "I understand citizenry anger directed at dictatorial Socialism and its threat to liberty, freedom, and the very fabric of American society." A week later, Representative Madison Cawthorn told his constituents, "If our election systems continue to be rigged and continue to be stolen, then it's going to lead to one place—and it's bloodshed." In October, during a conservative conference in Idaho, a man would ask, "How many elections are they gonna steal before we kill these people?" Below a video of the exchange on Twitter, a Republican lawmaker posted, "The question is fair."

Over Memorial Day weekend, Louie Gohmert addressed a QAnon summit in Dallas. Tickets started at five hundred dollars. A portion of the sales went to Defending the Republic, an entity run by Sidney Powell and Michael Flynn. *The Washington Post* later revealed that the group had raised over $14 million in donations since the election; much of the money was unaccounted for. In Dallas, having swapped out her

leopard-print cardigan for a leather biker vest with a patch that read NO
GOD . . . NO PEACE, Powell sidestepped any mention of Dominion Voting Systems, which was suing her and Rudy Giuliani. However, she
added Serbia, Germany, and Hong Kong to the list of governments that
had interfered in the vote, and she predicted that once Cyber Ninjas
completed its audit in Arizona, Trump would be "reinstalled." (The
audit extended Biden's margin of victory.) Flynn then took the stage.
During questions from the audience, a man brought up the recent coup
in Myanmar, where the military had arrested the democratically elected
leader, declared a state of emergency, and killed hundreds of protesters.
"I wanna know why what happened in Myanmar can't happen here," he
asked.

"No reason," Flynn responded. "It *should* happen here."

The former national security adviser went on to auction off a signed
baseball bat for eight thousand dollars.

INCREASING TALK ON BOTH the left and the right about the possibility of civil war left me somewhat bemused. Every civil war I'd covered
had been premised on real grievances, real oppression, real violation.
When I asked frontline soldiers on any side of a given civil conflict
why they were risking their lives, they almost always responded with
concrete, rational answers, be it the Talib whose village had been occupied by foreigners or the Yazidi whose daughter had been enslaved
by ISIS or the Syrian whom the regime had kidnapped and tortured or
the jihadist whose family was killed by a drone. Were large-scale violence to erupt in the US, it would be something different: a war fueled
not by injury but by delusion.

Most of the policemen in the SWAT team that I followed during
the battle of Mosul had been literally maimed by the people they were

fighting against. Ali had more than forty pieces of shrapnel embedded throughout his body after surviving multiple suicide attacks; a car bomb had made Hamadah's cheek and forehead severely concave, like a dented mask; ever since Mezher had been shot in the face, his jaw had been held together by four metal pins that deformed his mouth and slurred his speech; an ambush had deprived Mahmoud of a kidney and left a thick seam from his sternum to his belly button; Segar's head was patched with gashes from an IED; and thickly mottled tissue covered both of Faize's legs, the result of third-degree burns. Traumatic loss accompanied their wounds. Over the years, insurgents had murdered many of their friends, siblings, parents, or children. A young police officer named Bashar kept on his phone the video that ISIS had made of his older brother's execution. One day he showed it to me: a high-resolution, slow-motion beheading with a sword. "The Prophet tells us it's forbidden to kill prisoners of war," Bashar said. "If I catch someone from ISIS, I know I'll fear God's punishment. But if I watch this video, my heart will become like boiling water, and, even if it's forbidden, I'll have the strength to kill him."

A few weeks later, on the eve of the US presidential election, Bashar was in the aid station with me and Victor Blue when one of his best friends arrived in a body bag. A police officer unzipped the bag and removed a silver bracelet from the dead man's wrist. He handed it to Bashar, who fastened it on his own wrist. Then Bashar sat down, covered his eyes with his scarf, and wept. After a few minutes, he stepped outside. A procession of civilians was filing by. Bashar recognized one of his old neighbors: a petty criminal who'd joined ISIS when the group captured their village.

The man was dragged through a metal gate and into a compound with a narrow courtyard. Soldiers shoved him down, bound his hands, and began kicking him in the ribs, stomping on his skull, and beating him with their rifle butts. His nose was broken. He wet himself. Stepping on his ear, a police officer twisted his boot back and forth, as if putting out a cigarette. Blood pooled on the concrete.

I watched Bashar. He had not touched the man. He was the only person in the courtyard who had not touched him. When the man insisted, "I'm not ISIS, I swear to God," Bashar crouched down and said calmly, in a low voice, "You don't have a God."

Then he left the compound to rejoin his comrades. He did not watch the video of his brother's decapitation. He did not make his heart become like boiling water. I don't think he lacked the will. When the moment came, it was not revenge that he craved so much as simply for the horror to be over. Though their extraordinary bravery arose from extraordinary pain, the SWAT members weren't vindictive. They were just determined. Because they were struggling against specific, identifiable opponents who'd inflicted specific, quantifiable harm, their objectives were clear and their force intentionally deployed. Rather than commit a senseless war crime to avenge his brother's death, Bashar had returned to the front to help end the nightmare that had caused it.

When Patriots raised the prospect of civil war, there was no limit to the violence that might be perpetrated because there was no limit to the crimes that would provoke it. Both were products of the imagination. "Everything's gonna have to be annihilated," said Adam Fox. "It will be a bloody and desperate fight," warned Stewart Rhodes. "We're ready to stack bodies," George, the Pennsylvania Three Percenter, told me. In *The Turner Diaries*, William Pierce balances scenes of extreme carnage with descriptions of the fantastical Black and Jewish tyranny that requires it. One propels the other toward the book's inexorable conclusion: nuclear holocaust and global genocide.

Neither Fox, Rhodes, George, nor Pierce had ever experienced war, which might explain their lust for it. (In *Warrior Dreams*, James William Gibson points out that an underrepresented demographic among the clientele at mock-combat paintball parks after the Vietnam War was Vietnam veterans.) The problem for these men—and for the rest of us—is that, because the only real thing about their war is their own belligerence, their own fear, they can never win. They can only rage endlessly against elusive phantoms.

The eye patch that Stewart Rhodes affected always reminded me of a member of the Mosul SWAT named Kakawi. When I'd first met the policemen, they had all taken turns showing me their scars—rolling up their sleeves, dropping their pants, removing their shirts. Kakawi had sat cross-legged in a corner, sheepishly picking at the carpet. Finally, when I pressed him for his story, he smiled and recounted the time that a booby-trapped corpse exploded on him while he was on patrol. Then he reached up, removed his left eye—a glass orb—and held it out to me in his palm.

Stewart Rhodes had also lost an eye. But it had not been taken by the deep state, the New World Order, Antifa, or any of the other chimerical villains who so oppressed him.

It had been taken by Stewart Rhodes.

SECTION 60

Officer Brian Sicknick was the fifth private citizen to "lie in honor" in the Capitol rotunda. Rosa Parks had been the third, in 2005, and the evangelical pastor Billy Graham received the tribute in 2018. Graham—who criticized Martin Luther King's civil disobedience as un-Christian and objected to the historic march for voting rights from Selma to Montgomery, in which Parks participated—was a choice in keeping with the politics of the time. While eulogizing the pastor, Trump re-marked, "It is very fitting that we do so in the rotunda of the US Capitol, where the memory of the American people is enshrined."

Sicknick's other predecessors, Jacob Chestnut and John Gibson, had also belonged to the Capitol Police. On July 24, 1998, a man had entered the Capitol with a revolver, killed Chestnut and Gibson, and wounded a third officer, before being shot himself. The man was a paranoid schizo-phrenic who believed that President Bill Clinton was a communist agent, that cannibals had infiltrated the government, and that he was saving the country.

A ceremonial motorcade transported Sicknick's remains across the Potomac, to Arlington National Cemetery. (Prior to becoming an of-ficer, he had belonged to the New Jersey Air National Guard.) The week before Memorial Day, Gladys Sicknick suggested that lawmak-ers opposed to a bipartisan January 6 commission should visit her son's grave; none of the Republicans who voted against the commission are known to have followed this advice.

After being restricted to relatives during the pandemic, Arlington had reopened to the public, and I had plans to spend Memorial Day there with Vincent Bell's mother, Pamela, and his sisters, London and An-drea. It had rained the day before, but now the sky was rich and clear, the sun beamed, and it felt very much like the previous Memorial Day, when George Floyd had been killed and when I'd first met the Bells at the small Global War on Terrorism monument in Macomb County, Michigan.

I had seen them once since then, in March, at a coffee shop midway between Lansing and Detroit. Vincent and Pamela had promised each other, the last time they were together, that they would retire in 2021. Pamela had made good on her commitment and left her job as the deputy director of a social services center for homeless and at-risk youth. A few weeks earlier, though, she had been elected to lead a new branch of the NAACP in Macomb. "It's already started," she said, holding up her phone, showing me a backlog of messages.

Macomb had responded to the George Floyd protests in much the same way that other MAGA enclaves had. A police chief had suggested on Twitter that "real cops" should "take care of these barbarians," and after a Black family displayed a BLM sign at their house, their car tires were slashed, a rock was thrown through their window, and a bullet was fired into their living room. At a march held in solidarity with the family, a Warren city council member showed up with a Trump flag and a pistol, then assaulted a woman who had placed a BLM sticker on a Trump campaign sign.

At the coffee shop, Pamela showed me a local newspaper whose front page featured an article about two Macomb residents recently arrested for attacking the Capitol. "The same parents who showed up in D.C. are the ones who come home from work every day and have small children who go to school with classmates of color," she said. "When they hear what their parents say, they repeat it at school." Though her term with the NAACP had not yet begun, Pamela had already received several complaints from parents whose children had been victims of racist bullying. "We're going to be dealing with this for generations," she said.

ARLINGTON WAS ORIGINALLY a slave plantation owned by George Custis, a grandson of Martha Washington. When Custis died, he left his physical and human property to his daughter Mary. Mary's husband, a career army officer named Robert E. Lee, managed the plantation until 1861, when the newly formed Confederate States adopted a constitution that, "invoking the favor and guidance of Almighty God," ensured the preservation of slavery. After Lee decamped south to join the Confederacy, the Union seized his estate as a defensive position to protect its capital. By 1864, D.C.'s military cemeteries were at capacity, and the government began burying soldiers on Lee's former estate. By the end of the Civil War, Lee had risen to general in chief of the Confederate army. After surrendering to Ulysses S. Grant, he retired to Lexington, Virginia, where he became the president of Washington College. (His eldest son later sued the government for confiscating Arlington and was compensated today's equivalent of $4.6 million.) Arlington became a national cemetery, and the resting place for veterans of the Spanish-American War, the Philippines, both World Wars, Korea, Vietnam, and lesser-known conflicts.

Most of the Iraq and Afghanistan dead are buried in an area called Section 60. To get there, I followed a winding road through rolling hills covered with row after row of identical white slabs. Over four hundred thousand people lie in Arlington; the vast physical space that they occupy, measured by the grid points of their tombs, conveys a precise sense of scale that often eludes attempts to compute war's human toll. Only by walking through the statistic do you begin to grasp it. The same could be said for pandemics. On my way to Section 60, it occurred to me that the endlessly repeating headstones represented a hundred thousand fewer Americans than COVID-19 had killed during the past thirteen months.

I stopped to watch a long convoy of black SUVs drive by. It was the president's motorcade, bringing Joe Biden to the Tomb of the Unknown Soldier, for a customary wreath-laying ceremony. During his speech, Biden would insist that Americans were "called by God" to make the US "free and fair." A few days earlier, while reiterating his commitment to remove all US troops from the country by September 11, he'd described Afghanistan, conversely, as "godforsaken." The remark was a foreboding echo of Trump's dismissal of Syria as so much "sand and death." Liberal politicians who championed equality and justice at home seldom extended their values to the rest of the world. After securing landmark legislation for civil rights, Lyndon Johnson carpet-bombed North Vietnam with Agent Orange, napalm, and cluster munitions; Barack Obama expanded both health care for poor Americans and a drone campaign that killed untold Muslim women and children. On August 16, the day after the Taliban captured Kabul—installing themselves behind the president's desk, posing for photos, and crediting Allah for their victory—Biden would ask, "How many more lives, *American* lives, is it worth?"

No Americans had been killed in Afghanistan for nearly a year, and fewer than a hundred since 2014. During that same time, well over fifty thousand Afghan soldiers and police had died. Just how little Afghan lives mattered to Biden would become clear, however, as his administration declined to evacuate tens of thousands of longtime US allies, then left them marooned. In strikingly Trump-like fashion, Biden would characterize his catastrophic withdrawal not merely as an "extraordinary success," but as an unprecedented military, diplomatic, and logistical triumph. "No nation has ever done anything like it in all of history," he would claim. Like many people with friends in Afghanistan, I would become involved in private evacuation efforts. For those of us who looked to the Democratic Party as a countervailing force in American politics to the nativist cruelty of Trumpism, Biden's consistent and unapologetic disregard for Afghans would be profoundly demoralizing. "I thought I could never be more ashamed than when we elected Trump," a former political officer in the foreign service, and a lifelong Democrat, would tell me one night. "But this is even more gutting because these are people I admired." She would add, "What a shitty country we've become."

Whenever a president visits Arlington, the army honors him with a twenty-one-gun salute, and shortly after Biden's limousine passed me, cannons began reporting at regular intervals. A steady, pulsing roar also vibrated the air. That week, across the eastern US, trillions of cicadas had crawled out of the earth. Unlike annual cicadas, the members of this genus, unique to the region, lived for as long as seventeen years underground, feeding on sap and other root fluids. The last time they'd surfaced was 2004. Now the cycle was renewing—the insects tunneling from the soil, climbing up trees, shedding their skin, becoming adults. Males would have a couple of weeks to attract mates with loud clicking songs before they died, and the chorus everywhere was strident. Translucent exoskeletons lay around the trunks; innumerable eggs hatched in the bark.

Section 60 was already bustling when I arrived a little after ten a.m. Relatives, spouses, friends, and comrades gathered in small groups, some with coolers full of food and beer. Children chased each other around the graves. A middle-aged woman sat cross-legged in the lush grass, speaking softly to a headstone. Three men approached a tomb, kneeled for several minutes, and briskly departed. I spotted Pamela, London, and Andrea halfway down a row, unfolding plastic camping chairs. I'd been nervous about intruding on such an intimate experience, but they were characteristically warm and gracious. Every now and then, a cicada would alight on one of us; mostly, though, they kept to the trees. It was as if the dead were protected by a force that even the animals knew not to violate.

Pamela withdrew several objects from a bag and positioned them around the headstone: a teddy bear, a toy race car, a framed photograph of Vincent in his dress blues and utility cover. Every Memorial Day, the Bells told me, they met new people who came to visit his grave, and while we were sitting there, a stocky man with a military haircut appeared and introduced himself. He'd been Vincent's section chief in the artillery unit to which Vincent was assigned as a private first class. "He was one of the first brand-new Marines I ever got," the man said. Eleven years later, after he stepped on the IED, Vincent was evacuated to a base where the man happened to be stationed with a reconnaissance battalion. When a call came over the radio for an urgent O-positive transfusion, the man rushed to the aid station and donated so much blood that he fell ill for several days. He did not learn who the recipient had been until after Vincent died.

When the man left—he had three other graves to visit—the Bells fell quiet for a while. It was the first time they'd heard the story. The previous Memorial Day, they had told me how much it meant to them to be in touch with Marines who'd known Vincent. They also relied on the Marine Corps support network for "Gold Star" families—close relatives of service members killed in combat. Gold Star families, a concept that dates back to the First World War, are sacrosanct for all branches of the armed forces. Personally, I'd always been suspicious of the label, which seemed designed in part to curb the politically hazardous anger of survivors by assigning them a privileged social status. But the Bells, who never advertised or exploited their loss, derived real solace from the military's recognition of it. One of the items that Pamela had brought from Michigan and placed in front of Vincent's headstone was a gold star in a wood frame.

The extent to which the Bells valued their ongoing sense of connection to the Marine Corps had made the past year all the more painful for them. Throughout the Trump administration, some of the Marines with whom Pamela and London had become friends on Facebook had sought to engage them in arguments about race and Black Lives Matter. The exchanges had become increasingly adversarial, especially after George Floyd was killed, until finally Pamela had put an end to them. First, though, she'd given one of Vincent's old platoonmates a synopsis of her family history—Vincent's history. Through archival research and the website Ancestry.com, she had discovered that her maternal great-grandfather's parents, Mollie and Carter, were born into slavery on a plantation in Douglasville, Georgia. During the Civil War, Mollie and Carter escaped their bondage and fled north, where Carter joined the Union Army and fought in an all-Black battalion. After the war, they reunited and moved back to Douglasville. "I have a copy of their marriage license," Pamela said. "I have followed them through every census, the births of their children. Mollie had sixteen births, but only nine children, which tells me that the others may have been born into slavery when she was very young." One of Mollie and Carter's great-granddaughters was still alive, and still in Georgia. Douglasville now bordered the congressional district represented by Marjorie Taylor Greene. On January 6, during her speech from the Ellipse, Amy Kremer recounted attending a Trump rally in Greene's district two days before the election: the "thousands of people . . . two or three generations of families . . . elderly people in their wheelchairs . . . tears running down their faces, their children asleep on their shoulders."

When I asked what Vincent would have thought about January 6, Pamela replied, "He would have been angry. And he would have been confused." When Vincent was a teenager, Pamela belonged to the Michigan Certification Board for Addiction Professionals. The position required her to travel to D.C. twice a year and lobby Congress to increase funding for substance abuse treatment programs. She always brought Vincent with her. "We used to walk those halls together," she recalled. "Vincent was so good with directions, and he got me to all my meetings." The first time Pamela took Vincent to the Capitol, he was fourteen. He wore a pressed shirt and tie and gazed wide-eyed at the statues, paintings, and the high dome of the rotunda with its fresco of George Washington. The trip instilled in him a yearning to serve his country. "The Marines came to his school two years later, when he was a junior," said Pamela. "And that was it."

Late in the afternoon, the Bells folded up their chairs. Pamela collected the framed pictures and the gold star and put them in her bag. They would return tomorrow, without the crowds and without the journalist. Then Pamela would make the long drive with her daughters back to Michigan, where she had work to do.

AFTERWORD

The small town of Dahlonega, Georgia, in the Blue Ridge Mountains north of Atlanta, bills itself as the site of America's first gold rush. The area was home to the Cherokee Nation when, in 1828, a white hunter tripped on a yellow rock lying in the woods. Legions of prospectors soon arrived. The government divided the territory into "gold lots," which it distributed to settlers through a lottery system. In 1830, President Andrew Jackson signed the Indian Removal Act, authorizing the military and state militias to forcibly expel Indigenous people from Georgia and march them westward on the Trail of Tears. Thousands of Cherokee perished during the great replacement. Today, downtown Dahlonega revolves around its Gold Museum, which occupies a historic courthouse built during the boom times. Across the street, a row of redbrick buildings house local restaurants and retail businesses. When I visited in January 2022, the window display of an independent clothing shop featured DON'T TREAD ON ME and LET'S GO BRANDON hats and T-shirts.

I was there to see Chester Doles, the former imperial wizard in the

KKK. I had reached out to Doles after reading in *The Atlanta Journal-Constitution* that he was running for commissioner in Lumpkin County, where Dahlonega was the administrative seat. Doles's entry into politics reflected a broader trend. Across the country, right-wing extremists who'd assailed the democratic process over the past two years were suddenly participating in it. In Michigan, the American Patriot Council cofounder Ryan Kelley—whom I'd seen climbing the scaffolding outside the US Capitol on January 6—had launched a bid for governor. Jason Howland—whom I'd seen piling into the mob as it overwhelmed the police—was campaigning for state representative. Many more Trump supporters who believed that the election had been stolen were proliferating through the Republican Party bureaucracy, from the bottom up. "At the school board level, at the county supervisor level, at the precinct level—we're gonna take this back village by village," Steve Bannon, Trump's former chief strategist, told his millions of listeners on *War Room.* "Fix it at the county level," echoed General Michael Flynn. *ProPublica* reported a spike in sign-ups for local GOP positions, some of which directly impacted election administration.

Chester Doles had proposed that we meet at a fried-chicken restaurant on the outskirts of Dahlonega. He was sitting in a booth, eating a bowl of chili, when I got there. During his last stint in prison, he'd become a certified "master fitness trainer" and taken up amateur body building. Though he was in his mid-sixties, he still exuded a live-wire physicality that suggested an enduring explosiveness, prepped to spring. His white hair was buzzed to a low flattop, and he wore a sweatshirt printed with WE THE PEOPLE. On his hands, illegible tattoos appeared to cover over older ones.

He was accompanied by his campaign manager, whom he introduced as one of his nine daughters. He also had four sons and

thirty-four grandchildren. "Fighting the good fight," as Doles described it, was a family tradition. His great-great-great-grandfather,
General George Doles, had commanded a Confederate brigade at the
Battle of Gettysburg. Chester had joined the Klan Youth Corps when
he was five. "We had our own little uniforms—boots, patches, badges,
just like the Cub Scouts," he recalled. At eight years old, he helped his
grandfather distribute bumper stickers for George Wallace, the Alabama governor whose vehement defense of segregation had helped
push Martin Luther King and Rosa Parks to march from Selma to
Montgomery. In the nineties, Doles served as the southeast regional
coordinator for the National Alliance, the largest neo-Nazi organization in America. He was ordained a Christian Identity minister by
Richard Butler, the leader of the Aryan Nations, and, in 1991, worked
on David Duke's campaign for governor of Louisiana. In 2002, Doles
was a marshal at one of the biggest white-nationalist demonstrations
ever held in D.C., where sieg-heiling skinheads clashed with activists
from Anti-Racist Action. ("I knew Antifa before they even called
themselves Antifa," he told me.) He said that he viewed all of these
exploits as part of the same good fight that he was currently advancing
with his support of Donald Trump and bid for Lumpkin County commissioner. "Whatever banner I may have been under over the years,
the enemy has always been the same," Doles explained. "Left-wing
radical communists."

His priorities and those of the Republican Party were more in sync
now than at any point since Ronald Reagan, "the first president that
ever resonated" with him. January 6 had snuffed out whatever daylight
remained between them. "That definitely had to happen to make them
realize we're all on one agenda," Doles said. "It opened up a lot of
doors to me." Before the insurrection, Republican officials in Georgia
had studiously avoided Doles; now they seemed to recognize that

indelible battle lines had been drawn and he and they were standing on the same side. "I've attended Republican meet-and-greets, and they've been nothing but welcoming and gracious," Doles said. He mostly agreed with the politics of the Republican commissioner whom he was attempting to unseat. However, he told me, "I want to be in a position to be able to do something when this shit pops off. Because I do think it's gonna pop off. I really do. Whether we want it or not."

He envisioned a scenario in which some inevitable government affront would provoke a response, as Ruby Ridge and Waco had triggered the Oklahoma City bombing—except this time, a cascade of rebellion and reprisal would follow. "Timothy McVeigh was trying to spark a chain reaction of resistance," he said. "But the climate wasn't ready yet." The climate was changing. The lockdowns, the riots, Antifa, the election: "We'll have to be pushed into a corner, but we're definitely getting pushed there now." The grim future that Doles foresaw brought to mind *The Turner Diaries*, and when I mentioned the novel, Doles said that its author, William Pierce, had been a friend and mentor to him. Two months before Pierce died of kidney failure at his home in West Virginia, he'd visited Dahlonega and addressed more than two hundred National Alliance members in a meeting hall on Doles's property. Doles still regularly listened to archival recordings of Pierce's weekly broadcasts, and he described the sanguinary demise of America depicted in *The Turner Diaries* as "dead on the money." When I asked whether Trump running for president in 2024—and losing—might set in motion something resembling the events in Pierce's fiction, he nodded. "That would be a breaking point. I think that America would balkanize." Doles paused, and then added, "But probably only after blood runs knee-high in the streets."

His tone was similar to that of the man I had stood behind at the Washington Monument during Trump's speech on January 6—the man who'd said, "There's gonna be a war." There was no fury or resentment or sadness, only placid resignation. It was as if, having passed through all the preceding stages of grief, they had arrived at the final one: acceptance. Their country was dead. Now what?

While I was in Georgia, I had also hoped to meet with Ruby Freeman and Shaye Moss, the mother and daughter who'd been falsely accused of committing fraud in State Farm Arena. A torrent of racist death threats had subsequently upended their lives. The FBI had advised them to move. They had erased their social media accounts and changed their phone numbers and emails. Freeman had abandoned her business selling handbags from a kiosk in an Atlanta mall. Moss had gone to live with her grandmother, where, according to a lawsuit that she filed against *The Gateway Pundit*, strangers had twice "attempted to push into the house in order to make a 'citizen's arrest.'" The complaint said that Moss had "largely retreated from social and public life . . . She feels trapped by the unshakable fear that there are unknown people after her who want her dead." When I contacted their attorney, he informed me that the two women were unable to give interviews due to "security considerations." In a statement, Freeman wrote, "Just hearing my name scares me." She added, "I can't imagine ever going back to election work."

Freeman and Moss were not alone. In the wake of January 6, more than two dozen Democrats in the House of Representatives announced that they were retiring.

A couple weeks after I met with Chester Doles, the Republican National Committee formally excommunicated Representatives Liz Cheney and Adam Kinzinger. Citing their participation in the Congressional investigation into January 6, the party denounced their "persecution of ordinary citizens engaged in legitimate political discourse." Liberals responded with predictable alarm to the characterization of January 6 as "legitimate political discourse." But another clause in the resolution struck me as equally troubling. The paramount concern for Republicans, according to the committee, should be taking back control of the government in the November midterms, "on which the future of our constitutional republic depends at this critical moment in history."

As I write this, the midterms have not yet occurred. The presidential race is two years away. I am at my home in France. Watching my country from here, I am reminded of the scene outside the US Capitol toward the very end of January 6, after the building had been secured and the mob had been beaten back and the TV crews were chased away and night had fallen and the National Guard had shown up and most of the Trump supporters had returned to their hotels to go to sleep. On the west side, a couple hundred diehards lingered. QAnon and Trump banners were strewn across the bleachers. An enormous American flag had been unfurled down the scaffolding. Looters rifled through a mobile police command center. A few feet away, a solid wall of officers lined the steps. Men in military apparel faced them, screaming the same threats and insults that other men in military apparel had screamed four hours earlier. There were many more officers now, and they appeared to have the situation somewhat under control. But not totally. Not quite. The incredible thing was that it felt very much like it might start all over again. That was why we were standing out there in the wind and cold—because it could still go either way, and because no one knew which way it would go. Not the mob, not the journalists, not the soldiers, not the cops.

Rock music blared from speakers, and the anxiety and trepidation of the police was matched by the raucous energy of the Trump supporters. After all, whatever happened, they'd be OK. None of them was going to jail tonight. Or to the hospital. Or to the morgue. The

city was theirs, and so was the country. The crowd surged and re-
ceded, probing for an opening. A man passed me wearing a rubber
Halloween mask. Doubting what I thought I'd seen, I turned just in
time to watch him slip into the melee.

He held a coiled noose.

ACKNOWLEDGMENTS

This book expands on a series of articles that I wrote for *The New Yorker Magazine*. It would not exist without the steadfast support of David Remnick and Dorothy Wickenden. Above all, I'm indebted to my editor, Daniel Zalweski. Working with Daniel over the years has been a formative master class in writing and journalism, without which I would be a far lesser reporter. Every *New Yorker* article is a team effort, and much of the material here benefitted from the magazine's talented fact-checkers and copy editors, especially Alexander Barasch, Anna Boots, Teresa Mathew, Danyoung Kim, Micah Hauser, David Muto, Rozina Ali, David Kortava, Jessie Hunnicutt, Yasmine Al-Sayyad, and Hélène Werner.

Jelani Cobb was a vital source of encouragement and of inspiration for me. No one provided more trenchant feedback on drafts of this book than the photographer Victor Blue. Victor and I were side by side throughout the battle of Mosul, the uprising in Minneapolis, the Stop the Steal campaign, and the attack on the Capitol; my perspective on the historical events that we witnessed together was shaped to a large degree by our conversations—and arguments—during and after them. While on a

camping trip at Lassen Volcanic National Park, Zach Blue, Victor's brother
and a publisher at AK Press, schooled me on the origins of American antifascism. It was thanks to Zach that I went to Portland soon thereafter.
Nick McDonell, another Lassen camper, also provided crucial guidance
for this book. I likely would not have attempted to write the book without
the encouragement of Alice Whitwham. Before Alice was an agent and I
was a journalist, we were drinking companions—and thankfully still are.
I am deeply grateful to Scott Moyers, who skillfully shepherded these
pages into their current form. Helen Rouner, Kym Surridge, and Ewa
Beaujon made them better in countless ways.

Ironically, at every stage of my reporting on civic breakdown and division in America, I met Americans who were endlessly generous with their
time, wisdom, and stories. Everyone in Minneapolis would have been justified in dismissing me as an interloper; instead, Simone Hunter, Cornell
Griffin, Lavish James, Tony Clark, Corey Moore, and Cornell Griffin
warmly welcomed me into their lives at a moment of crisis. Similarly, in
Michigan, Pamela, London, and Andrea Bell could not have been more
gracious or kind. I would have been lost in Portland without Jay Knight
and Rico De Vera. I also learned much from Mac Smiff, Shane Burley, Hal
Bernton, Eric Ward, Effie, Ace, Sophie, and Morgan. Mic Crenshaw, Kent
Ford, Louise Erdrich, and Frank Paro opened my eyes to parts of my
country and its history to which I'd have otherwise stayed blind.

The sections of this book that address the wars in Afghanistan, Syria,
and Iraq derive from assignments for *The New Yorker* and *The New York
Times Magazine.* Except when embedded with the military, I conducted all
of that reporting with courageous local fixers or translators. In Afghanistan: Muhib Habibi, Naiemullah Sangin, and Shaheedullah Sangin. In Iraq:
Sangar Khaleel and Sardar Suleman Barani. In Syria: Osama Mohamed.
Joel Lovell gave me a chance and a career.

Nama, what can I say? You gave me a home.

A NOTE ON SOURCES

Nearly all of the scenes described here are based on video that I recorded while witnessing them firsthand. Any historical and political
context draws on the scholarly and journalistic work of others, of
course. Much of the background information on the origins and evolution of white paramilitarism in the United States comes from Leonard
Zeskind's exhaustive *Blood and Politics: The History of the White Nationalist
Movement from the Margins to the Mainstream*. For William Potter Gale
and the Posse Comitatus, there is no better authority than Daniel
Levitas and his book *The Terrorist Next Door: The Militia Movement and
the Radical Right*. *Bring the War Home: The White Power Movement and
Paramilitary America*, by Kathleen Belew, is a magisterial account of the
white-power movement in the seventies and eighties; James William
Gibson's *Warrior Dreams: Paramilitary Culture in Post-Vietnam America* is
another valuable treatment of the subject. Belew's analysis of how the
Vietnam War galvanized neo-Nazis greatly influenced my thinking
on the relationship between Trumpism and the Global War on Terrorism. So did Spencer Ackerman's *Reign of Terror: How the 9/11 Era*

Destabilized America and Produced Trump. Much of what we know about the political influence of the Kochs and the DeVoses comes from Jane Mayer and her authoritative *Dark Money: The Hidden History of the Billionaires Behind the Rise of the Radical Right.*

There are many excellent books on the rise of the Patriot Movement and the alt-right. Alexander Reid Ross's *Against the Fascist Creep,* David Neiwert's *Alt-America: The Rise of the Radical Right in the Age of Trump,* and Shane Burley's *Fascism Today: What It Is and How to End It* were particularly enlightening for me. To better understand the Bundy family, I relied on Leah Sottile's magnificent *Bundyville* project as well as Anthony McCann's *Shadowlands: Fear and Freedom at the Oregon Standoff.* In *Standoff: Standing Rock, the Bundy Movement, and the American Story of Sacred Lands,* Jacqueline Keeler offers a trenchant comparison of Patriot and Native American land revindications. The best account of the right-wing ferment during the 2016 presidential campaign that I have read is Andrew Marantz's *Antisocial: Online Extremists, Techno-Utopians, and the Hijacking of the American Conversation.* For what that ferment became over the next four years, and its historical underpinnings, I was grateful for *The Cruelty Is the Point: The Past, Present, and Future of Trump's America,* by Adam Serwer, and Jelani Cobb's revelatory commentary in *The New Yorker Magazine.* Mark Bray's *Antifa: The Anti-Fascist Handbook* was crucial to my understanding of antifascist ideas and activism in the US and Europe. I am also indebted to the podcast *It Did Happen Here*—coproduced by Mic Crenshaw, the former Baldie—an essential oral history of the battle between racist and antiracist skinheads in Portland and Minneapolis during the eighties and nineties. The definitive chronicle of neo-Nazism in Portland and the murder of Mulugeta Seraw is Elinor Langer's *A Hundred Little Hitlers: The Death of a Black Man, the Trial of a White Racist, and the Rise of the Neo-Nazi Movement in America.* In his podcast *Uprising: A Guide from Portland,* Robert Evans provides a detailed record of the recent protests in that city. I first learned about the origins of Oregon as an envisioned white utopia from the scholarly work of Walida Imarisha.

Superlative local news outlets were critical resources for me everywhere I went—in Minneapolis, the *Star Tribune*; in Michigan, the *Detroit Free Press*; in Portland, *Willamette Week* and *The Seattle Times* and Oregon Public Broadcasting. Antifascist activists were sources as well as subjects for this book. Dossiers on groups and individuals compiled by Rose City Antifa researchers offered the most nuanced and accurate portrait available of right-wing extremism in 2020. This book went to press before the publication of the Congressional report on January 6, but some details come from statements released by the committee during its investigation, which itself benefited from reporting by *The Washington Post, The New York Times*, and others.

The parts of this book that address Native American history derive largely from Pekka Hämäläinen's *Lakota America: A New History of Indigenous Power*, Dee Brown's *Bury My Heart at Wounded Knee: An Indian History of the American West*, Louis S. Warren's *God's Red Son: The Ghost Dance Religion and the Making of Modern America*, and Nick Estes's *Our History Is the Future: Standing Rock Versus the Dakota Access Pipeline, and the Long Tradition of Indigenous Resistance*. I also benefited from conversations with Frank Paro, the national cochair of the American Indian Movement. Most of my references to the life and legacy of Martin Luther King emerged from Taylor Branch's monumental King Era trilogy, particularly *At Canaan's Edge*. My historical framing of Michael Lynn Jr.'s advocacy on behalf of Black gun owners was informed by *The Second: Race and Guns in a Fatally Unequal America*, by Carol Anderson.

INDEX